# The Clintons Meet Freud:

## A Psychohistory of Bill, Hillary and Chelsea

**By Paul Lowinger, M. D.**

ISBN 0-9642614-6-4

Published by

Knoll Press
77 Belgrave Ave
San Francisco, CA 94117

*For my wife Margaret and our children, Larry, Wendy and
Leslie and grandchildren Claire and Julian who
both make a brief appearance in the book.*

# TABLE OF CONTENTS

# TABLE OF CONTENTS

# TABLE OF CONTENTS

# PREFACE

Many people played a role in the development of this book.  Special thanks are due to my friend, Webmaster Richard Petersen who suggested this psychohistory after I declined doing psychohistories of the Pope and Bill Gates. Richard posted it on www.zpub.com as it was written. Later, as the president of Z Publishing, he directed its publication with good will and editorial wisdom.

Other hands helped with this book including those who offered email suggestions in response to the preliminary versions which appeared on the web. My peer writers' group read and commented on the manuscript.

Librarian Susanna Bonetti of the San Francisco Psychoanalytic Institute provided ready access to psychoanalytic materials.  I depended on the University of San Francisco Gleeson Library for books, journals and documents so I thank its head, Dean Tyrone Cannon and the staff. I also used the San Francisco Public Library and the University of California at San Francisco Library.

The sources I consulted and quoted are nearly all in the public domain and appear in the footnotes and references. Some sources consulted directly are noted in the text including two who preferred to remain anonymous.

The production of the book was possible because of because of the copy editing by Jane Hermanau. Peggy Cartwright contributed vital computer support. Randy Harrison consulted on the project.

I was a student at the University of San Francisco's Fromm Institute of Life Long Learning headed by Robert Fordham while this book was written. The courses for senior citizens which were taught by retired faculty offered a unique catalyst.  There was feedback from the Fromm community to my lecture about Hillary's psychohistory. A University of San Francisco undergraduate course in the Department of Politics by Professor Ange-Marie Hancock was based on this psychohistory of Bill Clinton.

Paul Lowinger, M. D., M.Sc.
paulow99@yahoo.com

San Francisco
February 15, 2004

# INTRODUCTION

I retired in 1992 and so I had time to write. I did short stories, travel vignettes, book reviews and essays[1] but I needed a larger canvas and a longer range.

My affinities led me to choose Hillary and Bill. They are part of a pastiche that evokes my own identity, real and fantasized. I am engaged by their Sixties' passion for social justice, their quest for power, their political and sexual theater, their intellectuality, their martyrdom and their religious and charismatic intensity. The dialectic includes Hillary and Bill's opportunism, frenzy, cruelty, character defects, failures of nerve and their faithlessness. These paradoxes are epitomized by Walt Whitman in *Leaves of Grass*.

> Do I contradict myself?
> Very well then I contradict myself,
> (I am large, I contain multitudes.)

I write a Freudian story although I'm not a psychoanalyst. I like the elegance of Freudian theory which offers a richness, intellectual, literary and emotional that invited my psychohistorical effort.

Skepticism is the best way to look for terra firma in the wetlands of psychohistory and psychoanalysis, so you're in the hands of a restless guide, not a true believer. Still my friends say that they didn't know I was so Freudian. Well, I'm not really and certainly I wasn't when I practiced psychiatry and psychotherapy, and taught and did research for forty years. My own analysis was Freudian, but later I had humanistic therapy based on Maslow, Gestalt and Wilhelm Reich. I went to Esalen and I was in a therapeutic group. All were useful.

I did not visit the Clinton White House nor did I interview Bill or Hillary but I'll emerge from the closet of impartiality and list my biases. Although I admire both Hillary and Bill, I feel they both are ill equipped to cope with our mean spirited nation in the late 20th century. They share this limitation with other recent American presidents and leaders.

Many people have contributed to this effort. Emails about early versions of the manuscript posted on the web were often helpful. A peer-writing group read the text and commented.

## WHAT IS PSYCHOHISTORY?

Psychohistory begins with Freud's studies of Leonardo da Vinci and Moses and includes a book on Woodrow Wilson he coauthored with American diplomat William Bullitt. Many followed including Erik Erickson who wrote on Gandhi

# INTRODUCTION

and Luther. They write about the minds of Alexander the Great, Queen Victoria, Lawrence of Arabia, Lincoln, Hitler, Van Gogh, Loyola and Glenn Gould.

The study of an individual mind is the choice of a psychological viewpoint over a social perspective and it is a challenge to the usual way of looking at reality. The method is to produce a personal psychological script and to correlate this tale with life events and developments in the nation or the world. A biological dimension of psychohistory described by Abram is the influence of George Bush I's sudden thyroid illness (a "thyroid storm" in medical nomenclature) on the causes of the Gulf War.[2] Lowinger tells us that President Bush's desultory election campaign in 1992 might be the result of a lethargic depression caused by his poorly controlled hypothyroidism[3].

Psychohistory is a variant of Thomas Carlyle's Great Man theory of history, "Universal history, the history of what man has accomplished in this world, is at bottom the history of the Great Men who have worked here."[4] An opposite view was that of Otto von Bismarck, the Prussian politician who said, "A statesman...must wait until he hears the steps of God, sounding through events; then leap up and grasp the hem of his garment."[5]

In psychohistory, the explanation of the leader's behavior and national events depends on unconscious and conscious factors in the mind of the leader. The emotional meaning of experience is translated here primarily according to the psychology of Sigmund Freud with help from Carl Jung. The additional Freudian psychoanalysts, feminist psychologists, Jungians, social psychologists and the others whose ideas are useful are mentioned in the bibliography. Psychohistory uses individual mental development to explain both personal behavior and social events. Meanwhile critics like Susan Faludi reject the psychoworld where the "...search for 'character' is a lazy man's guide to quickie diagnosis of politicians based on third-hand potty-training reports...[6]

The unconscious is the part of the mind, which is hidden from awareness and is not accessible even to the imagination. Between the unconscious and the conscious lies a preconscious or subconscious, which can be reached by introspection. The unconscious is impervious to reality and morality and it is timeless as it mingles the emotions and ideas of a person's mind at different ages. We can glimpse the unconscious during dreams, sleep deprivation, psychosis, psychoanalysis, the use of psychedelic substances and in the creation of art. Repression, the force that separates the conscious from the unconscious mind will be described under Hillary's Ego Defenses.

Psychobabble is an unavoidable hazard in writing psychohistory but here it will be translated. Much psychological analysis of the heroes and villains of history leads to the mind of the writer. This is an effort to avoid such a pitfall and a warning to the reader. Another caution is to understand that biography is in the

# INTRODUCTION

words of John Leonard "...a cannibal feast of family dysfunction, vile apprentice-ship, open wounds, big scores, closet secrets, love gone wrong, grief and grudge."[7]

The portraits offered by psychohistory lack the authority of the therapist who deals with live patients as well as the precision of historians like Thucydides, Gibbon or Tuchman who record events and trends. Still the canons of history and psychology are used insofar as they further the task and otherwise they are set aside. The interchange of terms like psychohistory, psychobiography, psychology, psychiatry and psychoanalysis is not accidental since these overlapping disciplines all contribute to my study and are complementary here, even though elsewhere they may engage in turf wars.

What do these terms mean? Psyche was a nymph in Greek mythology who personifies the human soul or mind. Psychology is the study of the mind and behavior. Psychohistory is the use of psychology in the interpretation of history. Psychobiography is the study of a person's life using psychological methods. Psychiatry is a medical specialty dealing with the diagnosis and treatment of mental and emotional illness. Psychoanalysis refers to the theories of Freud about the unconscious, psychosexual development, free association and transference.

# PART ONE

HILLARY RODHAM CLINTON

"Like most mothers, I am the designated worrier in our family." *It Takes A Village* by Hillary Clinton, Simon & Schuster, 1996. p. 10

"I'm proud of my marriage. I have women friends who choose not to marry, or who married and choose not to have children, or who married and then divorced, or who had children on their own. That's okay, that's their choice. This is my choice. This is how I define my personhood - it's Bill and Chelsea." Hillary Clinton in *The Unique Voice of Hillary Rodham Clinton*, editor Claire Osborne, Avon Books, 1997, p. 48

"It took Hillary to raise a president." by Gail Sheehy in *Hillary's Choice*, Random House, 1999. p. 302

"I looked at some of the Icelandic Saga manuscripts...I even found a new heroine, Gudridur, who grew up in Iceland at the dawn of the last millennium, and who as a young woman sailed off in one of those open Viking ships to North America on one of the first expeditions ... She gave birth to the first known European child in North America...returned to Iceland and then decided to take a journey to see the Pope in Rome which she did. She returned to Iceland where she lived to a wise old age and she became a very important personage..." Hillary Clinton, Vital Voices Conference on Women and Democracy, Reykjavik, Iceland, October 10, 1999 in *Vital Voices* 1997-1999, Washington D.C., PREX 1.2 v 66

The psychohistory of Hillary Rodham Clinton is a challenge. The biographies of Hillary lack information about her early development although they offer some particulars. On the other hand, Hillary has written two books. *It Takes a Village and Other Lessons Children Teach Us* in 1996 is about Hillary's beliefs and experiences so it qualifies as a psychological script to be deciphered as it offers a potpourri of child rearing, child psychology and public policy about children. A brief public controversy about this book revealed that Hillary herself was the primary author. *Living History* in 2003 is a sequential autobiography explaining her life and politics as it targets her marital turmoil in the White House.

The free form *Village* book allows us to perform a kind of Rorschach on Hillary's unconscious mind while Living History floats on the surface of her narrative. Hillary's public appearances, remarks, publications and speeches are useful. The books and articles about both of the Clintons contribute to my study.

Understanding Hillary Rodham Clinton demands close attention so that her life won't be obscured behind a puffy Bill Clinton like the sun on an overcast day. There is also a tendency for the flesh and blonde Hillary to be hidden by icons: woman, wife, mother, daughter, attorney, politician, First Lady and Senator. Another hazard is the Hillary's biographers who demonize or glorify her so she appears one-dimensional as good or evil. My tool of understanding is psychohistory and particularly psychobiography.

The primary goal is to understand Hillary herself. However, the influence of Hillary on the culture and politics of the Nineties and onward is so significant that as her psychological story is told, we will illuminate ourselves and our times.


HILLARY'S OEDIPUS

Hillary was Daddy Hugh's girl but what does that mean? She was Curmudgeon Hugh Rodham's victim who wanted his love and approval even as she tried to escape his stinginess, irascibility and perfectionism. The victim survived and was marked by an identification with the aggressor. But Hillary also was "...always Daddy's Princess" according to Tony, her youngest brother who was interviewed for Jerry Oppenheimer's book, *State of a Union* about the Clintons. In this book, Hillary's cousin, Oscar Dowdy explains, "Hillary got the love and Hughie (the other brother) got booted...Tony got his share too...both of them (were) pretty envious of the attention she got. Hillary was just very smart and earned her father's respect...On Dorothy's (Hillary's mother) part there was a bit of jealousy of Hillary...Aunt Dorothy was always very, very defensive of Hughie because Hughie used to get the shaft from the old man... it was a protective mother thing."[8] Cousin Oscar Dowdy who is three years older then Hillary is the son of Hillary's aunt Isabelle, Mother Dorothy's younger sister so these families were often together on holidays and birthdays.

Hillary's Oedipus complex involved her attraction to and struggle with Gruff Daddy Hugh and her frustration and rivalry with Passive Mother Dorothy. This is the view of the 1993 Hillary biography by Norman King, which was elaborated on in the books by David Brock and Roger Morris. That Hillary was also Daddy Hugh's Princess is based on interviews with Hillary's brother Tony and her cousin Oscar in the Oppenheimer book. Like an ongoing psychoanalysis, these later revelations led to new insights.

Like Daddy Hugh, the adult Hillary became irritable, demanding and the family breadwinner. Hillary says in her Village book that when she brought home a report card with all A's from junior high school, Daddy replied that it must be an awfully easy school. We're not told what Dorothy Rodham said when she saw the grades maybe because her mother's approval wasn't important to Hillary or perhaps Mother Dorothy was also hard to please.

Mother Dorothy is described by Joyce Milton as "...stern and even slightly bitter" in her biography of Hillary.[9] In Jerry Oppenheimer's book, Oscar Dowd describes his aunt as "kind of cold, kind of standoffish...she had a difficult time being warm and truly affectionate...Dorothy's always mad at somebody. And it tends to last forever."[10] Oscar recalls the Rodham family Christmas as "plastic" and his wife Helen remembers that Mother Dorothy hated cooking and housework. Hillary celebrates a different family icon, mother-daughter cookie-baking in her book, *It Takes a Village.*

Everyone has a biased view of this family and his own life so everything said by the principals should be received with benign skepticism including the words of Dorothy, Hugh, Hughie, Tony, Oscar and Hillary herself. Psychoanalysis is about uncovering hidden and unconscious emotions, and also about changing behavior, but it is not a method for uncovering the truth although this may happen. Despite the similarity of psychoanalysis to psychobiography, it is the later that tells the story of the subject's behavior as well as its meaning. Beyond "just the facts, ma'am," this psychobiography takes us to the motivations of Hillary's mind, conscious and unconscious.

Dorothy has a fear of her own feelings and keeps an emotional distance from Hillary, so much so that in 1998, she tells biographer Gail Sheehy, "I don't talk to Hillary about anything deeply personal...her husband...her daughter..."[11] Dorothy's explanation about this is circular but informative when she says that although Hillary is sensitive, she doesn't over emotionalize, so "she (Hillary) doesn't go into one of these horribly overwrought kinds of tizzies. That's one thing I never did either."[12] "In a tizzy" is a phrase from the early 1900's defined as being upset, in a state. Avoiding a tizzy means using isolation as a defense so feelings are repressed (see Hillary's Ego Defenses). This process is quite different from the Dionysian emotionalism of Bill's family including Mother Virginia and Grandmother Edith who will be discussed later.

Daddy Hugh was from Scranton, Pennsylvania where he grew up and where he took each of his children for their Methodist baptism.[13] Family vacations were at a Rodham lakeside cottage in Pennsylvania. Emigrants from England, the Rodhams worked mostly as laborers in the coal mines and the lace factory, but also included civil servants, the owner of a hotel in the red light district, a respected doctor, and a Scranton political boss who served as a city councilman.

The solid, blue collar Rodhams stood in contrast to Dorothy's family, who were "marginal people" according to a researcher.[14] Dorothy was born to a fifteen-year old mother and a seventeen-year old father. Later they divorced and then Dorothy and her sister were sent from Chicago to California to live with paternal grandparents who were abusive and were on welfare during the depression years. Dorothy's father who got custody after the divorce largely disappeared from her life. Later her mother remarried but she wasn't given custody then because at the time of the divorce she had been considered to be abusive to her husband and was called violent by her own sister. Dorothy's mother was described in census records as illiterate at seventeen. Dorothy's father was described as a fireman or a chauffeur. Dorothy's parents were the children of immigrants from Canada and England.

Dorothy had survived childhood abuse with teenage parents who couldn't manage a family with two children, divorcing and sending eight-year old Dorothy by train alone with her three-year old sister from Chicago to Los Angeles to live with grandparents losing contact with her parents. The grandparents were verbally and physically abusive and she left their home at fourteen so she could finish high school. Dorothy learned to live passively with hidden and muted feelings. Her use of repression, denial and isolation were transferred to Hillary who suffered a kind of verbal childhood abuse from Daddy Hugh.

But it was an active Dorothy who said there was no room in the house for cowards when four-year-old Hillary ran home after a neighborhood attack by an "obnoxious girl." We learn from Hillary's youngest brother Tony that "our mother was pretty tough..."[15] so Hillary was forced to confront her attacker and hit back. She won the battle, and now had the respect of the children, according to biographers David Brock and Gail Sheehy and Hillary herself.[16] Sometimes Dorothy's memory of Hillary's plight is more vivid with her routs leading to successive tearful flights home from an older adversary, Suzie who was defending her turf as the only girl who played with the boys. The story of the counterattack is even more dramatic when the larger girl is knocked down or hit in the nose before an audience of neighborhood boys who now all wanted to play with Hillary.[17]

A curmudgeon was the way Hillary biographer, Norman King described Hugh[18] while another biographer, Roger Morris finds him guilty of the "psychological abuse"[19] of his children including Daddy's Princess, Hillary. Chief Petty Officer Hugh Rodham was a drill instructor who spent World War II training recruits at the Great Lakes Naval Station near Chicago while Dorothy was a secretary. Hillary's parents married in 1942 and she was born five years later. Afterward he became a successful businessman in Chicago who moved his family to Park Ridge, an upper middle class suburb from a city apartment three years after Hillary was born October 26, 1947. Tobacco chewing and fly-fishing Hugh, who had attended college on a football scholarship, was a regal presence in this family; Hillary says it was like the television sitcom, Father Knows Best. But the humor was lacking according to Dorothy, who said of Hillary, "She had to put up with him."[20] Of course, Dorothy did too. The Rodham marriage was described as "icy" and in "constant tension" by Helen Dowdy, the wife of Hillary's cousin Oscar.[21]

The current picture of Hugh as a genial taskmaster is a sanitized version of his behavior thirty years earlier. After his death, he was characterized as "confrontational, completely and utterly so" by Tony, Hillary's brother. Hillary recalls him as a "tough taskmaster"[22] who was empowering but then she was favored over her two younger brothers, Hugh Jr. born in 1950 and Tony in 1954. Cousin Oscar Dowdy explains, "Hillary was born with uncanny, extreme intelligence. Her dad recognized it...Tony and Hughie were regular kids, but Hillary was not a regular kid...He (Hugh) was proud as a peacock of her. Hillary knew how to get what she wanted out of him. She knew the right buttons to push."

Family symbols were Hugh's new Cadillac every year and the elegant Georgian suburban home on the corner, which was ice cold each winter morning because Hugh turned off the heat at night. Was this family purification or an atonement ritual led by Hugh, the high priest who wanted to turn off the libidinal night dreams?

The struggle between Daughter Hillary and Daddy Hugh, like most family feuds, went through several acts and intermissions, but was often one in which Hillary was in control. It reached the endgame with Daddy Hugh, then post-stroke and retired, moving to Little Rock with Dorothy and the sons, Hugh Jr., and Tony. Now Hillary was a corporate attorney and  married to Governor Bill Clinton but the focus was on seven-year old Granddaughter Chelsea. She needed Hillary's family nearby when it seemed that Bill and Hillary would be in the 1988 presidential race. Although Bill didn't run then, Hillary had taken over the Rodhams and installed them in her city far from Park Ridge or from Daddy Hugh's roots in Pennsylvania. Still, Arkansas was retirement country from the northern winters of Illinois for many who didn't make it to Florida. Passive Dorothy and powerful Daughter Hillary agreed, and so now the brothers, Hugh Jr. known as Hughie, and Tony went to college in Arkansas.

## HILLARY'S OEDIPUS MEETS FEMINIST THEORY

It is convenient to begin the description of Hillary's development with the Oedipus complex because this is a crucial aspect. An examination of the Oedipus complex is often the most direct route to hidden conflicts and the sources of anxiety. The fateful and incestuous union between the son Oedipus and the mother Jocasta and was also a symbol of the desire of the daughter for the father. The selection of a male centered myth for understanding women's development emphasizes the sexist bias of Freudian psychology. Sometimes the Oedipal phase of female psychosexual development is labeled the Electra Complex, named after the daughter of Agamemnon, who was responsible for the murder of her mother, Clytemnestra.

Freud and his followers debated for decades about how Oedipal events form the female personality, her sexuality and feminity itself. In contrast, the early explanation of the male Oedipus complex achieved a prompt consensus among these same Freudians. More recently women analysts and feminist psychologists have amended Freudian theory removing penis envy, vaginal orgasm, girl's castration fears, feminine passivity and the weakness of the female superego from the Freudian panoply. The gender-free constructs of id, ego, superego, the unconscious, ego defenses, bisexuality, the psychosexual developmental stages and transference remain.

A new Freudian psychology with the centrality of the mother in human development which blends with the older gender-biased Freudian ideas is the result. The preoedipal mother before the child is three has a greater influence on both sexes but the effect on girls is more important and more prolonged than on boys.

Freud's theory of personality was based on biologically determined instincts which were shaped during infantile development. This idea was revised in favor of a new object relations theory, derived from the recognition of narcissism, borderline personality (to be explained later in Slick Willie and the Genes) and a new psychology of women. Object relations theory means that the mother and other significant people enter the infant's mind and remain as objects. These objects influence the fundamental options about the gender behavior, sexual preference and the aggressive or life forces. In this land between biology and social influence, object relationship theory extends the role of culture.

Another important discovery was of a core gender identity for female and male infants so that both psychological feminity (and masculinity) have a biological origin. Psychological feminity was now removed from its earlier dependency on its being just a reversal of the male Oedipus complex by the new objects-relations theory and the recognition of core biological female identity.

Feminist psychologist Nancy Chodorow explains, "... psychoanalytic feminism makes important demands upon psychoanalysis and points to areas of potential expansion and revision."[23] She concludes that both the traditional ideas and the new theories can be used to understand the female (and male) Oedipus complex.

This feminist psychoanalytic theory is combined with some asides to older concepts such as penis envy, now cast in a secondary role in female development. An example of secondary penis envy is the announcement during a holiday gathering by Claire, my granddaughter who was then four and a half, "Penis, penis, penis, Julian, penis," as she looked in the direction of her two year old brother.

The investigation of Hillary begins with the questions about her image, character and behavior. "Very sharp, very Chicago," is the view of Ann Douglas' photojournalistic essay in *Vogue*. We immediately recognize Hillary's energy, intelligence, organizational and leadership abilities, political and professional ambition, charisma, social and religious motivations, and family commitment. The puzzle is reconciling these characteristics with her chronic anger and impatience, temper outbursts, anxiety as "the worrier," the victim of a philandering husband, the family breadwinner who cut some ethical corners, and the icy "Sister Frigidaire," a label from her high school newspaper. These are the complexities and polarities that we explore with Hillary's psychohistory.

How do the explanations of Hillary's problems fit in with the older Freudian and the new feminist Oedipal models? First, the Freudian Hillary. She was fixated in her love for her father according to the Freudian explanation of this universal and fateful event after her Oedipal disappointment when she discovers at three or four years of age that she doesn't have a penis. So penis envy moves the Freudian Hillary from the mother-love of the preoedipal years to a father-love which is never resolved.

Penis envy, a Freudian universal, means that Hillary holds her mother responsible for the loss or absence of the treasured organ which she will replace with the father's penis and by having his baby. (The word "treasured" is used with irony but in order to prevent misunderstanding, I also regard the female organs as treasures.) This wish for a penis is repressed and held in the unconscious where it mobilizes jealousy and death wishes for the mother. It is this  fear of the loss the mother and the mother's love that leads to the development of the conscience or superego. Freud said that the superego was weaker in girls because their fears did not cause a resolution of the Oedipus complex as effectively as did the boy's castration fears.[24] Not so, says feminist psychoanalyst Shahala Chehrazi who points out that the structure of the girl's superego is similar to the boy's superego although the content is different.[25] But Hillary's connection to Dorothy remained intact and Hillary's teenage social conscience and interest in community service and religion were manifestations of a strong superego.

The tie to Hugh continued, and then Elisabeth King and Don Jones appeared. Hillary remained uninterested in teen clothes, hairstyles and dating and her mother expressed some annoyance at sixteen-year-old Hillary's disdain for makeup. Hillary didn't shop, gossip or talk about sex like the other teens, observes Helen Dowdy, cousin Oscar's wife who was only a year and a half older then Hillary. Meanwhile, Hillary who calls herself "a tomboy"[26] was a good athlete, playing soccer, tennis, field hockey, volley ball and softball, which recalled her meticulous training by Hugh for hitting a curve ball. She was a good hitter and a shortstop who knew all about the Chicago Cubs.

At eleven, a view of Hillary as "teacher's pet" emerges from Donnie Radcliffe's biography. This was the time that her sixth grade teacher, Elisabeth King, transferred to a new school so that she could continue to teach Hillary for two more years at the intermediate level. Rick Rickets, her sixth grade boyfriend later recalled for a reporter, "Hillary was Mrs. King's favorite human being on earth."[27] A class picture in the Radcliffe biography shows Elisabeth with her hand on Hillary's shoulder. Such a school girl "crush" on a teacher and vice versa points to homoerotic feelings which may become conscious and sometimes overt at puberty.

This picture is given another dimension in the homoerotic painting, by Balthus. It shows a prepubescent girl lying across the knees of her music teacher whose hand is on her inner thigh just below her vulva while the eleven or twelve year old student reaches for the aroused breast of the teacher. The abandoned guitar, the clothes in disarray and the facial expression of the student "between misery and ecstasy - alarmed but also transfixed" informs us that "sex is naughty, pleasure and pain were coexistent...the state of arousal was close to the demonic." The words are those of critic Nicholas Fox Webber who writes in the *New Yorker* about this Modernist work, which is often considered pornographic.[28]

All the early phases of development, oral, anal and Oedipal, involve bisexual feelings, and these remain mostly unconscious. This is a look at Hillary's childhood and adolescent feelings, not an attempt to uncover a historical infatuation. Maybe these emotions were repressed and forgotten, or perhaps her unconscious presented them in disguised dreams or even in daytime questions like, "Do

I love Elisabeth? Does Elisabeth love me? What if Elisabeth was my mother?" The homosexual impulse often reflects the negative Oedipus complex beginning about age five when a rejection by the girl's father is accompanied by death wishes against him and a revival of the earlier love for the mother. Again this is an explanation of maturation, not a theory about female homosexuality. Here it seems to be a vehicle for Hillary's escape from her frustration in the unresolved Oedipal link to Hugh and Dorothy before her next important pubescent event, the appearance of Don Jones.

Don Jones was the new thirty year-old youth minister of Hillary's Methodist Church who arrived when she was thirteen. Don drove a fire-engine-red Impala convertible and played Dylan on the guitar. His views were those of Reinhold Niebuhr, the Protestant theologian who rejected religious fundamentalism, favored humility and placed the church in a struggle for social justice. But most important, Don Jones was a different kind of father because he was not a father-aggressor.

Don's emotional impact on Hillary's libido was to sublimate her teenage eroticism into art, theology and social concerns. Maybe she told her diary that she was in love with Don or pondered the question. Compliant Hillary, the teacher's pet, was to give way to the new argumentative Hillary. Today she has "...a temper you would not believe"[29] and that Hillary's staff is "terrified of her. Roger Morris says Hillary "...ate him (Bill) for breakfast" using the words of Bill's friend in Hot Springs.[30] She was elected to high school and college class offices, and by the late Eighties, she was mentioned as a candidate for governor of Arkansas to succeed Bill. But it was the thirteen-year-old Hillary who completed the transition from conformity to a controversial leader.

How does the feminist Oedipal Hillary differ from the Freudian Hillary? Hillary's basic gender identity is a response to her preoedipal mother and the security of this relationship was fertile for a transition to the Oedipal attachment to Hugh. Again Chodorow clarifies, "...women situate themselves psychologically as part of a relationship triangle in which their father and men are emotionally secondary, or at most, equal to their mother and women."[31] The relationship to father Hugh was not a threat to the relationship to mother Dorothy since Hillary was not a murderous rival; rather it was a part of family development.

The homosexual attraction to the teacher Elisabeth gives the preoedipal mother a new identity without Dorothy's defects such as her passivity in the face of Hugh's sadism and her aggression when she sent Hillary back to the Park Ridge streets to face the belligerent playmate.

Don Jones' arrival added to Hillary's experience of love for men, and so he amplified the Oedipal-Hugh attachment. Don showed Hillary and the other suburban teens the hidden and emotional world of art, politics and religion. They read e.e. Cummings, T. S. Eliot, and Stephen Crane and saw Picasso's *Guernica*, a mural about the Spanish Civil War. They met black and Hispanic youth including gang members from the inner city. Their projects included Bible study and baby-sitting for the Mexican migrant farm workers who lived west of Park Ridge. They went to hear Martin Luther King Jr. speak at Orchestra Hall in 1962 and afterward Hillary met him personally and shook his hand just as teenage Bill did with JFK in the Rose Garden. These are experiences of good and evil, the words, images and the passion of hell and heaven which revive the repressed, primal and unconscious forces of the Oedipal conflict.

Hillary's intellectual and religious stimulation in the long private sessions in Jones' office were a metaphor for and a reactivation of the sexuality of the Oedipal relationship. Were these new erotic feelings unconscious, conscious or even overt? Maybe all three. Thirty-five years later biographer Joyce Milton says that Don Jones's trips with Hillary and the other teens in his Impala made some parents "nervous" and then quotes Jones, now sixty-five who recalls that there was no "flirting" as though he knew the role of Eros in the minds of teen age girls.[32]

The Oedipal era with expressions like "I want to marry daddy," is typically is resolved at six and is followed by a latency period which lasts until puberty. Don Jones was the marker for earlier sexual events during the Oedipal period that Hillary may not recall or understand. Such events can be as ordinary as mutual genital manipulation while playing doctor with a younger brother or a sexual overture by an uncle or a cousin or even just hearing a story about this happening to a girlfriend.

The relationship with Jones was a visible token of her earlier Oedipal love for Hugh, which was not extinguished. The feminist psychoanalytic theory of Chodorow explains the female drama: the quality of a girl's sexuality is determined by her relationship with her mother.[33]

The mother's unconscious as well as her behavior are major factors in the psychological development of sexuality in girls. This cultural feminist explanation which begins with object relations theory contrasts to Freud's instinct-determined and biologically controlled Oedipus complex.

In addition to the psychocultural factors, women and men have different core biological identities from birth and earlier based on hormones, anatomy and the new findings about female-male brain differences. Freud's dismissive remark about women, "Anatomy is destiny,"[34] has come full circle with the discovery by psychoanalyst Robert Stoller that girls born without vaginas are fully female and feminine if their parents believe this.[35]

In the feminist psychoanalytic story, the resolution of the female Oedipus complex leads to a superego or conscience that is just as strong as that of the male in contradiction to Freud's view that it wasn't. But the content of the women's superego is different. It is more concerned with affectional and personal relationships and less with male abstracts and absolutes.

A feminist psychoanalyst Shahala Cherhrazi summarizes recent views about penis envy and women in 1986 so she is quoted directly.[36]

Over the past twenty years, research studies and substantial clinical material have provided new information regarding female psychology and development... The sociocultural attitudes and the phallocentric orientation that prevailed during Freud's time contributed to his theory of female psychology. The issue, however strong the possibilities for politicizing it are, is essentially a clinical one... The oversimplified and reductionistic interpretation of penis envy in the analysis of women often leads to a lowering of their self-esteem and an intensification of the neurotic image of themselves as deficient and damaged...

The girl's mental representation of her genitals at an early age (2-3) is less well established then a boy's at the same age, whose visible and protuberant genitals lead to a clearer mental representation. However, no matter how vague and incompletely defined the little girl's representation might be, it seems to reflect her awareness that she has "something there." That "something" is pleasurable and will later, under optimal conditions, become... highly valued... Furthermore, recent work suggests that early genital awareness is accompanied by an early or primary sense of femaleness. Core gender identity, an early (preoedipal) sense of femaleness or maleness is established by age two or three.

...the early theory emphasized what the little girl does not have rather then what she indeed has. If we reverse our focus, then it becomes evident that penis envy may be a phase-specific reaction since the little girl will soon come to value what she herself has, and relinquish the envy of what she does not have... Current views do not underestimate the trauma of observation of anatomical differences and penis envy, but they do suggest that at the time of its occurrence, the little girl already sees herself as a girl and has some awareness of her femaleness and her genitals. Her wish to have a penis, therefore, does not necessarily imply that she wants to be a boy, but that she wants a penis in addition to the vagina and clitoris she already has.

The factors that assist the reworking or attempted resolution of penis envy are: good enough relationship with the mother; awareness and appreciation of one's genitals; further cognitive development, which aids comprehension of the complex inner and outer genital; and most important, the resolution of the Oedipal conflicts, and identification with the mother...Current views reject a reductionistic equation of the wish for a baby with the wish for the penis. The wish for the baby can be seen prior to the penis envy reaction and is often an expression of identification with the mother, as well as inborn gender characteristics.

## HILLARY'S SADISM AND MASOCHISM

Sadism received its modern expression in the books by the Marquis Donation de Sade in the eighteenth-century while masochism appears in the nineteenth-century in the work of Leopold von Sacher-Masoch. Their names are used for sadism, pleasure derived from causing pain and for masochism, pleasure from suffering. Such behavior is ordinary and widespread and quite different from the exotic S and M of whips and chains.

Like a finch which has two songs, one for mating and another for territorial protection, traditional Freudian theory tells us that humans have two kinds of instincts or drives which originate in the unconscious: sexual instincts in the id and the survival or life instincts in the ego. An aspect of the life or survival instincts is aggression. These survival instincts are directed toward satisfying the need for food and shelter and are expressed by work. So in human behavior, work and love are everyone's conscious concerns which mirror the unconscious drives.

During childhood, the life instincts including aggression become sexualized while the sexual instincts are tinged with aggression. Freud says "...the two classes of instincts are fused, blended and mingled with each other..." so we enjoy the spectacle of love joined with death in *Romeo and Juliet* and in Verde's *Aida*. However, these instincts don't have free play because their expression is controlled by that part of the ego that represents both reality and parental rules, the conscience or superego where guilt is generated. I've returned to using instincts in describing the new feminist-Freudian theory of development because it's easier than its translation into the complexities of object relation's theory.

Sadism and masochism in which originate during the oral and anal phases of infantile development are altered by later experience. While the cruelty of sadism and the suffering of masochism appear to be separate in the person affected, they actually coexist, one overt and the other covert in a combination called sadomasochism.

Does Hillary's identification with Hugh's aggression lead to sadism?

Hillary's brother Tony says, "...my sister is tough as nails." But aggression is not sadistic which is cruelty or destructiveness experienced as sexually pleasurable. Hugh's aggressiveness toward Hillary can be called sadism, pleasure produced by causing pain, a mixture of Hugh's sexual and aggressive instincts. Hillary learned to play the victim role in Hugh's punishments followed by her rescue and solace. He taught her about life in visits to Chicago's skid row and the dark and dangerous Pennsylvania coal mines where he had worked. It was Hugh's implicit or explicit threat to leave her there that predetermined that he would rescue her, a frightening moral lesson from Mr. Reality Check. Hillary's identification with Hugh made this behavior her own so she became a sadist.

It is interesting to look at the Rodham family through the eyes of Helen Dowdy who married Hillary's cousin Oscar when she was sixteen and Hillary was fourteen. Helen, who was a frequent visitor in the Rodham home, says in Oppenheimer's book, " I wouldn't put anything past Hugh in terms of put-downs to anybody but Hillary...But the boys! Oh boy! That was a different story. I mean it was like night and day." A Park Ridge neighbor heard Hugh's booming voice, "yelling at the boys...Hughie and Tony" through the summers' open windows.[38] Grumpy Hugh's aggression was sadism on display and Hillary had learned to escape it and identify with it too. Sadism was learned by Hillary in a family process. Hugh didn't yell at Dorothy but there was an observable mutual antagonism between them. Subservient Dorothy called Hugh "an old fart" in one room while he watched television in the next room ignoring her complaints for years about fixing up their home.

Bill's names for Hillary include the dragon lady, Lady Macbeth[39], The Warden[40], Sarge and Hilla the Hun.[41] Her wrath is feared by her staff who are, "...intimidated she will fire them if they tell her the truth," according to interviewer Connie Bruck.[42]

In Arkansas, pitched battles raged at the Governor's mansion as Hillary screamed, "That sorry son of a bitch," when she woke to discover Bill was out "for a drive" at one a. m. according to the state troopers. As he arrived home, she shouted, "Where the fuck have you been?" Driving in a State limo with the First Couple was to see "...screaming quarrels and styrofoam cups, books, papers and keys thrown by Hillary." [43]

In the White House family quarters, Hillary continued to scream in her husband's beet-red face as a Secret Service agent saw her pick up a lamp and throw it at the President. These are reports from domestics, the Secret Service, Arkansas State troopers and other deep throats known to biographer Chris Andersen. Echoes of these events also appear in Milton's biography of Hillary and in Woodward's *Shadow*.

An objective observation about Hillary's sadism was made in April 1993 when Andersen tells us that the President appeared at a White House news conference with "a lurid two inch gash running from his right earlobe down his jaw line and a smaller cut on his neck...Press Secretary Dee Dee Myers ...reported that the President had cut himself shaving...later, the President offered a different explanation,  'I got hurt playing with my daughter, I'm ashamed to say...Rolling around acting like a child. I reaffirm I'm not a kid anymore.'"[44] Chelsea was thirteen and it seemed unlikely that she would be 'rolling around' with her father and that she could inadvertently inflict such a deep cut. Word had filtered down that the President and First Lady had another of their window rattling rows." Bill's masochism which complements Hillary's sadism is discussed later in Bill's Sadism and Masochism.

Hillary's sadistic impulses produce both pleasure and guilt. Her masochism is also experienced as painful and pleasurable. The two are part of the same emotion, sadomasochism. Her sadomasochism, like Hugh's is derived from aggression tinged with sexuality.  Although Hugh's sadism is a family legend, his masochism is only briefly visible in Hillary's account of his youthful prank when he broke his legs falling from a truck on which he was stealing a ride. [45]

Hillary defends herself and responds while she suffers as a victim of womanizing Bill, the sniping media and a hostile Congress. "Tough" Hillary retained the capacity to be hurt as explained by Robert Reich who saw her as a frightened rabbit when she came under attack during Bill's first term. (See Bill and Hillary in Group Process With Dick, Dolly, Gennifer and Robert)

The emotional energy for Hillary's aggression and sadism comes from the identification with Hugh as aggressor and sadist, but not entirely because we've heard about how Passive Mother Dorothy was "tough" too. Are Hillary's frustrations with Bill, the media, the Congress and her critics justified? Of course, but the psychological question is really how and why do aggression and sadomasochism play such a prominent role in her responses?

The Rodham marriage was a straightforward model of the fifties: a dominant husband and a stay at home, repressed wife. Passive Mother Dorothy says in Judith Warner's book that this was her "...accepted role...being afraid to say what was on her mind."[46] Hugh was called Mr. Difficult by Dorothy, and biographer Morris describes Hillary's home as one of "quiet cruelty and pain...warmth and vitriol...compassion and sarcasm..."[47] All this qualifies Hugh as a sadist and Dorothy as a masochist as their behavior is used to indicate the state of their unconscious minds.

Dorothy herself was a childhood victim of abuse by her own teenage parents. When they separated, she was sent alone by train at eight from Chicago to Los Angeles with her three year old sister to live with her paternal grandparents. Her grandparents were themselves so rejecting that she left at fourteen to work as

14

a babysitter with another family in order to finish high school.

Dorothy's sending Hillary back to the street in Park Ridge after she was attacked by another toddler is a variant of normal parental behavior, but perhaps it is also an indication of normal unconscious sadism. Daddy Hugh reassured little Hillary that although she might murder someone, he would still love her though he would disapprove of her act. The unconscious mind which is revealed in play and games here speaks of Hillary as the sadist and Hugh as the masochist.

Is masochism characteristic of women as Freud and his followers tell us or is there another view?

Masochism as characteristic of women is an argument between the Freudians and the feminists. Freud and his followers explained masochism and passivity in women as biologically determined with their origins in childbirth and motherhood. Today, feminist analyst Schad-Somers, who rejects the instinct theory of masochism, still finds that masochism is intrinsically female because of our culture, which depreciates women, while sadism is the male expression of a ubiquitous sadomasochism.[48] But the debate goes on and feminist psychotherapist Charlotte Prozan argues against the universality of women's masochism.[49]

## HILLARY'S MORAL MASOCHISM AND THE MONICA LEWINSKY PORNO FLICK

The issue of Hillary's masochism is reopened by James Bennet of the *New York Times* in "First lady backs up her man, once again"[50] as he reports her response to the Monica Lewinsky eruption (perhaps it should be called the Bubba emission). He says that "Hillary's just fine." We are told that Hillary "clearly had no illusions about Mr. Clinton's faithfulness" and now she is "in battle mode" as she was during the Gennifer Flowers expose. The "poor Hillary" mantra resumes later as Chris Andersen reports[51] her eyes as red and swollen from crying after Bill's grand jury testimony about Monica.

Arianna Huffington labels Hillary "enabler-in-chief" holding her responsible for Bill's eruption with Monica. It is worth clarifying that "enabler" is from the nomenclature of a Twelve Step program because columnist Arianna judges Bill to need membership in Sex Addicts Anonymous. Biographer Sheehy also calls Hillary is an enabler.

The prototype of masochism is the need to be beaten to achieve a sexual climax with the connection between the pain and the pleasure hidden in the unconscious. Another frequent kind of masochism is moral masochism where it is humiliation and failure in life that produces both the suffering and the unconscious pleasure. These are victims who bemoan their fate as martyrs: she says she is doing it for her marriage, the family and the children, and he says he can't let down his buddies, the company or the cause. The ego is besieged with guilt from a punishing superego or conscience and the solution to this dilemma is to be punished by life.

Nowadays, like Arianna, we are familiar with the enabler or co-dependent as a moral masochist who despairs but also facilitates the addiction of a spouse to violence, alcohol, drugs, gambling or casual sex. Like the chords in the blues, family themes are repetitive, so we recall that Bill's mother Virginia was an enabler for her husband Roger's alcoholism as Bill was growing up. So too, Mother Dorothy was an enabler for Daddy Hugh's cruelty. Masochism, including moral masochism, begins during personality formation in infancy and childhood when sexuality becomes linked with pain and suffering.

The question of Hillary's moral masochism goes beyond just her defense of an erring husband by a loyal wife. This kind of masochism involves Hillary's unconscious enjoyment of Bill's misbehavior.

The counterpoint of Hillary's suffering is in the innuendoes. She complains to Bill, " Look...I need to be fucked more than twice a year."[52] " Gennifer Flowers says Bill told her during their relationship that Hillary didn't enjoy sex and anyway Hillary was a lesbian, so Bill was frustrated.[53] Journalists report the gossip and some details about Hillary's ill-fated affair with her Little Rock law partner Vincent Foster, who committed suicide while he was a White House counsel. These emotions and events don't cause a masochism that began in infancy and childhood but they may channel its expression.

Beneath the level of reality in the secret recess of Hillary's mind, is her unconscious, where bittersweet dreams and fantasies are the response to Bill's affairs with Monica and the others. Hillary first denies the events, and then she sees them and next there is a kind of mental participation in them before she flashes back to real life and begins the battle to survive. This is a hypothesis but it is as plausible as a wife with an alcoholic husband who first looks the other way, then excuses him perhaps with compassion and finally picks up the pieces when he boozes again. You decide. The moral masochism is there.

The question is how much pleasure can there be for a serious, rational, religious woman in her husband's love affairs, some lurid and public but most only known by gossip. Her masochistic gratification is more complicated than the simple portraits in the media. Horror, anger, anxiety, dismay and fascination follow the infidelities during the Monica affair. The outward Hillary was observed by the New Yorker's Joe Klein as radiant with a roseate glow in a canary-yellow suit in the midst of the Monica affair while during the 1992 Flowers scandal she was "dressed to the nines." [54]

Does Hillary's mind create a threesome, a porno flick with her, Monica and Bill? That idea is not necessary to this argument about her moral masochism but it is illuminating. Masochism is a "radical aesthetic practice," according to postmodern critic Mansfield[55] while psychoanalyst Ross writing about *The Sadomasochism of Everyday Life* points out our fascination with the Bobbits, the Menendez Brothers, Tonya Harding and O. J. Simpson. I'd add JonBenet Ramsey and the Clintons.

What happened to Hillary to cause the moral masochism? The answer to this complex question goes back to the Oedipal guilt she feels about her desire for Daddy Hugh and her hatred for her rival, Dorothy. This traditional Freudian view is complementary to the newer feminist explanation of development where the attachment of a girl for her mother is primary and is the vehicle for her love for the father and other men. A feminist view postulates guilt both about Hillary's hate for Hugh, who has rejected the demands of her childish sexual love and her hate for Dorothy's excessive demands for control. This alternative hypothesis doesn't see Dorothy and Hillary as rivals for Hugh, but the causes of moral masochism are still there.

These explanations are about Hillary's emotional development going awry and laying the groundwork for moral masochism. Onto this fertile soil falls guilt about the homosexual feelings for the teacher and also the sexual response to Don Jones, the youth minister. Despite her powerful sublimations and active conscious outlets, her nihilistic feelings are masochistic, and so are her reactions of guilt and shame. The most direct evidence about her nihilism is her predominately negative feeling about herself and the world in her own words as explained in the next section of this essay.

## HILLARY'S ORAL AND ANAL DEVELOPMENT

The formation of character begins during the first year of life with the oral stage when milk from the breast or bottle and a mother's love are required for physical survival and growth. The explanations of disturbances in the oral stage involve overindulgence or deprivation.

Food is the first symbol of trust, so orality, the first of the Freudian stages of development, is described by Erik Erickson as producing a person's Basic Trust while an impairment during this phase leads to Basic Mistrust. These are the responses during the infant's first six months of passive incorporation or sucking followed by the second half of the first year with its more active incorporation process of biting. The predominance of Basic Trust leads to a character with oral optimism while Basic Mistrust results in oral pessimism. Erickson explains, "Whenever oral pessimism becomes dominant and exclusive, infantile fears...can be discerned in the depressive forms of 'being empty' and 'being no good'...which in psychoanalysis is called 'oral sadism,' a cruel need to take and get in ways harmful to others."[56]

Hillary's mind still exemplifies this lack of trust. There is a catalog of oral pessimism in the words of her *Village* book:  bone disease, bombing, sexism, misogyny, suicide, a distraught baby, powerlessness, skid row, death, math anxiety, hurry, a frightened grandmother, delinquency, accidents, desperation, difficult children, suffering, divorce, shortcomings, sexual abuse, a sharp tongue, parental indifference, a cold house, cowardice, teen drinking and smoking and drug abuse, teen pregnancy, murder, violence, fainting and the list goes on. The list of positives is much shorter and less graphic: sports, work, opportunities, support, discipline, guidance, love, prayer, parenthood and village. The question isn't what Hillary thinks or says about children, but how she says it.  Yes, this is an invasive and involuntary method, but it was Hillary who said, "I'm a Rorschach test." [57]

The anal stage is described by Erickson as Autonomy versus Shame and Doubt when he discusses the consequences of bowel and bladder training and the increased muscular coordination and activity.[58]  Conflicts about elimination and self-control in two and three year-olds may lead to anal fixation resulting in a person who is stingy, stubborn, compulsive, acquisitive and controlling. Control and perfection are the keys to Hillary's character like that of her parents, who are also controlling and perfectionistic. The list of words from Hillary's book illustrates the conflicts about this phase as well. Most of the words are in the category of Shame and Doubt while only a few reflect Autonomy. There is more information on Hillary's anal stage later in Hillary and Money.

The first stage of the anal phase begins with "the half liquid evacuations of the infant (causing) the first intense excitations of the anal zone.... The bowel movements and constipation, flatulence, diarrhea ...create ... a pleasurable desire at the anal zone," according to Richard Sterba who was one of Freud's original circle. He continues,  "Grown-up people, if they are honest enough to admit it, know and enjoy the sensual pleasure brought about by the passage of a large stool of a stick-like form...In the second phase of the anal period ...the chief pleasure is no longer experienced at the passage of the stool but in holding it back.... the stool even when evacuated, is regarded as an enormously important and valuable object.... extended to all the child's possessions..."[59]

A less ebullient phantasy of the anal stage appears in Kiki Smith's piece, Tale seen recently in an art show at the Whitney reviewing the twentieth century. This is a construction in which a naked woman who is crawling away from the viewer on all fours is trailed by a very long turd emerging from her anus. This picture is a contrast to the ultra clean and orderly Martha Stewart image as a cultural reaction-formation to the soiling of the anal stage. (Reaction-formation which involves turning an emotion into its opposite is discussed in the next section.)

18

## HILLARY'S EGO DEFENSES

An understanding of Hillary's behavior calls for an exploration of her ego defenses which are the way of regulating the three realms of the developing personality. First, there is the id or the primitive force of the aggressive and lustful unconscious instincts where Freud's Pleasure Principle prevails. Here the attempt is to maximize pleasure and decrease pain. This realm is the libido or the sexual energy. Second, a partly conscious ego uses the Reality Principle to balance the conflicting demands of external reality such as parents and society with the pleasure seeking id and a censorious superego. This is the province of reason. Third, the conscience or superego is often in conflict with id impulses and also with the demands of reality. More about the superego later but it is here that the sense of right and wrong uses guilt to control behavior.

The similarity to Plato's portrait of a tripartite mind is striking, "...her form is like a pair of winged steeds with their charioteer. In divine souls both steeds are good but in human souls one of them is bad..."[60] So the Athens of the Fourth Century B.C. anticipates the ego, super ego and the id.

The clash between the forces of the id, superego and reality produces anxiety and depression. The ego makes compromises using behavior called ego defenses often abbreviated to defenses to deal with the anxiety and depression from the conflict between id, the superego and reality. These defenses determine the strength of character. If they are solid, adaptable and work well, the personality is strong and healthy. If they are leaky and fragile, the person is anxious, fearful and depressed and maybe neurotic.

It is when a defense fails as a result of stress that depression and fear invade consciousness as in a neurosis. When repression is unable to control disturbing memories and impulses by keeping them in the unconscious, the result is that a person's emotions spin out of control. The defenses themselves can become a problem if they are in excess like denial which can produce a blind spot about danger in the environment.

Understanding Hillary's behavior leads to a study of her ego mechanisms of defense, which determine her actions, style, habits and her foibles. Her physical and emotional development, intelligence, traumas, parental and adult influences, social milieu and genetics all converge in the formation of these defenses.

Some of Hillary's defenses are best described in her own words from her books, speeches and interviews. Of course, her defenses don't explain all of Hillary's behavior.

*Repression*, the fundamental defense of the ego is the banishing of memories, feelings and ideas from the conscious into the unconscious where they remain excluded from awareness. This is a prominent mechanism for Hillary where it is based on the exclusion from her consciousness of her feelings of

Oedipal love toward Daddy Hugh as a sadistic lover and also the emotions about Mother Dorothy's inability to offer protection from him. This is a message from her *Village* book, "My strong feelings about divorce and its effects on children have caused me to bite my tongue more then a few times during my own marriage and to think about what I could do to be a better wife and partner." [61] This is a metaphor from her adult awareness about the process of repression.

*Denial* is a frequent defense which affects the perception of reality so that what is happening is not seen, heard or acknowledged. Anxiety is the trigger for denial and also for the other defenses.

"She had to know," is an observation by a Little Rock local about Bill's long and unconcealed affair with Gennifer Flowers while he was Governor.[62] Another example of denial is seen when Hillary stopped reading the newspapers in 1994 during the Whitewater accusations, according to Bob Woodward. Hillary spoke of denial metaphorically when she said to a television interviewer that what she and Bill did first in the morning when they awoke in the White House was, "Pull the covers over our head."[63] Other words of denial were, "I don't read what people mostly say about me."[64] Hillary's White House staff was under strict orders to sanitize their daily news digests, that is no sex, tabloid gossip and nothing about the Lewinsky scandal according to Anderson.[65] Denial grew in Hillary as a child who used it to avoid recognition of the events of her family's sadomasochism and its Oedipal drama. Clinton biographer David Maraniss says, "When it comes to Clinton and sex, she knew but she didn't want to know."[66] It was Hillary's denial that lead eventually led to Bill's impeachment when his attorneys "... favored settling with Paula Jones, but the First Lady wouldn't have it," according to Gail Sheehy.[67] (See *Hillary's Burden* for more details about this matter.)

*Projection* is an unconscious mechanism in which a person attributes to another person the ideas or feelings that are unacceptable to her. Frequent and intense projection is called paranoid and the ideas and emotions are closely guarded secrets. Hillary says, "If someone has a female boss for the first time, maybe they can't take out their hostility on her, so they take it out on me."[68]

Hillary is said by biographer Joyce Milton to have fired Barbara Feinman who worked on her *Village* book because she thought this writer had violated the secrecy about her séances with Eleanor Roosevelt and leaked the story to journalist Bob Woodward who then wrote about them.[69]

Hillary was the one who described Starr's investigation of the Lewinsky affair as part of a vast right-wing conspiracy. Latter it was David Brock, who exposed this conspiracy by multimillionaire Richard Mellon Scaife in a 1997 article in *Esquire*[70] and then in a book, *Blinded By The Right*. Paranoids have real enemies too.

Hillary often warned Bill against trusting people, saying, "Bill, don't be such a fucking Pollyanna. Some of these people you think are your friends aren't," are the words quoted by Chris Andersen from Bill's 1980 Arkansas gubernatorial campaign.[71]

It was Hillary's projection and her paranoid secrecy that led White House attorney Lanny Davis to speculate, "... that the whole chain of events that led to the Whitewater investigations, then led to Ken Starr, which led to the investigation of Monica and finally to the impeachment can be traced back to the Jeff Gerth, *New York Times* Whitewater story and Hillary's)... first instinct - to lock down." Later Jane Sherburne, Hillary's attorney, explained these events saying, "A lot of Hillary's reaction originated with that very private nature..."[72] The tortuous path of these events allows a glimpse into Hillary's unconscious.

Hillary's love affair with secrecy affected the planning phase of her health care proposal leading to its poor reception by Congress and the media, and so was a factor in its rejection. Hillary's approach to the obstacles of selling her health legislation was paranoid in its intensity. There is more about Hillary's failed health plan in *Hillary's Burden*.

As I read Hillary's *Living History*, it is the loss of her privacy that is the worst consequence of Bill's adultery with Monica.[73] Her preoccupation with secrecy/privacy is described in the section on Chelsea as Orphan and Hillary as Mother where it is called scotoptophilia.

*Isolation* is the splitting or the separation of emotion from an idea causing either the emotion or the idea to be repressed into the unconscious. "Hillary can separate personal emotions from the goal and task ahead in a way few women can,"[74] her friend Betsey Wright says to author Connie Bruck. Another example of isolation is when little Hillary asked Daddy Hugh, "Do you mean if I murdered somebody, you'd still love me? And he'd say, 'Yes, I would not approve of what you did...but I will always love you,' " according to biographer Radcliffe.[75]

*Intellectualization* is a mechanism of defense which substitutes words and ideas for feelings as a way of controlling unacceptable impulses. Hillary explains, "The idea that I would check my brain at the White House door just doesn't make sense to me."[76]

*Sublimation* is a defense in which socially unacceptable impulses from the unconscious are replaced by desirable goals. Serving the need of others and religious beliefs are solutions of the id-ego-superego conflicts. Destructive unconscious impulses are replaced by acceptable goals, compassion, religion and serving others. "I have a burning desire to do what I can, a desire to make the world around me...better for everybody," are Hillary's words.[77]

*Reaction Formation*, defined as turning an unacceptable impulse into its opposite, is one of Hillary's psychological defenses. Hillary's anger became manipulativeness and charm as she lunched and courted the editor of the Arkansas

Democrat in Little Rock in order to deflect his "nasty" criticisms of Governor Clinton. It worked according to Connie Bruck.[78]

*Identification With the Aggressor* is an ego defense involving Hillary's identification with gruff Daddy Hugh's psychological abusiveness so that she became "tough as nails" according to her brother.[79] Hillary says, "The harder they hit, the more encouraged I get."[80] Hillary's own staff are "...scared to death..." of her according to Connie Bruck.[81]

"She (Hillary) was a thrower - big time," of staplers, files and pens directed at Bill in the state limo during their quarrels about Bill's affairs, says a Arkansas state trooper who drove them. These attacks which were "...always initiated..." by Hillary, continued in the White House, according to Secret Service sources used by biographer Christopher Andersen.[82]

The aggressive Hillary appears during Travelgate according to White House aide David Watkins, who said, "...There would be hell to pay if we failed to take swift and decisive action in conformity with the first lady's wishes." Hillary is recalled as saying, "We need those people out. `We need to get our people in," speaking about the White House travel staff.[83]


## FRIGID HILLARY / SEXUAL HILLARY / BISEXUAL HILLARY / LESBIAN HILLARY

The Sister Frigidaire image from the high school newspaper opens a door on Hillary's frigid character. The formation of character is specially influenced by the forces of the sexual and aggressive unconscious instincts, which press the ego for gratification. Hillary's aggressive and sexual drives were unacceptable to her external reality and her conscience. The reaction is frigidity but this is more then just a defense because the character itself is altered in the interest of harmony within the ego. Hillary's mother, who didn't have "tizzies" also repressed her emotions. Hillary's solution was the development of the type of frigidity of character described in Otto Fenichel's *The Psychoanalytic Theory of Neurosis*.[84] Hillary alternates between her charisma and the icy nun image.

I watched Hillary's television biography and the 1992 Inauguration video that show her smiles alternating with visible coldness when her affect is contrasted to the emotions of Tipper Gore or Barbara Bush. It's like contrasting the affect or emotional tone of Al Gore, usually rigid and distant compared to that of Bill Clinton, predominately cuddly and warm. Novelist Erica Jong, a Hillary admirer and feminist writing in the *Nation* says Hillary is "...cold and too controlled...she gives off an aura of discipline and ferocious tenacity..."[85] Another feminist, Robin Lakoff, who studies language, finds Hillary's image in the mysterious, predatory and enigmatic Sphinx, a she-monster with the head of a woman and the body of a lion who silences and then consumes the men who confront her.[86]

Hillary, who dated in high school and college, had her first serious romance that lasted from her junior year at Wellesley to her sophomore year at Yale Law School with a student who appears as a " handsome black Irishman" in the Sheehy book.[87]    Like her, he was an upper middle class WASP, a northerner with Christian values, whom she met because they were both active in Republican student politics. They broke up after an intense relationship because he sought his future in the grass roots nonprofit world rejecting Hillary's sphere of power and politics.  Hillary was already a star as a class president, pictured in *Life*[88] magazine after her Wellesley commencement speech and then an activist at the Yale Law School.   Rupert is quoted on his physical attraction to Hillary and their satisfying sex life.  This was during the era when she went from a Young Republican attending the convention that nominated Richard Nixon (she favored Nelson Rockefeller) in 1968 to an interest in Chicago radical Saul Alinsky's community organizing and the Black Panther Party.  Her style had gone from pleated skirts and blouses to the bell-bottoms of the counterculture, and Rupert says they inhaled. Other college boyfriends are mentioned in passing but the Rupert melodrama is his kiss and tell entry into the Hillary story.  If one were to ask Hillary now, she may smile as she recalls a hunk who lacked Bill's ambition to be President.

Hillary's love life with Bill does not fulfill the intimacy of the sexy photos of their beach revel as they danced cheek to cheek in swim suits on a vacation during the Lewinsky crisis in 1998 or by their periodic hand holding.  Less rather then more is Chris Andersen's view of their sex life when he says, "...the Clintons had not shared the same bedroom - much less the same bed - for at least seven years."[89]

Maybe Hillary loves Bill and Bill loves Hillary (see the Sadomasochistic Marriage for details) but Hillary is heard to complain that she "gets laid only twice a year."  Bill's Good and Bad Women explains how Hillary went from the exciting Whore to the forbidding Madonna. Bill's failing erections are an issue too as explained later on in Bill as Impotent.

The question of Hillary's love interest in women has a psychohistorical importance whether it is true or not. Her image and behavior, her persona and the stereotypes about strong women call forth this issue, often as an accusation. There is a parallel to a rumor of Bill's homosexuality at twenty-eight when he ran unsuccessfully for Congress in Arkansas. Hillary campaigned with him during this hard fought race, and a rumor about her homosexuality also circulated during this election. In 1978 after Bill was elected Governor, there was talk that Nancy "Peach" Pietrafesa was Hillary's lover. This was a friend from her twenties in New England who went to Arkansas with her husband to work in the new Clinton administration.

Gennifer Flowers says Hillary is a lesbian in her book quoting Bill during their affair that ended in 1992. In 1996 Dick Morris, a friend of both the Clintons mentions Hillary as lesbian in a radio interview after he left the White House disgraced by his own sex scandal. During Hillary's Senate campaign, the tabloid *Globe* found a 1987 unauthenticated "kinky 3-way sex video" showing Hillary, Vince Foster and another woman.[90]

Hillary's longstanding lover is a woman who is a dean at an eastern university, I hear from the lesbian network who say this with gay pride.[91] A similar rumor in Jerry Oppenheimer's book is attributed to Mandy Merck, a lesbian and radical feminist and Bill's friend from his Oxford days, when she visited the United States in 1999.[92] As with Eleanor Roosevelt, the persistence and multiple sources of the lesbian issue make it a part of the psychohistorical equation.

Hillary watchers at the millennium continue the public speculation about her sexuality. Tom Junod says in *Esquire* that she has a "lewd laugh...a sexy mouth," and he asks if the men on the Senate campaign trail want to "do her."[93] He answers "yes" for himself, the mayor of Albany and the retiring New York Senator Daniel Moynihan. When Hollywood 's superstar Julia Roberts was asked by *Us Weekly*, "If you had to had to have sex with one girl, whom would it be with? The reply was, "Hillary Clinton 'cause I don't think she's getting her fair share."[94]

What can the known science about bisexuality tell us about a sexually ambiguous Hillary? Bisexuality as a potential in normal development was an early Freudian dictum that is widely accepted. Like a number of Freud's discoveries, it was foreshadowed by other students of human sexuality including Kraft-Ebing and Haverlock Ellis, but it remained a static idea until Freud explained the plasticity of infantile psychosexual development. It was Freud's discovery of infantile sexuality during the study of the unconscious, which explained how the different sexual identities come about.

Gender bending images appear in the Hillary jokes.

Why won't Hillary wear miniskirts?
She doesn't want us to see her balls.

What does Hillary do after she shaves her pussy?
Sends him to work in the Oval Office to work.

Gender words about Hillary call her "...hard ....direct ...precise ...controlled ...nonspontaneous ...cold ...impersonal ..." Her hair is "...helmet-like... clothes define her boundaries..." Those comments stand in contrast to Bill, who is described as "...soft ....intuitive... warm... caring... worries about his weight...he has fuzzy outlines...frizzy hair..." according to the linguistic analysis of Lakoff. The gender identity words used about Hillary are stereotypically masculine while the language about Bill uses female images.

There are few tools to measure gender identity like a verifiable scale of feminity and masculinity, so a linguistic commentary is helpful. There is little correlation between biological sexuality and gender identity: there are femme lesbians and femme straights and butch lesbians and butch straights, and their combinations and permutations are endless.

There are many unanswered questions in the study of sexual behavior, sexual preference and sexual identity, so we all wait impatiently for answers. But these sexual puzzles are also about nature-nurture and mind-body, so the explanations require research in genetics, biology, medicine and the social sciences as well as psychology.

Bisexual behavior is common so that 28% of women (50% for men) have homosexual responses, while 13% of women (37% for men) have homosexual orgasms at some time during their life according to Kinsey's work, which began in the Forties.[95] These studies of bisexuality have not been repeated although it is likely that these numbers would be larger today. In the Nineties, an encyclopedia of sexuality edited by Francoer summarizes several studies to conclude that 9% of women (10% for men) are entirely or mainly homosexual although half of the homosexual women have some heterosexual activity.[96]

The mainstream view is that a person's sexual orientation is either homosexual or heterosexual as the result of genes. This explanation is frequently amended by noting the influence of psychosexual development, the family and the environment. This common description is often correct, but it may be incomplete. Dividing people into gay or straight is confusing because some people change their overall orientation in the short term or the long term, or they do not limit themselves to partners of one sex. In fact recent biographies say that heterosexual Kinsey himself also had homosexual experiences.[97] Bisexuality is absent from the mainstream Western religions of the Jews, Christians and Muslims, but it survives in their folk and esoteric roots. In the Pantheon Zeus and Hera were sometimes bisexual; Dionysus celebrated androgyny, and the divine-seer Tiresais lived as both a woman and a man. In Hindu cosmology, Nirrtti is both male and female.

The milestones of a women's sexuality are menarche, her erotic life, pregnancy, mothering and menopause, although for some Jungians defloration is among the markers. Motherhood is a major marker of sexuality for the Freudians, who see a baby as fulfilling the woman's Oedipal need for the penis. As noted earlier in Hillary's Oedipus Meets Feminist Theory, the Freudian analyst Shahala

Chehrazi reports that the girl's wish for a baby represents her identification with her mother based on psychoanalytic observations of adults and children as well as recent studies of child development. Female identity is established in infants between two and three years and their occasional penis envy is a secondary reaction.

Marriage, pregnancy and motherhood are the traditional Freudian norms but feminist Hillary speaks for the sisterhood when she elaborates the today's wider options,"...women...who choose not to marry, or who married and choose not to have children, or who married and then divorced, or who had children on their own." Thirty years after the graduation of Hillary's Wellesley class of '69, journalist Miriam Horn found that 5% were traditional homemakers, 88% had married, one in three who married had divorced, one in three of the married women had been unfaithful, 23% were childless and one out of three had inactive or disappointing sex lives.[98]


## HILLARY AND MONEY

Hillary's Adult Oedipal theater performance in Little Rock was fourteen years as the new Queen, the law partner and First Lady of Arkansas, earning the family income while King Bill governed and philandered.  Bill was able to run for Attorney General in 1976 because they had Hillary's $18,000 law school salary to support them. They moved to Little Rock in 1977 from Fayetteville, where they were law professors after Bill was elected Attorney General, a post that only paid $6000 a year. Later the state salaries were raised and the Attorney General's salary was $22,500.  In Little Rock Hillary chose the Rose Law Firm, a conservative partnership serving primarily corporate clients. The less lucrative socially activist options of family law, consumer representation and criminal defense were rejected.

Governor Bill's salary remained $35,000 while Hillary's income from law rose from $46,000 to $98,000 during the 1980's while their additional income was over $100,000 a year according to Roger Morris. This was primarily from Hillary's investments including commodity trading, and her annual compensation for serving on corporate boards ranging from $15,000 for Wal-mart to the Lafarge Corporation at $31,000.

Hillary's investment profits began in 1978 with $98,540 from trading cattle futures, a 10,000 per cent profit in nine months on her original investment of one thousand dollars. Such a profit from this complicated series of trades without insider assistance is a one in two hundred and fifty million probability according to the economists who analyzed her account. She closed this account when she was pregnant with Chelsea, but a year later in a new commodity account Hillary made $6500 on a $5,000 investment. A $2014 investment in a cell-phone franchise in 1983 paid Hillary $45,998 when it was sold in 1988 according to Roger Morris.[99] By 1992 the Clinton's net worth was $931,000 in cash and bonds according to Chris Andersen.[100]

She was motivated to make investments, as a child by Daddy Hugh with whom she played investment games after he taught her to read the stock market tables in the newspaper. Hillary's investments and her commodity trades were her own initiative although her contacts with brokers and land developers were through Governor Bill.

The broker who handled Hillary's commodity account was a former Tyson executive whom she met through a Tyson attorney. Tyson Foods, an Arkansas institution and major polluter has been described as the largest family owned chicken farm in the world.[101] Meanwhile Hillary railed against "the unacceptable acquiescence in greed that occurred during the 1980's," according to Bob Woodward in *The Agenda*.[102] To dismiss her comment as insincere or contradictory is to ignore the anal compulsive Hillary who uses the defenses of isolation and intellectualization.

Bill showed less interest in investing leaving this activity to Hillary. He accepted her decisions about real estate developments like Whitewater, which lost money and by 1994 was the subject of an ongoing investigation by the Special Counsel. The contrast was between an organized Hillary and Bill who "...couldn't keep a checkbook...never paid his ...electric bill or his phone bill," according to Mary Fray, a manager during his 1974 congressional race.[103]

Day to day, Bill was so generally indifferent to money that often he didn't carry any, and an aide or a state trooper paid for soft drinks and incidentals as he traveled about the state. His friends say that Bill's style rarely included picking up a check in a restaurant or bar. An exception to Bill's disinterest in money was a profitable investment Bill made in 1977 when he was Attorney General with real estate developer Jim McDougal according to Brock who calls it a preview to Whitewater. After his presidency Bill earned millions of dollars for a book advance and speeches. (See Bill as Scapegoat in Perpetuity)

Bill and Hillary were both power and policy people, but Bill wanted to be liked, so he charmed and governed while Hillary practiced law and served on non-profit and corporate committees and boards. Hillary was like Daddy Hugh, who managed the family's financial affairs while Bill looked to Hillary to arrange money matters as his mother Virginia had done. Virginia had taken this job over as soon as she had discovered that husband Roger was unreliable as a drinker and gambler. Virginia, the nurse-anesthetist and Hillary, the attorney and were the strong earners and money managers while stepfather Roger who worked at his brother's Buick dealership, and Bill, the governor were weaker.

Hillary's creation of most of the family's income and savings is an aspect of the anal compulsive Hillary, a trait which results in her obsessive compulsive personality. She doesn't have an obsessive hand washing compulsion but she pursues her goals in a repetitive and tenacious way. This kind of compulsion is true of most parents about their children, most attorneys about their cases and all candidates about elections. But Hillary's style is a contrast to Bill's more relaxed way about Chelsea, his legal cases as Attorney General and even his elections. Hillary is a bulldog while Bill is an actor. Diversity encourages both life styles but these are observations not a beauty contest. Freud offers an explanation in Dirty Hillary and Clean Hillary.

Just as sex is Bill's Achilles' heel, so money is Hillary's. The legend is that Achilles' nurse dipped him in the water of the river Styx making him invulnerable everywhere except in the part of the heel by which she held him.

## DIRTY HILLARY AND CLEAN HILLARY

Freud's 1908 essay, "Character and Anal Eroticism" talks about orderly, obstinate and parsimonious traits which define the anal or compulsive character.[104] Obstinacy and parsimony are the most important in this definition but Hillary shares all three.

Orderliness and its cognates, cleanliness, reliability, conscientiousness, perfectionism and caution develop in the child as a response to the soiling experience during toilet training. Cleanliness can be understood as sublimation, an acceptable expression of "forgotten" or repressed infantile behavior. Hillary "...was an extremely - at times maddeningly - cautious candidate..."[105] as described by journalist Michael Tomsky. Her orderliness, reliability, perfectionism and conscientiousness are Hillary legends.

Her cleanliness expresses itself in the makeovers, makeup and hair styling as First lady in Arkansas after Bill's first term then later in Washington. This was a reaction formation to the many years that her hair was greasy, stringy and lacked any style according to observers like Bill's mother Virginia, Bill's lover Dolly Browning and Arkansas political campaigner Mary Fray.

Hillary's aversion to makeup during her teens, twenties and thirties also was a reaction formation noticed by both Hillary's mother and later Bill's mother. At the Rose Law Firm, Hillary's reaction formation was observed by the secretaries who noticed that she didn't pluck her eyebrows and sometimes she wore jeans or orange slacks in the office.

Hillary as Furry Freak vanished with the Makeover after Bill's loss of the governorship in 1980 so with the next gubernatorial campaign which began almost immediately, Hillary became a butterfly instead of caterpillar. The

Makeover included becoming Mrs. Clinton instead of Hillary Rodham and the '82 election campaign included baby Chelsea, who was born February 27, 1980. Hillary used makeup and lost weight "... wore her hair straight, lightened it, held it in place with a headband and began wearing contact lenses and knit power-suits...(and) adopted a phony southern accent..." according to Brock.[106] After Bill was reelected Governor in 1982, it wasn't long before she began campaigning in her new persona for Arkansas education reform by conducting hearings in every county.

While Bill was out of office, he was depressed; they lived in a modest house; Bill had a law firm sinecure and Maraniss says he talked of divorce. Hillary was able to organize his return to the governorship and so save the family. She was at the crossroads and had returned to active church going. Betsey Wright and Dick Morris were brought to Little Rock by Hillary to prepare for the next election. And she consulted a private detective about Bill's extramarital affairs that included a secretary at the Rose Law Firm where she had just been made a partner in 1979.

These are the conscious events and the motives for the Makeover. What were the unconscious consequences of the Makeover? Chelsea came to embody Hillary as the slob who affronted both Daddy Hugh's establishment and Mother Dorothy's passive resistance. It's a frequent psychological observation that behavior from a parent's childhood like bedwetting reemerges in a child. To Freudians this is the return of the repressed because behavior committed to the adult's unconscious reemerges in the child, while Nonfreudian psychologists see this as a kind of social heredity. Chelsea as the ugly duckling was Hillary redux.

Does anyone doubt that the choices and reactions about style, hair, persona and makeovers are both communal and personal as well as conscious and unconscious?

Reaction formation is one of Hillary's defense mechanisms mentioned earlier, which involves the turning of an unacceptable infantile impulse into an acceptable substitute. This reduces anxiety and keeps ego, id, superego and reality in balance. The infantile anal erotic wish, "I want to be dirty" becomes, "I want to be super clean." But Hillary's orderliness was balanced  by the opposite impulses, toward the counterculture with its utopian political goals and its unkempt hair and torn jeans. The cultural and the individual are woof and warp.

When the Clintons left the White House, it was trashed by lewd graffiti, the W's removed from computer keyboards, phone lines slashed and desks overturned according to some newspapers. Soon afterward, the General Services Administration said that there was no more damage then after the departure of any long-term tenant. But six months later, the Bush administration admitted there had been "vandalism" and historically minded writers recalled that in 1992 when

George Bush I left the White House,  telephones were glued to the desks.

What does this have to do with Hillary's anal complexes, perfectionism and messiness? (See Bill's Oral and Anal Development about his anality.) White House staff behavior reflects the impulses, conscious and unconscious of the President and First Lady, preppy for Barbara and George I and hippy with Hillary and Bill.  Both these administrations had issues about anality, and so do all the other Americans who are both tangled and tidy.  Housekeeping at the Clintons' White House at the end of their administration is not a measure of their nature or their politics, but it has a kind of Freudian accountability - a glimpse into their unconscious.

Obstinacy and parsimony like cleanliness are also linked with the sublimation of the infant's interest in her feces. Obstinacy is often visible as irascibility, rigidity, vindictiveness or even defiance. Parsimony covers behavior, which ranges from avarice and acquisitiveness to frugality and stinginess. Daddy Hugh is described as irascible and stingy. The connection between parsimony and excrement led Freud to the link in the popular culture between money and feces. The folkloric example offered by Freud is a Viennese Christmas tree ornament of a man excreting a gold coin from his anus, the Dukatenschiesser. In America, pay-day in the Army is "the day the eagle shits."

Hillary's obstinacy showed in her management of Bill's campaign for Congress. Maraniss mentions a worker who says Hillary's influence on the campaign staff was negative, "Our organization went to shit.  We lost the spirit over her."[107]  Hillary told campaign manager Paul Fray not to give $15,000 in cash to poll workers at the last minute in the marginal districts as was planned.  This was "dirty money " from the dairy industry to buy absentee ballots and conscientious Hillary was speaking from the moral high ground. Bill's loss in this normally Republican district was by a narrow margin.

Hillary's frequent use of profanity, that is, dirty language, as a medium of expression is consistent with the counterculture and feminism. A feminist who is a generation older then Hillary remembers that she felt "cleansed and healed" when she began to use the common profanities of everyday speech.  Hillary's proximity to dirty Arkansas politics is her choice of an environment that led to the Clintons' political power. Although her rejection of vote buying is clean and not dirty, it's in the same sandbox.  Clean and dirty words about Husband Bill, politics and money for campaigns are all energized from the psychology of anal development. Freud explains, "... cleanliness...gives exactly the impression of a reaction-formation against an interest in things which are unclean...and ought not be on the body." [108]

The obstinate Hillary in 1993 is described by Bruck, who quotes a health industry executive as saying, "She was so thin-skinned...that if you criticize one page of a thirteen-hundred-and sixty-four page bill (her health plan), you're the enemy."[109]  A Hillary booster, Montana Senator Max Baucus, said that Hillary's speeches in his state were unusually "...partisan...negative and...quick to judge."[110]   It was the obstinate Hillary who denounced Democratic Senator Cooper's health plan rather then seek an alliance with a proposal that Cooper himself called Clinton Lite.  Bruck says that it's hard for Bill to live with Hillary's "absolutism," a word from Connie Bruck's interview with Bill that could be either Bill's opinion or the interviewer's language.  An earlier judgment that Hillary should "just chill out" by a high school classmate was noted by Milton.[111]

The third trait of her anal eroticism is Hillary's parsimony which appears as acquisitiveness. The Starr inquiry, which spent over seventy three million dollars from 1994 to 2001, was focused on Hillary and money until Monica appeared in 1998.  This investigation of the Clinton's real estate investment was named Whitewater after a land development on the White River in Arkansas but also included Hillary's billing records at the Rose Firm and her roles in the Castle Grande Real Estate Development and the failed Madison Guaranty Savings and Loan.  Travelgate, which was also investigated by the Independent Counsel, was mainly about Hillary's role in the firing of the members of the White House travel office because of accusations of financial irregularities and the installation of a new travel agency from Arkansas.

The Whitewater books by James Stewart, *Blood Sport* and David Brock, *The Seduction of Hillary Rodham* accuse Hillary of wrongdoing although Brock offers the excuse that she married into the "Ozark mob." Gene Lyons, who exonerates her in *Fools for Scandal How the Media Invented Whitewater* was joined by journalist Lars-Erik Nelson in "Whatever Happened to Whitewater?" The Starr investigation convicted a former Arkansas Governor, Jim Guy Tucker, real estate developers Jim and Susan McDougal, Rose Law partner and Deputy Attorney General Webster Hubbell, and others before diverging into Bill's Monica Lewinsky affair. A Starr prosecutor said in court testimony that an indictment of Hillary had been prepared but was shelved.

The later sections on Bill's Ego Defenses and Bill's Oral and Anal Development will explain how Bill's anal phase led to his ambivalence while Hillary's anal stage led to orderliness, compulsivity and parsimony. How is this possible? The difference isn't absolute because Hillary is also ambivalent and Bill is compulsive and orderly. President Bill sometimes wore three freshly pressed suits a day and he had a newsworthy $200 haircut on the tarmac at LAX. In any case, these wildly speculative comparisons of Hillary and Bill's anal stages lack data about the differences in their toilet training and their underlying mental constitutions.

The qualities of Hillary's anal stage which are discussed in Hillary's Oral and Anal Development are based on her more-or-less free associations in the

*Village* book. This is an analysis by proxy that shows she has an anal character which is confirmed by her behavior which is orderly, conscientious, obstinate, acquisitive and controlling. She confirms this analysis saying, "I know in the Bible it says they asked Jesus how many times you should forgive, and he said seventy times seven. Well, I want you all to know that I'm keeping a chart."[112]

The anal stage of psychosexual development with its anal sadistic personality derivatives was the unconscious crucible of Hillary's sadomasochism. This sadomasochism remains a prominent feature of Hillary's life. Sadomasochistic behavior characterizes Bill too and also their marriage. (See Bill's Oral and Anal Development and Hillary and Bill in Marriage)

## JEWISH HILLARY /ANTI-SEMITIC HILLARY

A Jewish issue for Hillary arose during her Senate race when she was under political attack because of a kiss and hug she had given Yasir Arafat's wife Suhu during a visit to the West Bank. Then there was the allegation of an anti-Semitic slur by Hillary twenty-six years before the Senate campaign. Hillary biographer Oppenheimer says Hillary called Paul Fray "a fucking Jew bastard" during Bill's unsuccessful campaign for Congress in 1974 Paul, who was the campaign's manager, was described as a "a foul-mouthed... Southern Baptist" by Mary, his wife. He is said to have a Jewish father, a Jewish grandparent or a Jewish great grandparent. As the votes were being tallied on election day evening, Bill was behind, and there was a private meeting that erupted into a violent argument between Paul and Mary Fray on one side and Bill and Hillary on the other. Bill said little as they argued about Hillary's unwillingness to let Paul spend $15,000, dirty money from the dairy industry to buy absentee ballots as the votes were being counted in Fort Smith, a crucial city in a very close race. Hillary opposed this spending on moral grounds although the Republicans were said to be stealing votes this way, an Arkansas electoral tradition.

It was a meeting charged with recriminations, the Frays saying that Mary would have had more time for the campaign if she wasn't obliged to be the nanny for Bill's girlfriends. Hillary attacked Paul and Mary for setting Bill up with women and the quarrel resulted in objects being thrown and a broken window according to the account by Sheehy.[113]

During the fracas Paul Fray "accused" Hillary of being Jewish saying that, "...when Jewish people get together and things don't go right, they get hot and go at each other's throats." Hillary, the newby, a Northerner and an assertive woman from a big city was attacked by Paul, the Arkansas good ol' boy as "Jewish" although she's not. This incident occurred when Paul heard Hillary call him "a fucking Jew bastard." No one mentioned this racial slur until the Senate race, when Hillary denied it and other witnesses to their noisy argument didn't recall it, although Paul offered to take a lie detector test.

Hillary was Daddy Hugh's Fifties American Princess in her suburban Chicagoland home but during the New York Senate campaign, she gets a casting call as a Jewish American Princess with a story in the *Forward*. a national Jewish newspaper. It discovered that Hillary's maternal grandmother, Della Howell married Max Rosenberg, a Russian Jewish immigrant in Chicago in 1936 after Della's eight-year marriage to Hillary's maternal grandfather, Edwin Howell had ended in divorce. Court records show that Della bit and scratched Edwin when he wouldn't take her out because he was too tired and anyway he couldn't afford it. This story of Della's violence was confirmed by her sister. After the divorce, Edwin was given custody of eight-year-old Dorothy, Hillary's mother who was sent with her three year old sister, Isabelle to live in Southern California with their paternal grandparents. [114]

Della attempted unsuccessfully to regain custody later when she was married to Max, who was a successful businessman. Biographer Oppenheimer learned that Dorothy was told by her mother that Max would send her to college when she returned at eighteen from California to Chicago, but he wouldn't and it was then that Dorothy developed a life-long dislike for Max. She would say things like, "Oh, all those Jews are so cheap...that Jew has to watch every dime..." in family conversations. She echoed her mother Della's language, who was heard to say to Max, "you cheap Jew bastard" during their marital battles.[115] Despite Dorothy's anti-Semitic sentiments, Max and Della spent time with Hillary in her home. They took her and her brothers on excursions in Chicago and Hillary had a warm relationship with both Della and Max.

It seems probable to Hillary's first cousin, Oscar Dowdy Jr. that Hillary's alleged anti-Semitic slur stemmed from her mother Dorothy's views. However, Hillary's Daddy Hugh liked Max, who gave Hugh and Dorothy their first apartment rent-free during the post-war housing shortage in a building owned by Max. Later Max helped Hugh start his drapery business.   (See Hillary's Burden for more about Hillary's mother.)

Racial slurs like dirty or foul language point to anal psychological developmental issues for the listeners as well as the speakers including Hillary. "Don't shit where you eat" is a folk aphorism which expresses the irony of biographer's Sheehy's observation that if Hillary and Bill and the Frays had eaten a meal together after the confrontation about the lost congressional election, they would have parted as friends and forgotten the slurs they exchanged. Hillary's Oral and Anal Development and Hillary and Money deal with some of these issues.

## HILLARY'S SUPEREGO

Hillary's conscience or superego has already been discussed in several sections of this essay. Its manifestations are never far from visibility in Hillary's role as a mother, a feminist, the First Lady in Arkansas and Washington and as a political leader. Her superego developed in her unconscious while she was a toddler from her Oedipus complex and castration fears in the Freudian model. According to the newer feminist psychology, it follows her identification with Mother Dorothy and a balance with Daddy Hugh. Along either route there are questions about the course of her superego development and its content.

The superego as well as the ego and the id are metaphors, so our psychological structure is like the shadows that dance on the wall of a Platonic cave, where we are confined. Plato tells us in *The Republic* that the world is like this cave so our reality is the shadows on the wall cast by the distant daylight from the long entry tunnel.

Hillary is conscientious and contentious as she sublimates her impulses of hate into works of social welfare that help woman, children and the poor. She likes to control and to make money for her family. She worries and is sensitive to criticism. She loves Bill and Chelsea and protects them. She is a forthright and brusque planner, a pragmatic strategist who doesn't waste her time or resources. Her love extends to her staff, who receive her support and the celebration of their birthdays but who are afraid to criticize her. The confusion in this description between what is form and what is content in Hillary's superego is self-evident. Sorting the vignettes of her behavior into categories isn't really going to help visualize her superego. After all we really don't have a map of the superegos of other well-known personalities like Bill Gates, Ruth Bader Ginsburg, Oprah and Newt Gingrich although we feel we more or less know them.

The *Talk* interview by Lucinda Franks encouraged Hillary to fantasize about her life and her marriage. Her freest associations occur when she's asked whether her marriage is an arrangement and if she chose Bill for her own benefit. Her answer, said to be delivered as a "scoff" is, "Yeah, right! Like I picked him - this big gangly guy with goldish hair looking like he just came off the boat, like some Viking."

Vikings were pirates who invaded Europe from northern bases attacking cities as far inland as Paris before the first millennium. They didn't usually settle the territories they conquered although they stayed a couple of years in North America at Vineland and are said to have founded Russia and Normandy. Hillary says she studied the Icelandic Sagas where she found Gudridur, a heroine who sailed for Vineland about 1000 A. D., where she gave birth the North America's first European child.

Perhaps the Viking is Hillary who explored the new world of being co-president, won political office while First Lady, attacked President Bill with flying missiles, some of which hit the target, sacked the White House travel office, failed in her attempt to found a new national health care system, but did pass a major education bill in Arkansas. A confirmation of the identity shift from Bill as Viking to Hillary as the Viking is her reference to Bill as having goldish hair. The biographers tell us that as children and for some years afterward, Bill was a brunette and Hillary was a blonde. Now Bill's hair is gray and Hillary remains a blonde. "Just came off the boat..." suggests Hillary whose grandparents were immigrants from the British Isles and Canada, while Bill was from a family that had lived in Arkansas for four generations after moving west from Alabama.

It was Hillary as Viking who chose Bill according to the legend that begins with her opening line in the Yale law library, "Look, if you're going to keep staring at me, then I'm going to keep looking back, and I think we ought to know each other's names. I'm Hillary Rodham."[116] Hillary's reference to Norse Mythology introduces the Viking sagas as metaphors: Bill as Odin, the All-father, a powerful but flawed god of battle who broke his promises or as Thor, the thunder god with a prodigious appetite; and Hillary, as a Valkyrie maiden who decides which of the heroes will enter Valhalla where the white armed Valkyries will serve them. Do the Valkyries, charming in Valhalla but sinister spirits of slaughter on the battlefield, include Hillary, Gennifer, Dolly and Monica too?

Hillary's *Talk* interview becomes even more self-referential as she explains Bill by saying, "There was a terrible conflict between his mother and grandmother...for a boy being in the middle of a conflict between two women is the worst possible situation. There is always a desire to please each one." She says a psychologist gave her this idea, but isn't Hillary's inner psychologist also talking about a girl in the middle of a conflict between Sadistic Daddy Hugh and Masochistic Mother Dorothy? Hillary attempted to please both Powerful Hugh with his goal of perfection and Martyr Dorothy who tidied up defensively for the family. There were other hard choices and terrible conflicts for Hillary: a post law school career in Washington versus love in Arkansas, maybe heterosexual love versus homosexual love, and maybe even Bill versus Vince.

## HILLARY AND NARCISSISM

Narcissism is Freud's allusion to Narcissus from classical mythology, a beautiful youth who fell in love with his reflection in a pool and drowned as he sought to embrace the beloved image. Narcissism was used by Freud to describe the infant's primary union with the mother that later plays a major role in the formation of personality during maturation. Freud's discovered narcissism after his earlier description of the epoch of the sexual and aggressive instincts during

Oedipal development. Then narcissism became a second track for the growth of personality. This parallel channel of development led to contentious debates among the Freudians but after a while narcissism was recognized as an important ingredient in the formation of character.

By the 1930's, unchecked narcissism was recognized as a character disorder and as a significant problem in the analysis of neurotic patients. These narcissistic patients, who were more difficult to treat, were later called borderlines.

Narcissism is a disorder with strong feelings of grandiosity and entitlement, demands for constant attention, self-centeredness and a lack of empathy for others, difficulties in love relationships and a diffusion of identity. Anger, depression and suicidal impulses accompany the frustrated narcissist. A lack of a central identity damages the fulfillment of both love and work, the two major life tasks, according to Freud.

A narcissistic character is the result of a narcissistic wound that is caused by a mother's or a caretaker's inability to meet the infant's needs. An event such as a catastrophic illness or the loss of a parent does not itself cause such a narcissistic wound but may be its symbol. Some of these wounds heal and some do not. Narcissism is not learned, but it often develops in a family environment where there are other narcissists like Daddy Hugh. He is described by Donald Rodham, his first cousin, "Hugh was a blow hard...'the Big I Am-I Am Hugh Rodham. I Am Important. I have a company and I could care less about anybody else. ' "[117] Daddy Hugh wasn't a full blown narcissistic character, but here are the elements that encouraged Hillary to learn to cast herself as self-important. Hillary, who has a normal share of narcissism, escapes the status of a narcissistic personality that categorizes Bill. (See Bill as Narcissus for more on this.)

Narcissism is part of normal personality development, while a narcissistic character or personality is abnormal although such classifications are artificial reflections of a mental life which is fluid and not at all clear-cut.


## HILLARY'S ESCAPE FROM CHICAGOLAND

Hillary needed to escape from Chicagoland and so she went off to Wellesley at eighteen and never lived there again eventually moving her parents and brothers to Arkansas away from Chicagoland. Of course, Chicagoland is the mythical territory of Chicago Tribune publisher Colonel Robert McCormick. It comprised the states of Illinois, Indiana and Wisconsin, but it was often extended to a Middlewest stretching from Ohio to the Rocky Mountains. The decadent Eastern seaboard was specifically excluded.

The center of this Middlewest Nation is Saul Bellows' "... showpiece... of the lakeside, the seething ...immigrant slums...square miles of ruin...wounds...corruption...violence...creative energy...a world city." Sherwood Anderson calls it, "Chicago triumphant; factories and marts and the roar of machines...horrible, terrible, ugly and brutal." This is Carl Sandberg's "Hog Butcher for the World, Stacker of Wheat, Player with Railroads" which attracted settlers from all over the world. Like the others, Dorothy and Hugh from the English immigration soon became aware of the industrial slagheap onto which the workers are periodically discarded by the chances of the economic cycle.

The greensward of Park Ridge could not tranquilize Hillary's restless mind. It was a borough of the dreaded Chicagoland with its smoke and odors of dark factories and bloody stockyards from which teenage Hillary planned her escape. It was also the suburban prison of wide lawns and narrow minds in the words of Ernest Hemingway, who fled from Oak Park, another Chicago suburb.

Hillary needed to elude her fate as " ...an all-American, rugged Midwesterner with childbearing hips, stocky legs...a strong back and a utilitarian body inherited from the Middle American gene pool that is designed to deliver a baby one day and carry sacks of corn and grain...the next," according to biographer Elizabeth Wurtzel.[118]

Dread of the Middlewest is a strange idea to me as a native of Chicago where I lived on the edge of Lincoln Park not far from where Hillary was born. Bellow affirms my olfactory memory when he says, "The stockyards are gone...but the old smells revive in the night heat...the old stink still haunts the place." I fled the Middlewest too, first to New York for a year, then to the South for two, summers on Cape Cod and finally to California in my fifties. Hillary's first escape was to New England, then Arkansas and the District of Columbia and to New York in 1999. Much of this aversion to Chicago is covert, partly unconscious although the emotions emerge. "Hillary hates cold weather" one columnist says.


## HILLARY'S PSYCHOPOLITICAL CHOICES

Are there public policy consequences for Hillary's unique mental life?

How do Hillary's creative tensions mirror her politics in the culture of the nineties? This dialogue was opened by David Brock in *The Seduction of Hillary Rodham* where he says she was the naive victim of Bill's "Ozark mob," referring to her involvement in seamy Arkansas politics, Whitewater and commodities trading.

Hillary's governmental policy commitments follow her early social activism: children's needs, education, health and the social safety net for the poor. Her life long campaign is directed from the war room of her mind, where the large banner reads, "It's children's rights, stupid" although education, health and the social safety net each have subsidiary logos. The choice of children as her fulcrum to move the world is a solution in which springs from Hillary's own childhood of powerlessness. Children's rights are Child Hillary's reaction to Hugh's sadism and Dorothy's masochism. Daddy's girl felt abused by Hugh and couldn't depend on Mother Dorothy although her identity comes from both. The family Oedipal drama in Hillary's unconscious mind is a story which begins before the Oedipus phase and continues after it into what Freudians call latency, the years from six to eleven or twelve, when puberty and adolescence begins.

Hillary, the child advocacy attorney, says it all,

The first thing to be done is to reverse the presumption of incompetency and instead assume all individuals are competent until proven otherwise...I have seen a lot of situations in which families have abdicated their responsibilities to their children...some parents do not deserve continued authority over their children...anyone who has dealt with abuse knows...you've got to make a very tough decision...Decisions about motherhood and abortion, schooling, cosmetic surgery, treatment of venereal disease or employment...should not be made unilaterally by parents. Children should have a right...to decide their own future if they are competent.[119]

As a sixth grader Hillary circulated a petition to allow a classmate to wear nylons to a dance.

Hugh's aggression and Dorothy's passivity were mirrored by Hugh's argumentative Republicanism and Dorothy's secret Democratic votes. Hillary was a Goldwater girl when she started at Wellesley but soon moved leftward, and four years later, when she spoke at graduation in 1969, she attacked both the established order and the other speaker, Republican Senator Brooke.

As Arkansas' First Lady, she spearheaded a major reform of the state's educational system which required an additional sales tax. She held hearings on school reform throughout the state and eventually the bill passed with the addition of a teacher competency test, which was the price for voter approval. The teacher's union and the civil rights leadership unsuccessfully opposed the testing of teachers as demeaning and racially biased against black teachers. Teacher testing remains an issue for some educators like Bob Schaeffer who say that these tests do not measure competence or classroom educational quality and are responsible for a decrease in the number of minority teachers.

The educational reform in Arkansas led to advances for one of the poorest educational system in the nation with increased teacher salaries, kindergartens, smaller class size and new educational programs such as foreign language and advanced math in the high schools. Hillary's child welfare agenda was also expressed by a new nursery school program based on an Israeli model using parents as educators. Health was added to Hillary's agenda in the White House where she headed the task force that wrote the proposed legislation for Bill's major campaign issue after the economy.

Not all the people want child welfare, education and health care legislation because its price tag means new taxes and also because they have come to represent Big Government. Such programs are seen as the opposite of the traditional family role in the care of children, the local control of education and a fee-for-service medicine advocated by the Republican Party and particularly the Radical Right. On the other hand, no one favors their opposites, ignorance and illiteracy, child neglect and death and disease, but they are there too in the sibling envy and murderous rage of the voter's unconscious. This sadism may be expressed in political behavior as voters receive pleasure from  aggression against children's needs, the poor, education and health care. Of course, the voters also feel guilt but that's masochism, a kind of pleasure too.

Hillary's activism touches psychological depths and political complexities that exceed Barbara Bush's campaign on literacy, Nancy Reagan's Just Say No to Drugs and Rosalynn Carter's mental health agenda. The similarity to Eleanor Roosevelt is compelling but FDR's policies were often different from Eleanor's and FDR had not campaigned saying, "Buy one, get one free."

Does Hillary as a victim affect Hillary as a policy leader?  Was the 1993 attempt at a new national health policy affected by the balance between the Hillary who was a cold sadomasochistic aggressor and the Hillary who was charismatic, compassionate and innovative?  Was Hillary selected to lead the campaign for managed care because it was risky and might fail?  If it succeeded, Bill would get the credit for helping people and fulfilling his major campaign promise on health care. If it failed in Congress, which is what happened, the blame would be Hillary's, and Bill would move on to meet his goal with lesser initiatives like the immunization of preschoolers, children's health insurance, making private health insurance portable between jobs, insurance coverage of preexisting illnesses, and making HMO's liable for consumer lawsuits.

Why didn't Hillary make the more radical single payer program her legislative goal? This is the Canadian Health Care Plan that eliminates the insurance companies and is truly comprehensive in its coverage. The general understanding was that Hillary preferred this plan but she rejected it as politically unfeasible. So her perception of a congressional rejection of the simpler single payer solution obliged Hillary to masochistically give up her reasoned preference for an expediency that turned out to be illusory. This a repetition for Hillary who won the successful struggle for education reform in Arkansas by a compromise that required an increase in the regressive state sales tax. The use of the teacher competency test to sell the package was a maneuver, politically devious in its covert racist appeal to white voters in a Southern state where blacks are only fifteen percent of the population. In a sadomasochistic maneuver, Hillary sacrificed some civil rights credentials to get the white votes for a higher sales tax and better schools while Bill retained his popularity with the black voters and became the education governor. The unconscious was also operating in synch with the political world. A health crisis in Arkansas about Medicaid funding worsened while Bill was Governor, but Hillary stayed out of the fight that time. Sometimes there is a choice.

## HILLARY AS CINDERELLA

A portrait of Hillary emerges from the books by Monica Lewinsky, Dick Morris, Dolly Kyle Browning, Gennifer Flowers and Robert Reich. These books are discussed later in Bill and Hillary in Group Process With Dick, Dolly, Gennifer and Robert and also in Monica Talks About Bill.

Hillary tells Robert Reich to communicate with Bill about his agenda on worker's rights via private memos to her on blank paper with only a date and his initials. This is Hillary, the secret manipulator who uses a back channel to control policy as she did in manipulating Daddy Hugh in her childhood Princess role. (See Hillary's Oedipus) Mother Dorothy and Daddy Hugh were manipulative too. By the time Hillary was First Lady of Arkansas, she was really in control of the Rodhams, so Daddy Hugh and Mother Dorothy and her brothers moved to Arkansas from Illinois.

Dick Morris also allied himself with Hillary's strength in the White House as he contended for Bill's ear and the control of policy decisions. He met with Hillary's staff, "the girls," in addition to his meetings with Bill's staff, "the boys." Another time when Hillary stopped going to Bill's policy meetings, Morris briefed her in separate sessions.

Reich's book portrays Hillary as the little girl who shows "hurt and anger...just beneath the surface..." covered by an aloofness "that can't take sympathy well." Reich calls her a vulnerable "rabbit" after she "chaired the health plan... a mistake."[120] Hillary's defenselessness is like Mother Dorothy's weakness in the face of Mr. Impossible, another name for Daddy Hugh. It is a paradox that Hillary the manipulator is also Hillary the fearful. But why was Hillary's vulnerability concealed, asks Reich, when it could have served to humanize Hillary, the "strong woman" who needed friends in the press? Later, this media sympathy did occur during the Lewinsky events when Hillary's favorable ratings rose from a low of 42% in 1996 to 65% in 1998 as she was portrayed as sympathetic and brave. Hillary's little girl weakness is deeply repressed, so it remained for George Stephanopoulos to tell us that Hillary cried at a strategy meeting because she felt "alone."

Here we leave a sympathetic understanding of Hillary for the cruel words of the Wicked Stepsisters, Dolly and Gennifer. Dolly Kyle Browning portrays Hillary, whom she renames Mallory as a Cinderella, "...dowdy-looking... wearing a misshapen brown dress-like thing...to hide her lumpy body...fat ankles and thick calves covered with black hair...wide feet...hair on her toes...a definite odor of perspiration...greasy hair...eyes bulged out of focus... dark thick eyebrow which crossed ...her forehead..." Gennifer describes Hillary as, "...a fat frump...hair hanging down...big thick glasses...ugly dress...a big fat butt...behaving oddly...buzzing around." Bill's mother Virginia, another rivalrous Southern woman, had a similar if more muted response to Hillary, "No makeup. Coke-bottle glasses. Brown hair with no apparent style."

This is Cinderella before the arrival of the Fairy Godmother and Prince Charming when the dirty ragged char girl is transformed into a Princess: wife, influential attorney, policy leader, cultural icon, intellectual, author, mother and a styled First Lady. By 2000, Sheehy says she is "...Cleopatra in full regalia, gowned to the floor in a pyramidal coatdress of black satin...golden hair, swept high shimmers Bill is the Prince but the human persona of the Fairy Godmother is a mystery, maybe Eleanor Roosevelt.

Then, why dredge up the sludge? Because within the rivalrous, hurting and hurtful, frigid and over-controlled Hillary is the needy little girl, beautiful and worthy who is searching for love. Of course, the two Hillarys are a paradox but both need to be acknowledged.

There is a national hate-Hillary faction, which describes her as a cultural and political threat to both civility and the Republic. Bill called this a "right-wing venom machine." The anger and fear of this cabal is about Hillary as a person, a frenzy about her ambition, intrigues and manipulativeness. During the New York Senate race, she was said to be planning a run for President in 2004 or 2008, a dreaded scenario. The attack is on her although it includes her agenda for children, education, health care, women's rights and her pro-choice feminism.

Hate-Hillary is a female crusade led by Reagan speech writer Peggy Noonan whose polemic about Hillary calls her "...arrogant and opportunistic...(she) never graduated from the sixties."[121] Congressional investigator Barbara Olson's Hillary biography says the danger is from her "...corporatist, managerialist, quasi-socialist view of the world" and her White House of "miniskirts, hair spikes and T-shirts."[122] NBC 's talking-head Laura Ingraham's book is titled *The Hillary Trap: Looking for Power in All the Wrong Places*; biographer Joyce Milton says Hillary is "abrasive"[123] and columnist Camille Paglia calls Hillary "bitch."[124]   Men like Gary Aldrich accuse Hillary of saying that the Secret Service and FBI are "trained pigs."   After Hillary's election to the senate in 2000, a leading Republican, Senator Trent Lott says that "if this Hillary comes to the Senate...maybe lightning will strike and she won't." The Hate Hillary's are in tandem with the "Clinton Crazies" who attack Bill as a Satanic murderer. (See Bill as Oedipus)

It is the psychological Hillary that ignites her opponents. The jokes are frequent like, "What's the Hillary Clinton KFC Special? Two small breasts, two large thighs and two left wings." The ire aroused by Hillary is like the misogyny that also guided the private and public anger against Eleanor Roosevelt and sometimes flared up against other First Ladies as their popularity waxed and waned. It was easier for some enemies of the New Deal to attack Eleanor's social activism instead of the popular FDR. Some Reagan opponents preferred to attack Nancy 's use of astrology for White House scheduling. Jimmy Carter's detractors said that Rosalynn shouldn't attend Cabinet meetings.

In the millennium, Hillary is a new countercultural foe. As Bill fades from the screen, his image morphs into Hillary as the target.  Twelve years of the conservative Reagan-Bush era and their military victories in Grenada, Panama and during Desert Storm didn't heal the wounds of the Sixties. Bill Clinton's adoption of Reagan-Bush policies such as welfare reform, the death penalty, the limitation of First Amendment rights and even the defeat of Serbia didn't make many veterans of the culture wars feel any better. In fact they felt worse as the hard core Right (and Left) offered toward new conspiracy theories.

Hillary as threat was the subject of a conference sponsored by the publishers of *American Enterprise Magazine*. They charged that her Secret Service escorts had "manhandled" the press as they were filming the crowd who booed her during the New York St. Patrick's Day parade in 2000, but Columnist Marie Cocco said that this scenario was unlikely.

The attack on Hillary is an attack on the Goddess who is called Mary, Eve or Athena in the West, Astarte in the Near East, Kali in India and the Queen Mother of the West in Taoist China. Hillary's leadership and her anger polarize a public that includes her partisans, while others join in opposition. It is this dichotomy that gives energy to the hard core Hillary haters. This not just along party lines, liberal versus conservative nor is the division only between the counterculture and the establishment. It is grounded in Hillary's persona reflecting her narcissism, sadomasochism, bisexuality and an unresolved Oedipus, all aspects of the Goddess that are projected by Hillary's unconscious.

A Jungian, Erich Neumann says,

...the maternal tree, whose roots go down to the underworld, suddenly shakes its riches down upon a Cinderella, and a celestial growth, whose hidden powers come from the world of the ancestors and primordial images, unexpectedly unfolds the richest flowers of psychic life. But it is inherent in the mysteries of the Great Goddess ... that she grants life only through death, and development toward new birth only through suffering...no birth and no life without pain.[125]


## HILLARY'S DREAM

When Senator Clinton spoke to the National Press Club in 2001, she was asked if she would seek the White House in 2004, she replied that she was "having too much fun being president..." quickly correcting this to "being a first term senator." On this kind of error, the press are all Freudians.

Presidents need a dream to stoke the fire in the belly during the years of campaigning. Hillary is member of this tribe, and she has a presidential vision. Her mother Dorothy wanted her to be a Supreme Court Justice. We don't have Daddy Hugh's words, but he trained her to be a shortstop who could hit a curveball. Hillary dreamed of the White House and so wed Bill, who plainly said that was where he was headed.

I am on a vision quest for Hillary's dream. I must be a surrogate for a reticent Hillary who says during the Senate campaign, "I am a well-known unknown person." Dreams are myths and so we had the pleas of the Elders led by New York Congressman Rangel for Icon Hillary to run, then the attack-dog opponent Mayor Giuliani falls to cancer and marital woes and finally a lackluster and boyish Congressman Lazio emerges as the opposition candidate. President Bill is supportive, offering benefits to New York's major communities of Puerto Ricans, Jews and seniors. Bill pardoned Puerto Rican prisoners although Hillary said she didn't want this support perhaps fearing a negative reaction from the suburban voters. Bill tried personal diplomacy to help Israel toward peace first with Syria and then with the Palestinians promising more dollars for military security. Hillary had lost some ground with Jewish voters after her remark about a Palestinian state and a kiss for the wife of Yasir Arafat. Seniors were more secure as both Bill Clinton and Al Gore emphasized the security of Social Security.

Hillary's dream was not of clouds, chases, cheese, cold, faces and water. Eight-year-old Hillary dreamed of being president. This is the manifest content, but what of the dream's latent or hidden meaning? What should a woman president do that is not just her platform for peace, health care, children and women? The answer is in the unconscious of Hillary's sadomasochism: suffer herself, punish and banish her enemies, and revenge the indignities, slights and insults. Most of the Cinderella stories don't kill, torture or exile the wicked stepmother and stepsisters but this dark side of Hillary's dream is hidden. Some Cinderella stories eventually dress the wicked stepsisters in finery and they come to live in the palace, but in a Russian version, Cinderella takes revenge so the wicked step-mother and sister are driven into the cold and freeze to death.

That Hillary's senate candidacy and perhaps a forthcoming presidential bid waited until midlife may reflect menopausal zest, a midlife surge of creativity and growth. (See the chapter on Bill and Hillary's Change of Life) Midlife Jimmy Carter and Rosalynn were newly creative after their four years in the White House becoming writers and builders of housing, world peace and democracy. The Clintons' midlife crisis, his really, but one for her and their marriage too, offered a surge of menopausal creativity for Hillary in a time of disaster. Maybe Bill too will have menopausal zest.


## HILLARY'S BURDEN

What are the conclusions of this evaluation of Hillary's psychology?

We learn that she isn't in full control when she is angry, cold and isolated. At times, the opposite is true, that her control is excessive and she lacks flexibility. Her anger and her withdrawal, whether justified or not, are determined by her Basic Mistrust and her Shame and Doubt, which result in sadomasochism and a frigid character. Hillary explains her need to control anger during her New York senate campaign when she says to interviewer Michael Tomsky, "I ... believe that it is just more difficult for women candidates to express their strong feelings about things affecting them...I don't want anything I say to feed into the kind of, ah, climate in which people engage in insults." [126]

It must be acknowledged that there is not enough information about how these trends developed. Her mother Dorothy was eight when her parents separated and divorced. Dorothy's parents, Della and Edwin are called immature and neglectful parents by Hillary's biographers. After the divorce Dorothy, age eight and her three-year-old sister were sent to live with their paternal grandparents traveling alone by train from Chicago to Los Angeles. Her grandfather ignored Dorothy, and her grandmother was verbally and physically abusive so she left when she was fourteen to do childcare for a family so she could finish high school. Sometimes such events are reflected in a later generation with Chelsea saying to the school nurse, "Call my dad, my mom is too busy."

There is a public meaning to the kaleidoscope of Hillary's image makeovers beginning with a successful professional career woman using her own name to a cookie- baking- tea-serving hostess using Bill's name. The first makeover was during Bill's campaign for reelection as Governor after his defeat in 1980 at the end of his first term, and there were other makeovers later. These periodic events reflect more than just political expediency. They are attempts to escape the public consequences of her anger, coldness and isolation, real or perceived. Hillary is an energetic and magnetic leader who offers a public policy for social welfare, but despite these qualities, her anger, pessimism and coldness are not lovable. Is this judgment true? Yes, but would this judgment be made about a man? No, is the answer to that question. Still her public image is not only politics, misogyny or anti-feminist bias. They are there but that's not all.

Finally, what are the legislative and political results of Hillary in the White House?

First, the defeat of the Clinton health care reform, planned by Hillary, involved the complementary sadomasochism of both Hillary and Bill. Hillary's health plan failed by February 1994, early in the first term without even a vote as Congress including many Democrats became increasingly resistant to it. Bill delivered a health care message in September 1993 but there were no arm-twisting presidential phone calls to the Hill for Hillary's health bill.

Journalist David Gergen, a White House presidential counselor for eighteen months during the first term, tells the story of the health plan as a White House imbroglio pitting Hillary on the Left against a Right led by Treasury Secretary Bentsen, Secretary of State Christopher, and Gergen himself. This was the time when the North American Free Trade Agreement known as NAFTA was on the table, and Hillary and her advisors, Carville, Stephanopoulos and Begala believed that "...NAFTA was a disaster...and... would once again postpone health care reform, their number- one priority health care reform for his (Bill's) first term." Then in December 1993 the stories about the Arkansas state troopers' procurement of women for Governor Bill began to appear, and soon the First Couple were barely speaking to each other. Bill's political muscle went into the passage of NAFTA. Hillary's team was told to "shut up on health care...it was NAFTA time," Connie Bruck explains.[127]

Neither Washington nor Vienna is simple and linear so it was also the assignment itself of health care to Hillary that was a " 'mission impossible, ' " according to David Gergen. His book asks, "Might he (Bill) have passed a bipartisan reform plan if the shadow of his past had not hung over his relationship with his wife?" Gergen's explanation is that "...the relationship between the President and the First Lady...operates like a seesaw. If he goes down in the relationship, she goes up."[128] This first arc of this seesaw refers to the Flowers revelations that almost derailed the 1992 campaign which was followed by the state troopers' procurement exposure. The reason for Bill's mistake, the assignment of a doomed mission to Hillary lies in Bill's Sadism and Masochism to be explained in a later section. Recall that even FDR's New Deal couldn't pass a comprehensive health care plan, the Wagner-Murray-Dingell Bill.

It was the masochistic Hillary who withdrew her failed health plan from Congress as NAFTA passed in November 1994 with the support of some of the same members of Congress who opposed to Hillary's health proposal. Gergen speaks of the health plan when he says that "...he (Bill) did not...personally marshal the resources of the administration for its success." It was then that a sadistic Hillary said no to the settlement of the Jones case. Sometimes even the pragmatic Hillary makes mistakes under the control of her unconscious.

Second, it was Hillary's opposition to a settlement of the Paula Jones lawsuit against Bill in 1994 that led to his impeachment. Four years later it was settled for $850,000. Her decision not to allow a settlement of the Jones case, which had been recommended by President Bill's legal advisors, is mentioned by several of her biographers and by Bob Woodward in *Shadow*. This was an almost fatal mistake but what was going on in Hillary's unconscious?

The Paula Jones case was about Paula's alleged harassment while she was an Arkansas state employee after she had refused oral sex for Governor Bill in 1991. It was the legal discovery process in the Jones case about Bill's sex life, which led to a deposition by Monica Lewinsky after her affair with President Bill was leaked to Jones' attorneys. Although Monica denied having sex with Bill, it was President Bill's false statement about not having a sexual relationship with Monica that led to his impeachment for perjury.

Hillary's unwillingness to settle the Jones case reflected three of her ego defenses. Her *Identification With the Aggressor* revived the combativeness of Daddy Hugh. She used *Denial* about Bill's behavior as Mother Dorothy used denial and passivity in the face of the curmudgeon, Daddy Hugh. Her *Projection* was Hillary's own paranoid attitude toward a hostile world, and her secrecy was a part of this paranoia. The hidden emotions that were being defended against were the sadism and masochism described in Hillary's Oral and Anal Stage.

Third, it was Hillary's excessive secrecy amounting to stonewalling about the Whitewater events that led to the appointment of the Special Prosecutor, first Robert Fiske and then Kenneth Starr.

Biographer Sheehy calls this "the 'fuck you, Jeff Gerth' strategy" as Hillary and her spokeswoman Susan Thomases stonewalled the *New York Times* reporter who wrote the original 1992 Whitewater story. White House co-counsel Lanny Davis and Hillary's attorney, Jane Sherburne, recommended the release of all the documents about Whitewater and the related financial matters. President Bill also agreed to full disclosure when the *Washington Post* began to pursue the Whitewater story with a Watergate-like intensity according to White House counselor David Gergen, who remembers that Hillary said no.[129] Hillary recalls that her "gut instinct... was to resist giving someone free reign to probe..."[130]

Hillary's silence on Whitewater was based on her unconscious scoptophilia.

(See Hillary as Mother and Chelsea as Orphan for an explanation of scoptophilia.) Scoptophilia is not just the secrecy of paranoia. It is the fear and avoidance of one's emotional secrets being exposed and watched, not just the privacy of the financial records of Whitewater, but also the deeper unconscious sadomasochistic complexes of the anal developmental stage. In the realm of Hillary's unconscious, the exhibitionism of a First Lady helping her candidate husband in Arkansas and Washington and then as a senatorial candidate herself is paired with her intense personal secrecy. So it is also for many public figures in politics, the arts, sports, business and elsewhere.

In the White House, Hillary sought healing, self-understanding and inspiration from feminists, therapists, theologians and scholars like Jean Houston, Mary Catherine Bateson, Doris Kearns Goodwin and Michael Lerner.   (There is more about this in Hillary and Bill's Psychotherapy.) Whether these White House visitors were psychotherapists for Hillary is speculative. Hillary and Bill had marital counseling in Arkansas in 1989 and also during the Monica events according to Bob Woodward.[131]  But a prescient note from Hillary's law school experience is that one of the teachers at the Yale Child Study Center, where she studied for a year was Anna Freud.

After I read this to a writer's group, a psychologist grimaced and said, "Your theories are slippery, like ice cubes, so they can't be grasped - criticism is impossible," and then she was silent.

# PART TWO

## CHELSEA VICTORIA CLINTON

### CHELSEA AS ORPHAN AND HILLARY AS MOTHER

Pregnancy had eluded Hillary until she was thirty-two, when Chelsea was born by Caesarean section on February 27, 1980, five years after her marriage. She explained, "Bill and I had wanted to start a family immediately after we married in 1975, but we were not having much luck. In 1979, we scheduled an appointment at a fertility clinic right after a long-awaited vacation. Low and behold, I got pregnant during that vacation...we might have had more children if we had taken more vacations..."[132] Like Hillary, many of her Wellesley classmates had also deferred childbearing and a fifth of them had also struggled with infertility. According to biographer Sheehy, Hillary has endometriosis, a uterine disorder that predisposes to infertility.

Hillary describes ordinary difficulties in nursing Chelsea, "There I was, lying in my hospital bed, trying desperately to figure out how to breast-feed...It seemed to me I ought to be able to figure this out. As I looked on in horror, Chelsea started to foam at the nose...a nurse appeared...(and) said, 'It would help if you held her head up...like this.'"

Sometimes advice comes more easily in the Village from a tribal sister then from Mother Dorothy or Mother Virginia. Hillary's words about her attempt to nurse Chelsea gives us a keyhole into the unconscious mind of Hillary with a link to the broader vista of Hillary's oral pessimism during her own infancy as well as its resurgence during Chelsea's infancy.

Even more problematic to Mother Hillary was Mother Virginia of Arkansas. This was the Virginia who had tried to run Hillary off years earlier but now she had given birth to Virginia's only grandchild. (See Bill's Good and Bad Women.) After the delivery, Bill and Hillary felt safer with Virginia at arms length waiting for admission to Hillary's room from 11:34 P.M. to 1:30 A.M. ostensibly because Bill was bonding with Chelsea.

Another cloud over Hillary's Village was Virginia's experience a generation earlier when she left Baby Bill to go away to school for two years and then, after she returned and married she faced an attempt by her own mother to take the custody of her baby. (See Bill as Oedipus) Hillary is not Molly Bloom from Joyce's *Ulysses* who speaks in the language of free association so an oblique view is needed to limn Mother Hillary's unconscious mind.

A forty-nine year-old Hillary discusses about her frustration at not becoming pregnant again as she talks about adopting a child in 1996. We know Hillary was pregnant once, but maybe there were the frustrations of an unrecorded miscarriage or two. Her reported endometriosis may have had an effect on her fertility and stress also affect fertility Stories and legends give emotion a role in fertility, although there are no psychobiological studies of its place in fertility.

Both parents were involved in Chelsea's life. At times it was more one than the other, so when Bill said he might be unable to go to Disney World if he ran for president, seven year old Chelsea said, "Well, then Mom and I will go without you." Nine-year-old Chelsea who witnessed some of the noisy arguments between her parents, asked, "Mommy, why doesn't Daddy love you anymore?" When the school nurse asked Chelsea who to call for permission to give her an aspirin, she replied, "Call my dad - my mom's too busy."

Bill is credited for carrying photos of Chelsea in his wallet and for being tearful at her high school graduation. But Hillary, who cried on Chelsea's first day of school in each grade, was told by nine-year-old Chelsea not to take her to school on the first day.

When Chelsea was seven, Mother Dorothy moved to a condo in Little Rock with Hillary's younger brothers and Daddy Hugh, who was now post-stroke and retired. Dorothy would take care of Chelsea while Bill and Hillary traveled as they planned the run for president in 1988. Then a tearful Bill withdrew as a candidate saying he wanted to spend more time with Chelsea, and Hillary cried too. They both responded to political godmother Betsey Wright, whose investigation produced a list of women including Gennifer Flowers who could talk about an affair with Bill if he ran for president. This was also the time of another crisis, Bill's "serious" love affair with Marilyn Jo Denton Jenkins according to two biographers, Milton[133] and Sheehy. The Clintons were close to divorce, but they stayed together and probably had marital counseling in 1989.[134]

A mommy grade for Hillary is problematic but I will assign the one that is implicit in the words of her many biographers. Nearly all of the biographies see Hillary as a concerned mother, so they give her an   A - to a B + including the Clinton-averse Brock.  But Chris Andersen gives her only a C+ to B -, calling her overprotective, while she receives a C- from Joyce Milton and a D from Barbara Olson, both of whom say that she didn't spend enough time with Chelsea.

The most striking attitude of Mother Hillary was her secrecy about Chelsea which  she believed to be necessary for a normal childhood in the White House. It was the subject of well-publicized meetings between Hillary and Jackie Kennedy about raising children in the White House. Bill agreed and no reports, interviews or gossip about Chelsea were allowed, just photos holding hands with her parents. The pictures of Chelsea as a physical link between an impeached Bill and an aggrieved Hillary were particularly noteworthy.

Sometimes it seems as though Hillary's role with Chelsea is a clichéd script without depth or variability; there are few surprises, and even they are shallow and lack resonance. At age thirteen Hillary didn't allow Chelsea to have her ears pierced. Chelsea's personality was largely unknown, and America didn't hear her voice until she spoke on television in Tanzania. A student journalist was dismissed for writing a story about her at Stanford soon after she entered at seventeen.

I have no quarrel with privacy for a presidential child but this is a  parenting style that invites psychological study.  The focus of this decision is Hillary's paranoid defense that projects her anger and fears onto others who are then seen as being dangerous. Secrecy is the observable face of Hillary's paranoid defenses. A stimulus to this defense is that Chelsea has received death threats.  (See Hillary' Ego Defenses)

Three psychoanalytic terms need to be explained here to clarify the Chelsea-Hillary relationship.

*Displacement* occurs when an emotion is severed from its original connection with a person or event and is attached to a substitute person or object. It is an ego mechanism of defense, which isn't frequent enough to make Hillary's main list of defenses.

*Screen Memories* are the conscious manifestations of infantile amnesia that reemerge as adult fantasies in place of the original repressed memories or events of childhood.

*Scoptophilia*, named by Freud, is the sexualization of looking and being looked at, which are the usual courtship preliminaries to love and sexuality. It may become an end in itself and so interfere with a fulfillment of love as in pathological shyness, a reaction to scoptophilia that is seen more often in women then in men. Men's scoptophilia is exemplified by a voyeur peeking at women undressing or an exhibitionist who shows his penis to women in public. Exhibitionism in women involves the display of the whole body for erotic and narcissistic satisfaction.

Hillary's need to keep Chelsea's life private is a displacement  from Hillary's own secrecy about herself. But that's not the whole story about the blackout of news and photos of Chelsea.

Hillary's secrecy is a kind of screen memory  for her own childhood amnesia about looking at forbidden sexual desiderata and seeing or imagining the primal scene, that is, parental sex. This is no longer conscious in the adult Hillary, who like, other adults, has amnesia for her childhood sexuality. Some of her emotions about this unconscious imagery are displaced to Chelsea who like all of Freud's children is charged with forbidden sexual energy.

Let's look at Chelsea with her own Oedipus complex, which is hidden both from her and from Mother Hillary by the forces of repression. "She's a Daddy's girl," it was said about little Chelsea. Meanwhile, Chelsea's own conscious sexual flirtations, secrets and her real and fantasied lovers and girlfriends express her scoptophilia as she is watching and being watched.

A graphic description of a young woman's scoptophilia appears in James Joyce's scene in a Dublin park in *Ulysses*,

> Gerty smiled assent and bit her lip. A delicate pink into her pretty cheek but she was determined to let them see so she just lifted her skirt a little but just enough and took good aim and gave the ball a jolly good kick and it went ever so far...it was nothing else to draw attention on of account of the gentlemen opposite looking. She felt the warm flush, a danger signal always with Gerty MacDowell, surging and flaming into her cheeks. Till then they had only exchanged glances of the most casual but now under the brim of her new hat she ventured a look at him and the face that met her gaze there in the twilight, wan and strangely drawn, seemed to be the saddest she had ever seen.[135]

Hillary's scoptophiliac tendencies are provoked by her screen memories of a forbidden sexual father or his surrogates, a teacher like Elisabeth, or a Don Jones, her youth minister. Hillary's desire to both revive and overcome this attraction is accompanied by the even more powerful need to avoid it by not looking at it.  Hillary's conflict about looking and not looking at secrets is the expression of an emotional conflict in her unconscious in which denial is a prominent defense.

There are more floats in this parade.  To look is to devour according to a psychoanalytic equation.  "He devoured her with his eyes," is often said. This expression is derived from the symbolic connections between the eye and the oral aggressive phase of development. The eye according to Freud is also a phallic symbol because of its identification with the penis in the primal scene. The eye has a bisexual character because it is also identified with the vagina.

Pagan and biblical folklore speak of a powerful Evil Eye that causes infertility or illness, so many wear charms that protect against this danger.   The eye's oral aggressiveness is expressed by The Wolf in Little Red Riding Hood, who says he has such big eyes, the better to see her, and then he says that his mouth is so big, the better to eat her. The dangers of scoptophilia and the Evil Eye are elaborated in the hate-Clinton mythology of former FBI agent Gary Aldrich, who says in *Unlimited Access*, "When 'Queen Hillary' walks down the hall you're not supposed to look at her...She doesn't want the staff 'seeing' her."[136]  A Hillary-friendly journalist Beth Harpaz tells us that the media were not allowed near Hillary when she ate lunch in a New York restaurant during her Senate campaign.[137]  A Biblical response to the scoptophiliac experience is being turned to stone like Lot's wife, who violated God's injunction not to look back as she fled Sodom with her husband.

The secrecy about Chelsea hides her real behavior and her character from a curious public who saw only the photos of a homely, awkward and dowdy teen in the White House.  Hillary's preoccupation with her own privacy is a partial explanation for the secrecy about Chelsea while Hillary's own scoptophilia also plays a role. Of course there were security and child-rearing considerations too.

Camille Paglia tells us that Chelsea looks like  "...an orphan...abandoned...a castaway on a desert island...a hostage..." She compares sixteen year old Chelsea to Hillary at the 1996 convention who was   "...all turned out and stylish (while) Chelsea seemed to be deliberately trying to upstage her mother by looking like a spinster in mourning."[138]

Chelsea went to Stanford at seventeen, and she was better groomed by her junior year, a makeover. As a senior she had "...a halo of honey-golden curls moussed into waves, heavily powdered face and a handsome figure...perfect teeth shining out of a heart-shaped highly lipsticked mouth...a big friendly grin..." as she is regarded by journalist Beth Harpaz during Hillary's Senate campaign where Chelsea greeted the voters.[139]

Chelsea did enter the news during the impeachment after Bill's apology when she broke up with her boyfriend and went to the emergency room with "stomach pain" caused by stress. This was in the tabloid press and eventually the mainstream media carried it, perhaps because Chelsea was now nineteen. Soon Chelsea was off on world visits with Hillary and then she went with Bill to the Balkans. These were better gigs then trying to bridge the Clinton family gap on Martha's Vineyard but one wonders what was really on Chelsea's mind.

In the summer of 2000, Chelsea campaigned with Hillary and went to Japan with Bill, who was attending the Group of Eight meeting. She announced that she would take the fall semester off so she could campaign in New York with Mother Hillary and be at the White House with Daddy Bill during his last months. She had enough credits to graduate with her class in 2001 but the *Globe*, a tabloid, said that Chelsea missed her life in California and Jake Gyllenhaal, her current love interest.[140] Meanwhile, the *Star* said she was in the East because she was uncomfortable on campus, where she was called a lesbian like her mother since she spent her time with girlfriends.[141] The *Star* says she believes her mother would be better off divorced and Chelsea "went ballistic" at her Dad about a woman who flashed her breasts when Bill signed her T shirt on a Lake Placid street after his 54th birthday celebration.

Like Princess Di and Jackie O, Chelsea's privacy was violated. The media images about her are contradictory and sometimes demeaning, but there is a personal psychological meaning about Chelsea here too.

The conflicting words of the tabloids hint at Only Child Chelsea's attempt to manipulate her parents. Chelsea is saying, "Dad, be good and don't hit on the bimbos or even think about them if you want me to be your geisha during the last days in the White House and on the presidential legacy trail." Chelsea, who's been to Japan, knows a geisha is a costumed entertainer/conversationalist/wife-substitute for the CEO who needs a night away from home. The message to Hillary is, "Mom, Dad isn't worth the pain. I'll campaign with you in New York and protect you from the lesbians. Get a divorce after the Senate race and we'll be together or else I just could go back to Dad." Then a younger Chelsea's speaks in a teen-age voice to both parents, "It's your fault I don't have a boyfriend, you're both too gross. Maybe I'll just be a lesbian." The brass ring for Chelsea is control, an inter-generational family value for Parents Hillary and Bill and her Grandparents, Dorothy and Hugh Rodham and Virginia Kelly and Bill Blythe as well as Virginia's other spouses including Roger Clinton.

The observations of Chelsea's controlling behavior as a child and adolescent directed at her parents are a small visible slice of the Oedipal iceberg. Chelsea in her classic Freudian unconscious wants to marry Bill and have his child even as she rages murderously at her mother for her lost penis. In the feminist revision of Freud, Chelsea's unconscious is allied with her mother, and so she seeks to repeat the intergenerational drama by loving a man like (or unlike) her father and having a baby with him. In the feminist Freudian model, she has a career as an end in itself, a requirement of her conscience or superego while in the classic Freudian portfolio she's a housewife or a conflicted career woman. This template is not a Procrustean bed because ego development is not a formula, and many variables are present including life events, genetics, and the idiosyncrasies of parents and other relatives. Chelsea's unconscious is awash in paradoxes like Father Bill, warm and soft in contrast to Mother Hillary as hard and cold. (See Lakoff's language analysis in Frigid Hillary/Sexual Hillary/Bisexual Hillary/Lesbian Hillary)

None of this analysis suggests that Chelsea isn't intelligent, friendly, poised, cheerful, mature, She is an outstanding student, a dutiful daughter and a good girlfriend for college swimmer Matt Pierce and others whom she dated for a while. Now Chelsea is an adult and a historical judgment cannot be made until she talks to the interviewers or appears in her own book, and then she will be ready for her own psychohistory.

## CHELSEA AS ADULT

Did the World Trade Center disaster benefit any Americans? Yes, maybe Chelsea Clinton, who was in New York during 9/11 and got to write about her reactions in *Talk*. This was her first publication and marked her emergence as a public figure in her own right at twenty-one as she went off to Oxford. Also 9/11 gave her a reason to call on her former boyfriend for "hugs" which he delivered. So maybe he benefited too. The other beneficiaries were Chelsea watchers who before Chelsea's article had only second hand accounts and rumors for a psychological picture of Chelsea.

Chelsea says in *Talk* that she was innocent before 9/11 using a neologism, "innocences" to describe her state of mind.[142] Although she'd seen the victims of war, famine and natural disaster in her travels with Hillary and Bill, these sights hadn't really affected her personal outlook. Before 9/11 she was "feeling good about where I was in my life and where I was going." She had graduated from Stanford in June 2001 and was moving on to Oxford in October to study international relations.

Chelsea was staying with her best friend Nicole Davison in an apartment near Union Square in lower Manhattan a few miles from the World Trade Center on 9/11. Her friend went to work but phoned shortly afterward to say that a plane had crashed into the World Trade Center. Chelsea turned on the television and watched the second plane hit. Now Chelsea was fearful and lonely and wanted to talk to her mother in Washington but couldn't get through.

After watching the 9/11 spectacle again on TV, she left the apartment in a "panic" looking for another phone so she could try the call to her mother again. She wandered south toward Ground Zero hoping to find an available working phone since everyone was fleeing north, but she couldn't find one. As she saw the streams of people, many ash-covered, tearful and frightened, she became more depressed, erratic, emotional and confused. On the terrifying streets, she heard an explosion; she saw fires and someone said that one of the towers had fallen.

Although later she didn't remember where she had been, immediately afterward she recalled a few landmarks and people said that she was only twelve blocks from Ground Zero.

Chelsea describes the symptoms of a Post-Traumatic Stress Disorder (PTSD) when she says, "...I find myself returning to the day itself." Her "...sense of security is gone and...for some moment of every day, I have been scared...by...an uncertainty about my place in the world.." Many who were at Ground Zero or nearby on 9/11 had similar reactions so Chelsea is not unusual, but this is a unique opportunity to study Chelsea.

PTSD is defined by persistent anxiety, depression and emotional numbing in response to the exposure to a man-made or natural disaster with flashbacks that revive the trauma. At Oxford, Chelsea's initial response to the 9/11 tragedy included an aversion to peace demonstrations, a preference for the companionship of Americans instead of foreigners and a sense of personal dislocation. After a few months, she was more comfortable at Oxford and told a reporter in March 2002 that she loved England.[143]

Those who developed PTSD after Vietnam were a minority among the veterans who served. (PTSD was neurocirculatory asthenia in the Civil War, shell shock in World War I, traumatic war neurosis in World War II and recently Gulf War syndrome when it was lumped with the effects of wartime toxic exposures.) The vets developed panic attacks, depression, rage reactions and flashbacks soon after Vietnam or later on. Their condition lasted for months or years, while Chelsea's symptoms were present for about two months at the time of her *Talk* article.

The people with the most vulnerable ego defenses are the most likely to succumb to PTSD. For example, the successful use of Denial as an ego mechanism may block PTSD along with other mechanisms like Repression, Intellectualization and Sublimation. Ego defenses can't be measured, but their failures are often observable in situations like Marilyn Monroe's suicide or a troubled Princess Di, who developed anorexia. (See Hillary's Ego Defenses and Bill's Ego Defenses for explanations.)

PTSD offers an understanding of the life experiences of the victim because it often signals a personal loss or severe stress earlier in life. I don't know what that event was for Chelsea but typically PTSD occurs on a stage set by childhood trauma. Chelsea's Oedipal development is unresolved and this unconscious complex may be significant in the development of her PTSD. Later in this chapter, a theory about her Oedipus based on Chelsea's words in *Talk* is presented. (Also see Hillary as Mother and Chelsea as Orphan) In other words, it is possible to look backward from Chelsea's PTSD to the vulnerabilities in her earlier life experiences and her ego development that led her to PTSD.

What do Chelsea's words reveal?  Her fear and confusion led her to seek tranquility, so she calls her mother in Washington on the morning of 9/11 but fails to connect until that afternoon. Chelsea's difficulties in phoning her mother symbolically contrasts to the simplicity of her call to her father in Australia and his arrival home at Chappaqua the next day.

On Thursday of that week, she tours lower Manhattan with Bill during tear-stained hours of high emotion as they meet with the families who are searching for their lost loved ones. Chelsea is "overwrought," and she explains her "horror" in her first-ever interviews on camera.  The following week Chelsea goes to Ground Zero with Bill; Hillary has already been there three times, once with President Bush. Chelsea is "proud" of Bill and "unspeakably proud" of Hillary.

This the Chelsea that told the school nurse when she needed an aspirin, "Call my dad - my mom's too busy." And at seven when Bill said he might not be able to go to Disney World if he ran for President, she said, "Well, then Mom and I will go without you." Like Hillary and Bill and most everyone else, Chelsea's Oedipus complex is never really resolved so it remains a potent force as she manipulates the players in her life.

The orthodox Freudian Oedipal explanation says that Chelsea's unconscious seeks a sexual connection and a baby with her father or his surrogate to replace the missing penis. But feminist psychoanalyst Shahala Chehrazi says the solution of a girl's Oedipal dilemma is to identify with her mother and as she satisfies her sexuality, she has a baby in a further identification with her mother. In the first scenario, mother and daughter are murderous rivals while in the second they are allies. Mr. Hugs is real enough, but he is also a surrogate in both scenarios. These scenarios are unconscious and influential in the solution of Chelsea's changing Oedipal needs.. (See Hillary' Oedipus Meets Feminist Theory for more about this.)

Another game in the 9/11 casino is Chelsea's phone call to her boyfriend requesting "hugs," a euphemism best translated by what Monica Lewinsky, another Gen-Xer calls "fooling around." They have agreed to a separation as Chelsea goes off to Oxford for two years and he returns to Stanford for his senior year. Reason trumps love when Chelsea says their separation is rational. No matter what was decided or how the decision was made, this is Chelsea's theater. So she writes a script of sacrifice in the interests of what? Order, study, ambivalence, lower phone bills, a new lover and absence that make the heart grow fonder. All and each may be the rationale for a decision that's really an emotional act.

Chelsea's sadomasochism enters as she seeks hugs from a soon-to-be ex-boyfriend when the flames of the Twin Towers trigger her libido. Her first calls were Oedipal to Mommy and Daddy but then this blazing sexual stimulus leads her to hugs. So Chelsea shares vicariously in the pyromania of the forest ranger in 2002, who burned a letter of rejection from her husband thus causing a notable forest fire. In the unconscious, Freud tells us that fire mobilizes forbidden sexual feelings and a need to put out the fire by urinating on it.[144] This is a sado-masochistic event for both the fire setter and the fire observer.

The renunciation of future intimacy with Mr. Hugs is another facet of Chelsea's sadomasochism and maybe Mr. Hugs' too. It is sadism because Chelsea's infliction of no contact with Mr. Hugs involves his pain and her sexualized response to it. And it is her masochism, too, because her hurt is also sexually stimulating. Her sadism and masochism involve suffering by Chelsea both as victim and perpetrator while Mr. Hug's pain amplifies the overall S and M effect. (The theory of sadomasochism as an unconscious mechanism affecting behavior is in Hillary's Sadism and Masochism and Bill's Sadism and Masochism.)

This behavior doesn't mean that Chelsea is a sadomasochist although this condition is prominent in the personality of both her parents. For Chelsea, it is one of several mental mechanisms. But trends stemming from Chelsea's unconscious sadomasochism may become an influence on her future behavior.

Chelsea's article offers the reader personal details and emotions as well as a look at her personality so she is seen apart from her mother's scoptophilia. Hillary's scopotophilia is the fear of the sexualized process of looking and being looked at. Chelsea was a part of this process as a teenager who was hidden with the rationale that this would protect her privacy. Chelsea isn't a scoptophiliac and her words say that it's all right for her to look at anyone and for anyone to look at her. (Scoptophilia is explained in Hillary as Mother and Chelsea as Orphan)

Chelsea's emotions after 9/11 are predominately depressive as is usual in PTSD. She has gloomy thoughts, fear, loneliness, and tears, and her venues are funerals, memorial services and the morgue. A month later at Oxford, homesickness contributes to the mood depression, and Chelsea writes in an essay in James Steyer's book that "I am at Oxford now, further from my family then I have ever been. I miss my parents all the time."

There is no anger or hate from Chelsea amid the words and emotions of her turmoil. It is striking that the terrorist acts of 9/11 have not produced rage or hostility in Chelsea. Chelsea identifies with America however America is angry and vengeful toward Osama bin Laden, who personifies the hated terrorists. America wants Osama dead or alive as President Bush said. America's bombing of Afghanistan began three weeks after 9/11, while al-Qaeda, the terrorists' network is targeted by American forces inside the U. S. and elsewhere. This is the anger that leads some Americans to demonize Arabs, Islam and Muslims.

Chelsea's anger shows obliquely as she visits the New York family of a high school friend, August Zach, who has joined the Marines and will report as a lieutenant to Quantico in November. Some, maybe even Chelsea, said it was a waste

58

of his Cornell degree to join the Marines. Now Chelsea feels he is protecting her and America, and she asks, should I enlist in the Marines? Without conscious irony, her strained answer is that she and the others outside the military are also serving by pursuing their studies and careers in fields like banking.[145]

Why does Chelsea avoid her anger about 9/11? The reason is Chelsea's personality. She never developed a temper like her parents who were often outspoken in their anger at each other as well as their enemies and sometimes their friends too. Chelsea's anger turns inward, so when she was angry with a boyfriend and her Dad during the Monica crisis in 1998, it was said that she went to the emergency room for stomach pains that were psychosomatic. (Hillary and Bill's anger are discussed in the sections on their ego defenses, their sadism and masochism and also in Bill's Death Instinct.)

High tempers were well developed in both the Clinton and the Rodham families. There were plenty of psychological factors as well as reasons in reality for these parents and grandparents, both men and women, to express anger and rage.

What was different about Chelsea? She had an ego defense, *Inhibition* that blocks awareness of unacceptable emotions, anger in her case. Ego defenses develop along with other attributes of personality but they also have a constitutional basis. When more is known about Chelsea, it will be possible to' profile her ego mechanisms of defense and the psychosexual stages that influenced their development.

Chelsea's Inhibition explains her lack of visible anger, but she needs to justify her passivity. The young are "powerless," she says, but then she releases her generation, "Give blood, mentor and celebrate America's greatness." This is an anemic update of "make love, not war," the slogan of her parents' youth. Chelsea's new patriot in the 01's is summarized by the cry, "I regret I have only one pint of blood to give and one hour a week to mentor for my country." A display of the flag and these homilies lead Chelsea to return to the African proverb that forms the title of her mother's book, "It Takes a Village To Raise a Child," and then Chelsea's brief tangent with activism and anger is gone.

Humpty Dumpty, Mother Goose's best-known rhyme focuses Chelsea's concerns so she quotes it:

Humpty-Dumpty sat on a wall
Humpty Dumpty had a great fall
All the king's horses and all the king's men
Couldn't put Humpty together again.

Chelsea says the fallen Humpty Dumpty stands for her worry about the damage of 9/11 and the overwhelming problems of reconstruction.[146] Beyond these visible and conscious manifestations of 9/11 are Chelsea's unconscious Oedipal and sadomasochistic responses.

Humpty Dumpty was an egg, a symbol of the earth and of life in many tales of creation. The rhyme has a firm hold on the popular imagination, for it has appeared in several European languages for thousands of years. The words are recited by adults and children using rhyming, warm emotion and sharing to transcend death and loss according to psychoanalyst Stewart Gabel.[147]  Humpty Dumpty addresses the conscious and unconscious pain of universal tragedies. It uses symbolism, metaphor and humor to mobilize psychological defenses against such sad and fearful events. Healing for Chelsea begins with this verse.

A darker and narrower interpretation of the power of Humpty Dumpty's fall is offered by psychoanalyst Tom Petty, who says that it is symbolic of the destruction of a child's rival, often a new sibling.[148]  Nine year old Chelsea asked her mother, "Why doesn't Daddy love you anymore?" in 1989 as if to place blame, maybe on her mother for Daddy Bill's straying from Hillary and from Chelsea too.  It was then that profligate Governor Bill was having a "serious" romance with Marilyn Jo Denton Jenkins that threatened a Clinton divorce as described in Gail Sheehy's book about Hillary.

The Humpty Dumpty metaphor is also about Chelsea's Oedipus complex where Daddy Bill lies broken beyond repair by the Monica scandal, and irreparably damaged like the Twin Towers on 9/11. It's Gotterdammerung, the Twilight of the Gods for Chelsea, whose PTSD hides her Oedipal anxiety and so fulfills the purpose of a neurosis, to protect the functioning of the ego. Chelsea identifies with Mother Hillary according to the feminist Oedipal theory of Chodorow and Chehrazi. (See Hillary's Oedipus Meets Feminist Theory) Both she and Hillary found new Oedipal objects, Hillary the Senate and Chelsea a new boyfriend, Ian Klaus, a Rhodes scholar at Oxford like Daddy Bill. Hillary's surrogate, Mr. Senate, is combative like Daddy Hugh while Chelsea's new boyfriend is "cute, " and their relationship is "serious."[149]

Notice that Chelsea is her own person psychologically. She has two conditions that neither of her parents have: PTSD and significant mood depression. These are her responses to stress. Chelsea doesn't have Hillary's scoptophilia. Her sadomasochism is a tendency rather then the established pattern that is seen in both her parents. Nor does she have her parents' narcissism.  Bill's and Hillary's overt hostility and anger seem to be absent or still latent in Chelsea.  But Chelsea, who won academic awards in high school and honors in her history degree at Stanford, has Hillary and Bill's perfectionism and intelligence.

There is not enough information about Chelsea to predict the outcome of her PTSD and depression after 9/11, but it seems that the forces of self-healing have prevailed, maybe with psychotherapy and an antidepressant like Prozac. Of course, a new boyfriend played a role but it's hard to find one when you are deeply immersed in PTSD and depression. By March 2002, the *New York Times Sunday Styles* reports that after an initially "rough time" at Oxford, she "...has blossomed into someone who does not mind the limelight and certainly does not mind having a good time..." A photograph of her at the Versace couture show in Milan shows her with boyfriend Ian Klaus, a fellow student from California according to *Times* reporter Sarah Lytall.

# PART THREE

WILLIAM JEFFERSON CLINTON

"Our mothers's spirits stay with us always," 'A powerful memory of constant love' by Bill Clinton, syndicated column in the *San Francisco Examiner*, May 10, 1996. p. 23A

"...I spotted a dark haired young man, about fifteen years old...He seemed so sweet, so innocent.  I realized suddenly that I was in love with him - something decidedly strange because in my dream I was my twenty-four-year old self and Clinton was a fifteen-year-old boy. " *Dreams of Bill*  Edited by Julia Anderson-Miller and Bruce Joshua Miller, Citadel Press, 1994, p. 173

"He's like a God in their eyes!"  An anonymous woman from Little Rock talking about Arkansas' opinion of Bill Clinton in 1999.

"In Clinton, the inner conflicts - both the personal psychodrama and the policy debates - rage on."  *The Agenda* by Bob Woodward, Simon and Schuster, 1994, p. 401.

"Jack Stanton could be a great man if he weren't such a faithless, thoughtless, disorganized shit."  Susan, a stand-in for Hillary is speaking of Jack, Bill's surrogate in *Primary Colors* by Joe Klein, Random House, 1996, p. 21.

## BILL'S PSYCHOHISTORY

"I remember, as a small child, watching my mother on a railway platform... sobbing and waving goodbye to me...she sank to her knees." Bill Clinton writes[150] as if from an analyst's couch. Little Bill stayed in Arkansas with his grandparents from the age of two to four[151] while his mother went to New Orleans for two years of training to become a nurse-anesthetist. His mother describes this scene in virtually the same words in her autobiography leading one to wonder about whether Bill cribbed the lines and so underlined their salience.

Bill's separation from his mother has a great deal to do with his character and his Presidency. How does the turmoil of his early years affect the paradoxical picture offered by his biographers?  He is described as hesitant, indecisive, and passive in the face of opposition; cowardly; desiring to please; chameleon-like in reinventing himself; deceptive; often late; unreasonably angry; sexually profligate, and addicted to food and exercise. Yet he is also described as having strong religious beliefs, a need to help, great energy, many accomplishments, intellectual, ambitious, perfectionistic, understanding, courageous and charismatic. These are the contradictions of his "personal psychodrama" which Bob Woodward says are baffling in *The Agenda,* a book about Clinton as president.

The information about William Jefferson Clinton comes from a variety of sources with varying authenticity. The accuracy of the personal details and the events in the books by his mother, brother, friends, journalists, biographers, muckrakers and former lovers are less important then the story itself, the emotional climate and the mythos of Clinton's life. The sources including his own words present an affective unity even when their viewpoints diverge. *Leading With My Heart,* the book by his mother, Virginia Kelley, is a unique opportunity for a psychohistorian, a mother's story about a national leader.

## BILL AS OEDIPUS

Oedipus, the complex that defines the path of love in the family also identifies the converse, the route of hate. A national Oedipus complex is an analogue to the one in the family and so we have the hate of the "Clinton crazies." They attack Clinton as a cocaine cartel leader, a drug smuggler and a Satanic murderer in books, magazines, on videos, radio and the internet according to Philip Weiss' survey in the *New York Times Magazine*.[152]  The hate-Bill reaction was heard largely from the hard right of national politics but in 1999, author Christopher Hitchens, a socialist and *Nation* columnist, called Bill a serial rapist, a pathological liar and a war criminal.[153]

64

Love and hate in the national Oedipus complex are also seen in the irrational and excessive transference about President Bill, as though all America was in therapy with Psychoanalyst Bill. The surplus of love and hate here exceeds the quantity that can be attributed to Bill either as a political force or as a symbol. Of course, Political Bill affected everyone with peace or war, the economy and the list goes on. Icon Bill was a role model and ego ideal so during the Monica era, the public asked, "What will the children think?" Nonetheless the surfeit of emotion about Analyst Bill as president-father-mother was from the national unconscious. Here resides an unconscious reservoir of the unresolved infantile love and hate reactions that we have about our own parents. Other presidents like Reagan, Nixon and JFK elicited similar over-reactions.

Transference is the emotional reaction of the patient to the analyst based on the patient's unresolved emotions about her or his parents. This reaction is separate from the patient's reaction to the analyst as a real person. Transference  as resistance slows therapy and has to be worked through, but it is this very transference that leads to the cure as the patient's problems are mobilized, understood and resolved during the analysis. Transference was one of Freud's main discoveries as he encountered strong emotions of love and hate toward him in his earliest patients based on their unresolved emotions about their own parents. It was the intensity of the love and hate of the transference that caused Josef Breuer, Freud's first collaborator, to end his study of neurosis during the 1890's and leave the field to Freud.

What does it mean to describe Clinton as Oedipal? It refers to the role of Oedipus in the family drama of King Laius; the father murdered by the ill-fated son, who then marries his mother, Queen Jocasta. The son, who is destined for this role by the Gods, is punished by self-inflicted blindness. After wandering in life-long exile, he enters a sacred grove from which he goes to a consecrated afterlife. A sacred Greek legend was the basis for Sophocles' *Oedipus Rex*, which Freud read as a map of personality formation.   The universality of this explanation of development is still debated, but its power in the life of President Clinton is beyond any clinical doubt. The evidence is in the story written by his mother, who describes the childhood traumas and intimate details of the President's development, including even the location of the parental bedroom in relation to that of the son.

Clinton's Oedipal story is in the portents, expectations and cues of his mother Virginia as Jocasta. The ill-fated queen is the surrogate for the citizens who wanted the magical economic benefits of the Gods denied them by Bush in 1992, who represents another aspect of the murdered King Laius. Virginia describes herself as a workaholic nurse-anesthetist, colorfully costumed, vividly made-up, hard drinking, flirtatious, assertive, impulsive and controversial. This self-portrait is similar to the one in the biography of Bill Clinton by Arkansas journalist Meredith Oakley who adds that Virginia was "not a pretty woman" but she was a "striking figure."[154]

The final event in which Clinton vanquished his King Laius was a struggle at age fourteen when he told his stepfather, Roger Clinton, never again to hit his mother. He was now taller and stronger then this alcoholic man who was argumentative and paranoid. Bill recalled this episode, "...one of the most difficult things for me was being fourteen and putting an end to violence." There was an ongoing argument between Virginia and Roger that led Roger to strike Virginia. "I just broke down the door of their room one night when they were having an encounter and told him that I was bigger than him now and there would be no more of this when I was there."[155]

Virginia tells us that Bill was already "father, brother and son" in the family where he "took care" of his mother and his younger brother. Husband Roger often wasn't available, so Bill as a teen was Virginia's "date" in the Hot Springs nightclubs where he danced with her and listened as she spontaneously sang with the band according to biographer Chris Andersen.[156] Bill's was a "special child - smart, sensitive and mature,"[157] according to Virginia and these powers were amplified as an only child until the age of ten.

The unconscious fantasies of a son who possesses the mother after killing the father produces a reservoir of guilt and anxiety in the son, especially if this drama is confirmed by family events. Clinton's mother was married to his father, William Jefferson Blythe, while he was serving in World War II, and Bill Clinton was born three months after his father's death in an auto accident in 1946. Oedipus killed his traveling father at the crossroads in an encounter fated by the Gods while Bill Blythe died alone from an accidental tire blowout in a speeding car on a lonely highway.

Bill Clinton's father was en route to Arkansas to meet Virginia, Bill's mother, so they could travel to the new home that Bill Blythe had found in Chicago. Bill often heard the story of his father's death while traveling from Chicago to Arkansas, and he tells us, "I had to live for myself and for him too...that ...shaped my childhood - that great memory.[158]

Was Bill Blythe's death on that urgent and fateful trip a consequence of Virginia's pregnancy with Bill are Virginia and Bill guilty of Father Bill Blythe's death? Of course not, that isn't rational, but neither is the mind of the child as he learns of his role in his father's death. As Virginia mourns, she is embarrassed or maybe ashamed because her new baby named William Jefferson Blythe III is fatherless. She has a vision of herself as a disgraced unwed mother, and this is the time that Bill's care passes to his grandmother for the first four years of his life.

Presidential biographer Maraniss tells us that Bill's birth August 16, 1946, eight months after William Blythe and Virginia were reunited December 10, 1945 "spawned rumors" because of Virginia's "flirtatious nature."[159]   Virginia explained that Bill's birth had been induced weeks ahead of schedule by the doctor because of concerns about her condition. Author Sheehy disputes the story of Bill's induced delivery based on an interview of the nurse who delivered Bill. His birth weight of 8.6 pound ruled out prematurity so the question is unresolved.[160] Unknown to Virginia, Bill's father, William Jefferson Blythe, was still married when he married Bill's mother in 1943 so that  their marriage wasn't legal.

Clinton's mother influenced his Oedipus complex, but what does this mean? In Sophocles' drama, there was no initiative by Jocasta toward her son Oedipus, but Virginia's seductive behavior influenced little Bill's unconscious mind and so affected his Oedipus complex. This influence goes beyond the Virginia of his childhood image as a musical, caring and sexy woman. The overtly seductive parent of the opposite sex who figured in Freud's first Oedipus theory in 1895 was replaced in the early years of the next century by a parent whose eroticism was unconscious but equally powerful for the child.

Michaelangelo's *Piéta* shows the Oedipus Complex in stone portraying a Virgin Mary and Jesus at the same age as their naked bodies merge into a loving physical and a mystical union. Psychoanalyst Oremland says that this sculpture is an aging Michaelangelo's statement about his reunion with his own mother.[161]

Virginia was unconsciously seductive toward her son who was her romantic or sexual object and a successor to her real loves, her father and Bill's dead father. The seductiveness is seen in Virginia's "shrine" of photos and awards to Bill in her living room[162] and her struggle for control of Bill with her mother, Edith Cassidy when Bill was four. (See Bill's Separation Anxiety)

Virginia's own unresolved Oedipal experiences as a child can be understood this way. Virginia's mother, Edith, who was called Mawmaw in the family was "...vindictive, manipulative...(with) ...nightly screaming fits..." of jealousy when she lunged at Eldridge Cassidy, Virginia's father who was called Pawpaw. He invoked Virginia futility pleading, "Please, the baby has to go to school tomorrow. Please."[163]

The Oedipal rage between Mother Edith and Daughter Virginia exceeded even harsh discipline as Edith's sharp switches bloodied Virginia's legs. The contrast was with the kind and good Father Eldridge about whom Daughter Virginia said, " I loved my father as much as it's possible for a daughter to love her father." As Father Eldridge was attacked by Mother Edith's harsh words, Virginia wondered, "Why don't you stand up to her, maybe even strike her...that might teach her a lesson." Virginia decided about the time she got to high school that she "wasn't going to cater to my mother's bullying," but she didn't announce it, "I was gutsy, but not crazy."[164]   Her rebellious behavior in nursing school was a deferred attack on her mother after she left home and is described in Bill's Sadism and Masochism.

Virginia's own Oedipal frustration in attempting to possess her good father and destroy her bad mother was revived in her mother-son relationship; thus fulfilling Freud's meaning. She possessed her son and so won a victory in the Oedipal struggle with her mother about her father. After Bill's Presidential inauguration, Virginia muses in the[165] Queen's Bedroom of the White House, "I wish my daddy could have been there to see his daughter... on the Queen's bed." [166] Like mother, like son, the Oedipus complex is hard to resolve.

The labyrinth of Virginia's Oedipal drama included her marriage to Roger, an attractive older man whom she first met when he was in business with her father. In this venture, Roger supplied the bootleg whiskey that had been confiscated by the police in Hope, a dry town and Father Eldridge sold it in his grocery store from under the apples. Virginia was a nursing student then but she says this "hadn't been intended as an introduction for a date or anything like that."178  She adds that she didn't know about the partnership and she had forgotten about Roger until she encountered him again as a young widow in 1947 when Bill was a year old. Roger, called The Gambler by Virginia, was Bill's stepfather during the stormy seventeen years they were married.

Virginia shows her Oedipal frustrations as anger when author James Stewart portrays Mother Virginia and Son Bill, then a first term Governor, "With her skunk-stripe hair, thick makeup, and eyeliner, she would charge through the office...bumping Rudy Moore (chief of staff) out of the way. 'Get the hell out of here, Dwire (Virginia's name then) said. 'I want to talk to this little brat.' From behind the closed office door, the staff could hear her yell at her son, 'I'll be goddamned if you can pull this shit on me."167

In addition to her immediate annoyance, Virginia was expressing Queen Jocasta's reaction to her role in Oedipus' tragic actions. The Queen had allowed her newborn baby to be taken away to the forest by King Laius' servant to be put to death after a prophecy that Oedipus would kill Laius. Oedipus was spared this fate by being given to a peasant family; however, he returned as a young man to kill King Laius and marry Queen Jocasta as the new king. In the play, the Queen committed suicide when it was revealed that Oedipus was her son.

Is the Oedipus complex universal? It appears to be present in some form in most of the societies studied by anthropologists and psychoanalysts although agreement about this is lacking.  Frantz Fanon, psychoanalyst and Third World liberationist, questions its universality in Africa. The best argument for some kind of Oedipus everywhere seems to be a universal prohibition against incest. The superego, the location of cultural rules and standards is thought to be an heir of the Oedipus complex. Incidentally, Freud never argued that the Oedipus complex was universal although other psychoanalysts did. All this and more is explained by Andreas Bernoldi writing about Africa.[168]  Meanwhile, Alan Roland reports that psychoanalysts in Japan propose an Ajase complex that focuses directly on the mother as a substitute for the Oedipus complex with dependency relationships that are called amae which are the center of Japanese psychological functioning.[169]

## BILL'S PRIMAL SCENE

Virginia is unusually revealing about the family's psychosexual panorama when she says that Bill's childhood bedroom was directly across the hall from the one she occupied with her second husband, Roger. The primal scene is a psychoanalytic dictum about the effect on the small child who sees parental sex as an attack of an aggressive male on a passive female. The emotion of the coupling and the mystery of adult sexual organs excite and confuse the child. The parental bedroom was the source of noisy accusations of infidelity by a drunken Roger and attacks on Virginia. A curious and precocious Bill could hardly have avoided this kind of primal scene as it was combined with Virginia's frustration and parental conflict.

More about the sexual problems of this family are revealed when Virginia tells about Roger's lack of in sexual interest in her. She complains about her husband's inability to impregnate her more then twice in 17 years of marriage, one a miscarriage, although they wanted very much to have another child. She says, "I don't recall ever using any kind of birth control…a husband's nightly alcoholic tantrums can work wonders in that regard."[170] In addition to the effect of alcohol on reducing the sperm count, Roger may have been periodically impotent, a condition which is not rare among alcoholics. Virginia tells us that he spent time with other women and says that the family found Roger at a lady friend's house after a search when Roger's father was on his deathbed.

The other side of this equation is Virginia's sexual disinterest in Roger. "I'm a single mother," Virginia thought in 1960 when husband Roger's drunken rage had led to the confrontation with fourteen year old Bill that stopped the abuse. By the time Bill graduates from high school, Virginia says of Roger, "...our marriage was basically over...I hardly even looked at him."[171]  Virginia's frustrated marriage was the kind of family secret that made a traumatic impact on Bill's immature psyche.

We know a good deal about Bill Clinton's sexuality from his promiscuous reputation as reported by his biographers. Gennifer Flowers wrote a book about their twelve-year affair. Dolly Kyle Browning wrote a "thinly disguised" novel "loosely based on a true story" about their thirty-three year love affair, which, she said, began when she was eleven and Bill was thirteen. Later she confirmed that this affair became an "extramarital relationship" in a lawsuit she filed against President Clinton. The Monica Lewinsky affair is documented by Ken Starr's report and Monica's own book.

Maybe as one observer says, there are similarities to his role model, Jack Kennedy, who needed sex at least once a day with a variety of mistresses, lovers, secretaries and prostitutes to avoid headaches. Sexuality is a drive based on biology, but its individual expression varies so the usual list of adulterous Presidents since World War II includes Roosevelt, Eisenhower, Kennedy, Johnson, Bush I and Clinton. Reagan and Nixon are added to this roster in Cawthorne's lively book but Truman, Ford, Carter and Bush II escape. [172]

Did Bill Clinton's reputation for sexual promiscuity increase his voter appeal? I haven't seen any polls on this question but I believe this was probably true and so Gary Hart is the only presidential candidate to be punished for sexual indiscretions. The Paula Jones and Kathleen Willey episodes titillate and disgust. The Gennifer Flowers and Monica Lewinsky affairs, the denials by Bill and Hillary, and then the apologies by Bill attest to the libidos of the Nineties' voters. Prurience and resolution outweigh disapproval.

## BILL AS A BISEXUAL IN LOVE WITH HIS STEPFATHER

Bill's primary Oedipal struggle about his sexual love for his mother and his death wishes toward his stepfather are accompanied by a secondary or negative Oedipal reaction as he identifies with his beloved stepfather against his errant mother. Virginia says she flirted openly with men in the nightclubs because her husband preferred to spend the evenings gambling in the club's back rooms. At least once, Roger attacked a man because she danced with him. She spent much of her free time with men at the racetrack. She tells us that she was innocent of her husband's constant accusations of infidelity, but Dolly Kyle Browning says Virginia had an affair with Dolly's father when they were both married. Dolly speaks through her novel where the locale is Mississippi and the thinly disguised Arkansas characters have new names. Gossip perhaps, but it carries the same emotional valence as Dolly's own affair with Bill Clinton in this novel, narrative-fiction based on her story.[173] Author David Brock says Virginia "slept around" without giving us any details.[174] I heard the same comment in 1998 from James Morgan, Virginia's biographer in Little Rock who said, "You have to remember that she was single for many years."

When Bill was four or five, Virginia and Roger, the stepfather, were rivals for Bill's love. The original positive Oedipus complex is followed by the negative one which helps to neutralize it, but both remain active in the child's dreams, fantasies, imagination and games as other objects of love and hate are substituted for the original Oedipal figures.

Little Bill and his stepfather had a close relationship especially when Roger dated Bill's mother, and Virginia tells us that this was one of the reasons that she married him. Bill was three during their courtship and four when they married. Despite Roger's alcoholism, abusiveness and their confrontation, Bill and Roger remained close until his death from cancer when Bill was 21. Bill's negative Oedipus complex was fostered by his emotional response to Roger's noisy accusations of Virginia, so their truthfulness is less important then their sexual and emotional content. A contributing factor is Bill's jealousy on hearing that his mother preferred other men not just to husband Roger but also to son Bill.

A strong and persistent reverse Oedipus complex can create homosexual feelings for men who are father surrogates although this is not apparent with Bill. This is not a psychoanalytic theory about the development of homosexuality, which is mainly biological or constitutional, but simply a look at the psychosocial and family issues of normal bisexuality.

Bill isn't gay or actively bisexual, but the negative Oedipal complex may have provided him with empathy for homosexuality that led him to give more government help in the AIDS crisis. He is the first President who had a direct relationship with an openly gay friend and activist, David Mixner, who raised money and organized gay voters for Bill in both his presidential campaigns. Although Bill made an unsuccessful attempt at equality for gays in the military early in his first term, he later opposed gay marriage.

Rumors accused Bill as a twenty-eight year old bachelor of being gay during his unsuccessful 1974 Congressional campaign against the incumbent Republican, although Hillary had just arrived in Arkansas and Bill was said to have a girlfriend in each county. In 1998 during the Lewinsky scandal, listeners on KSFO, hate-Clinton radio in San Francisco, were asked to imagine Clinton playing " bear and otter," gay argot for a large hairy man cavorting with a slim hairless one like George Stephanopoulos so bisexuality has a role in the Dionysian persona of Bill Clinton at least according to some in the Radical Right.


## BILL'S GOOD AND BAD WOMEN

The role of Hillary Rodham Clinton in Bill's life as his wife and the mother of his child are described in some detail by his mistress, Gennifer Flowers. The veracity and narcissism of her memoir are of concern, but her words and those she heard from Bill during their relationship are part of the psychohistorical climate of Clinton's gubernatorial sexuality. Flowers recalls Bill describing Hillary as Hilla the Hun or Sarge and saying that she preferred women to men, but that he really "admired" her mind and the things she tried to accomplish.[175]

This is the classic psychoanalytic dilemma of the Madonna (not the pop performer) and the Whore for a man who is impotent with his wife but potent with a mistress. His wife represents the mother, a tabooed sexual object, while the bad woman is permitted sexually. Bill's mother image is split by the power of the Oedipal prohibition into a good mother-wife who becomes forbidden as a sexual object and a witch or bad mother who is allowed because she is degraded by the sexuality denied to the wife.   Bill's first solution to his Oedipal dilemma was to escape from the taboo against Mother Virginia's steamy Southern sexuality into Hillary's cooler Yankee persona.

In an Oedipal confession, Virginia says she wanted him to choose an Arkansas beauty queen like her self-image rather then Hillary, the hippie intellectual Chicagoan with coke bottle glasses. Virginia casts herself as a Freudian Queen Jocasta when she speaks of the  "...the young ladies in his (Roger's but also Bill's) life...all beauties in the classic Hot Springs beauty-pageant mold...the image of womanhood my boys grew up with starting at home with their coifed and painted mother."[176]  She recalls "... my first meeting with Hillary...electrifying...I ...had never...any dealings with ...Yankees." Bill spoke up to Virginia about his love for Hillary but she says that "...emotionally we had a long, long road ahead of us."  Later Virginia has a "biblical conversion" at Arkadelphia driving between Hot Springs and Hope and writes a letter asking Hillary's forgiveness which goes unanswered but sending it lets Virginia "live again."[177]

But after a few years of marriage, Bill's libido returns to the Arkansas beauty queens and groupies like Gennifer, Dolly, and Monica. Why? The Madonna/Whore dilemma was back with a new cast and now Hillary was the taboo Oedipal good mother. Hillary had blended with Virginia and had gone from Whore to Madonna in the unconscious of Bill Clinton.


## BILL'S CASTRATION ANXIETY AND MASTURBATION GUILT

A boy's sexual impulses toward his mother are terminated by castration anxiety, the response to real or imagined threats of genital mutilation like, "If you play with yourself, it will fall off."  Castration anxiety is often linked to masturbation guilt. The defenses against this anxiety are crucial to the newly forming personality and their form is influenced by the specific threats and the style of the parents.

Bill Clinton's masturbation guilt is visible when he fires Surgeon General Jocelyn Elders because she suggests teaching about masturbation in schools as part of sex education. Despite this physician's distinguished career and service in Clinton's Arkansas and Federal administrations, she was asked to resign because she spoke permissively about masturbation!

Bill Clinton's castration fears include his learning early in his life about the danger of love when his real father Bill Blythe was killed in a car wreck as he was driving from Chicago to Arkansas so he could take Virginia, who was pregnant with Bill, to their new home in a suburb of Chicago. Hillary explains this feeling by saying, "(He)...viewed his father's death as so irrational - so out of the blue - that it set a tone for his own sense of mortality...an intense sense of ...what he might miss at any moment."

Castration anxiety is often experienced as both a verbal and a physical attack on bodily integrity. Joe Purvis, a kindergarten contemporary recalls that five year old Bill was jumping rope in cowboy boots when he was tripped by a classmate who tightened the rope so Bill fell, breaking his leg in three places. The five year olds shouted at tearful Bill to get up and when he didn't, they hooted, "Bill's a sissy." When the teacher saw what happened, she sent for Bill's grandmother who took him to the hospital where he stayed for two weeks.[178]

This was at a time when Bill was already called a "sissy" because he was fat and clumsy. These are the words and the image of failed masculinity and then the accident actualized the fear of the loss of the penis. Soon the emotions of this trauma if not the memory itself are repressed into the unconscious but they don't go away. The omission of this episode from Virginia's tell-all book also suggests its special emotional significance.

Another physical assault was at seven when Bill was attacked by a "big ram" who had him down in a pasture on the family farm, Virginia writes, He was rescued and then fled to his mother's arms. Later Bill recalls this experience for a reporter, "...a ram butted me cutting my head open. I was too young, fat and slow to run even after he knocked me down the second time. He must have butted me ten times. It was the awfullest beating I ever took and I had to go to the hospital for stitches." This was a likely renewal of castration fears and perhaps anxiety dreams too. Bill blames himself for being unable to escape the attack of the castrating father as ram. His low self-esteem is accompanied by self-blame. How Bill's blaming conscience (also known as the superego) works will be discussed later. Seven-year-old Bill had both strong inferiority feelings and a persona as a leader.

Virginia tells us the attack by the ram happened on a 400 acre farm near Hot Springs, to which Roger, the alcoholic stepfather had moved the family after he failed as an automobile dealer in Hope. Virginia says they soon moved into Hot Springs because Roger didn't know anything about farming. She undoubtedly told Bill so, too.

## BILL'S SEPARATION ANXIETY

Separation anxiety following the loss of a parent or a parent's love is another character-forming experience. It is akin to anxiety about castration, so it may reinforce Oedipal fears.  Age seven was a time of separation anxiety when Bill's mother had to be away from home more often because of the increasing demands of her work as an anesthetist. This wasn't Bill Clinton's first episode of separation anxiety, as will be explained later, but its coincidence at seven with the castration anxiety of the ram's attack makes understandable the consolidation of his ego defenses especially repression and denial, a topic to be spelled out in detail in Bill's Ego Defenses.

Virginia, who was on twenty-four hour call to give anesthesia, was working more by the time Bill was seven, so she needed to find a substitute mother. Virginia explains in her book that a neighbor, Mrs. Walters, an older white woman, came along then, and she is the one who taught Bill the Golden Rule.  Is this just a Southern lady's appreciation for a good nanny or are we also learning that embattled Virginia's rule was that of the Old Testament, an eye for an eye and a tooth for a tooth?

The mother image, which was split earlier between grandmother Edith and Virginia, is split again. Mrs. Walter is at home, benign and religious, while Virginia, aggressive and mobile, is in conflict with stepfather Roger. The stepfather's constant accusations of infidelity against Bill's mother are another threat to the security of Bill who may have believed that something was wrong with his mother. This view was in contrast to the kind housekeeper, who was always available and exemplified the local Bible Belt morality in contrast to his racy mother Virginia, who smoked, drank and gambled. According to Virginia, Mrs. Walter stayed for eleven years, and then her daughter Maye took over as housekeeper.

Another version from Roger Morris' book, *Partners in Power* is that the surrogate mom was Earline White, an African American.  Her husband worked at Ray Clinton's Buick dealership where brother-in-law Roger also worked.

Earline in a 1998 interview with the author says she began work for Virginia when Bill was seven and stayed until he was eighteen when he went off to college.  Earline said that little Bill and Roger always minded and were never difficult. If they needed a reminder, she swished a little switch. Bill told her she could find a better paying job in town and she did. Virginia was said to have been angry with Bill.

There was also more then one nanny in the story written by Bill's younger brother, Roger Clinton, Jr. in his *Growing Up Clinton*. He says a black woman, Earline White, took care of him from an early age, but Miss Walters, another housekeeper whom he called Waffers was also there from his early years so that they "really raised me."   Virginia's remembrance of only a white nanny, Mrs.

Walters, as Bill's example of living Christianity may be Arkansas elegant or just plain racism in Hot Springs a largely white town. Ms. Walters is the only one in both Virginia's book and Roger Junior's book without a first name so perhaps here is a place where the fact checking by their coauthors fell short.

Like a good and bad mother, Bill also had a good and a bad father. Bill Blythe was dead and an idealized symbol, while Roger, the live stepfather, was an abusive alcoholic. The biography by Allen and Portis quotes Bill, "It's a very difficult thing to be raised with a myth...I felt...in a hurry in life because it gave me a real sense of mortality...I thought about it all the time because my father died at twenty-nine..." [179]

Despite his later flaws as a husband and father, Roger was a handsome older adventurous businessman of thirty-six who arrived in toddler Bill Clinton's life as Dude when twenty-four year-old Virginia began her romance with him. He was interested in Bill and helped pay for little Bill's travel to New Orleans with his grandmother so he could see his mother Virginia while she was away studying anesthesia. The good stepfather Roger helped in the resolution of Bill's Oedipus complex. But there was also ambivalence about the early attractive Roger versus his later negative persona. And there was also a lifelong ambivalence about the good father Bill Blythe versus the bad stepfather Roger Clinton. Ambivalence produces the frequent indecision in Bill, as Governor and President and more will be said later about how this ambivalence began at home even before Roger entered Bill's life.

A year after fending off Stepfather Roger's attack on Mother Virginia, Bill, now fifteen, wanted to help his weakened stepfather, so he legally changed his name from Blythe to Clinton. Bill's conscious motive was to support his stepfather, who was depressed about Bill's mother divorcing him but Bill also wanted to help his half brother, who at age five was starting in school. Bill felt he and younger brother Roger should have the same name legally. Bill had already used the Clinton name during school. Virginia, who had remarried her divorced husband Roger after three months of separation, was pleased at this gesture that she thought might help Roger's low morale. But at an unconscious level fifteen-year-old Bill is announcing that he is the father of five-year-old Roger Clinton and the husband of Virginia since his name is now legally Clinton.

The first and crucial separation episode for Bill occurred when his mother went to New Orleans for two years to study anesthesia leaving him as a two year old with his grandparents in Arkansas. Virginia says she was only gone a year, but most of Bill's biographers say it was two years. "It almost killed me to be away from Bill," she said and cried after their visits.[180]

Bill Clinton writes about his memories of separation at two from his mother for two years. "I remember my mother crying and actually falling down by the rail bed. And my grandmother saying, 'She's doing it for you.'"[181] This separation was necessary to assure Bill's future, according to his mother since her earning potential as a nurse was limited, and it also "saved my life" by giving her a focus that helped her shut out her later marital problems.[182]

Bill's maternal grandmother Edith wanted Bill's mother out of town so she could take over the baby, her only grandchild, and she really did come to hold "sway" over Bill. Grandmother Edith disliked Roger, Virginia's new beau, and it was when Bill was four that Virginia's decision to marry Roger led to a crisis. Edith announced she would take Bill's custody away from Virginia even though Eldridge, Virginia's father opposed the plan. After Edith consulted an attorney, the plan was abandoned, but Bill was the object of an emotional struggle between his grandmother and his mother. His grandmother had taken care of him during his first four years, including the years when his mother was in New Orleans and then after her return to Arkansas, when she worked different shifts in local hospitals and was often out of town on weekend parties with Roger.

The struggle for Bill was finally resolved when Virginia's seventeen year marriage to Roger began, but the tension continued. Neither Virginia's nor Roger's parents attended the wedding. Bill's grandmother Edith hated Roger because he was a gambler and alcoholic while Roger's family disapproved because he was still married and behind in child support payments while he court-ed Virginia. Roger's courtship included Bill so "if Roger Clinton loved anybody in this world, it was Bill," Virginia writes. Hyperbole perhaps, but the tangible symbol of the connection between Roger and Bill was Roger's playful German Shepherd, Susie that they both loved.

Virginia says that the emotional struggle over four year old Bill between her and her mother was one that he probably remembered years later. Hillary calls this struggle "abusive" during her interview in *Talk* in 1999.[183] This announcement by the First Lady highlighted the conscious enmity between Grandmother Edith and Stepfather Roger as well as the latent Oedipal rivalry between the Matriarchs, Grandmother Edith and Mother Virginia. Virginia's family history book tells us that the open antagonism between Edith and Roger continued unabated till they both died when Bill was 21. Virginia says that her conflict with Edith was muted over the years as Edith aged, was widowed, became morphine-addicted, under-went withdrawal and finally lived in a nursing home.

Bill's second separation took him away from his grandparents' home when Virginia married Roger. Bill's compensation for this emotional loss was the new house on 13th street in Hope, where he lived with his mother and his new stepfa-ther Roger, who bought him a Lionel Train. Little Bill was loved by his new father, but events were to interfere with this idyll.

Separation anxiety in a child is usually resolved in time with tension, irritability and insomnia, hardly earth shaking events. But not all separations are innocuous or brief, and it is the later behavior that tells us retrospectively what happened in the mind of the child. The unconscious residual of such events is often a lifelong cautiousness or inhibition about sudden change, or just the opposite, risk taking and daring, or Bill Clinton's combination of both. For example, Clinton dared to promise gays full integration in the military, but the fear of the political consequences of this change frightened him, so he withdrew his promise. Bill had received support from gay voters whose concerns included the harassment of gays and lesbians in the service and the discharge of career military men and women who were gay. Bill's risk taking was there, but his fear of the loss of Congressional support was overwhelming.

When Bill's initiative in appointing Lani Guinier to head the Justice Department's civil rights division in 1993 was threatened, his separation anxiety again took control, and he canceled her nomination. She was a law professor and a former NAACP attorney who was called a "Quota Queen" because of her law journal articles about how to make voting more democratic using a kind of proportional representation called cumulative voting. She was denied an opportunity to defend her views before a Senate committee but finally had an emotional ninety minutes in the Oval Office with the President, whose eyes were moist while her nomination hung in the balance as she explained her writings. He seemed satisfied then but twenty minutes later Bill phoned her to tell her he had withdrawn her name. When Lani recalls the experience in her 1998 book, *Lift Every Voice*, she questions the President's leadership, integrity and motivation but didn't Bill's separation anxiety play a crucial role in the decision? The answer is yes because Bill feared separation from his white voters.

Bill's fear of abandonment was resolved by being the abandoner of gays in the military and then of Lani. The fears of America's first rock and roll president defeated his leadership for gay liberation and African American electoral reform.


## SLICK WILLIE AND THE GENES

What about the Slick Willie image? Arkansas journalist Paul Greenberg in the Pine Bluff newspaper popularized this appellation but it was already in the local folk culture with a pre-Clinton bar called Slick Willy near the state capitol in Little Rock.

Bill Clinton's character problems are mentioned by the *Washington Post's* Bob Woodward in *The Agenda* and by his other biographers too. The use of deception in promises, manipulation, self indulgence, and addictions to food, casual sex and exercise, the failure to take and hold a position in the face of criticism, and a lack of a dominant focus to his politics are offered by biographers as evidence of Clinton's character disorder.

Hillary entered the pop diagnostic quiz in 1999 with the Lucinda Franks interview in *Talk* saying that the struggle over four year old Bill between Mother Virginia and Grandmother Edith is the cause of his promiscuity because the worst situation for a boy is to be in the middle of a conflict between two women.

Journalist Edith from concludes that Clinton has "no 'self'" while Andrew Sullivan calls him a "sociopath." *Harper's* editor Lewis Lapham says that Clinton has "...the emptiness of a soul that knows itself only by the names of what it seizes or consumes." Hillary biographer Gail Sheehy says that Bill has a multiple personality calling this by its synonym, dissociative disorder, and attributes this opinion to an unnamed White House doctor.[184]  Of course, these character faults are common in life and politics and Presidents Kennedy, LBJ, and Nixon come to mind.

The mental health professionals who make one-shot diagnoses of Clinton in their books are Doctor Paul Fick, who calls him an adult child of an alcoholic, and Doctor Jerome Levin, who says he's a sex addict.  A psychiatric diagnosis may be of value in coding patients for health insurance reimbursement or for the selection of a medication, but it doesn't offer a theory of behavior or thought.  The rigidity of this nomenclature offers little room for personal or presidential individuality.

Like a child in a candy store, I found the temptation to sound bites hard to resist, so here goes.  George W. Bush is a dyslexic; Clinton has a borderline character disorder and an underlying sadomasochism as will be explained later in this essay. Bush Senior is cyclothymic with a mood, which swings from normal to periodic depression and torpor. Reagan, the president who couldn't remember during the Iran Contra investigation had Alzheimer's disease. Carter was an obsessive compulsive who micromanaged his presidency. Ford, who was appointed vice president by Nixon and succeeded him, was the passive president. That Nixon was a paranoid president is confirmed by his words on his White House tapes.  Kennedy was a speed freak, the substance-abusing president who injected amphetamines. Lyndon Johnson was both manic as he promised the Great Society and depressed as he selected the targets for bombs in Vietnam and sometimes these symptoms ran together. I was able to resist the temptation to diagnose the First Ladies but you get the idea.

Clinton's personal characteristics translate into psychiatric jargon as an addiction to exercise, food and casual sex, the lack of a central identity, narcissism, unstable interpersonal relationships that are used exploitively, inappropriate anger, and a distortion of his superego or conscience. These are the symptoms of a borderline personality disorder, which affects 2.5 % of the population, six million people.

"Borderline" originally meant a condition between neurosis and schizophrenia but now "borderline" often refers to the border between a neurosis with its anxiety, fears or obsessions and a grossly disordered character with a defective conscience and a lack of controls like a criminal or an alcoholic. Borderline is a diagnosis, which began to be used, by psychoanalysts and psychiatrists in the Fifties to replace the older and pejorative mental hospital labels: asocial or sociopathic personality, constitutional psychopathic inferiority, and character or personality disorder. These terms in the frequently changing nomenclature of the American Psychiatric Association[185] (APA) are all part of a debate. Psychiatrist Fritz Redlich who wrote about Hitler says that anyone using the term borderline needs to define it to clarify what it means to the writer. The definition of narcissistic personality appears later in the section on Narcissism. It overlaps with the definition of borderline although the APA attempts to distinguish them.

"Borderline" and "narcissistic" as diagnoses don't reveal much about Bill, but they do point to underlying genetic and biochemical factors in addition to the psychodynamic and family issues. (However, Thomas Szasz, the psychoanalyst who has written on the myth of mental illness, would be outraged at a psychiatric diagnosis being applied to Bill or anyone else.)

Behavioral genetics is a new field described by Dean Hamer and Peter Copeland with preliminary results suggesting genetic influences on risk taking or novelty seeking behavior.[186] Virginia tells us that Roger was attractive for her when they met in Hope because he seemed "dangerous," a gambler, a drinker, and an older divorced man from glamorous Hot Springs with its nightclubs, gambling and gangsters. (Like Roger, Mother Virginia was also a drinker, a nightclubber and a gambler.) These tendencies in his mother and Father Bill Blythe's frequent liaisons and marriages and unacknowledged children suggest a genetic factor in Bill's addiction to risky activities such as casual sex.

Novelty seeking behavior is accompanied by frequent casual sex and a preference for the less common varieties of intercourse like oral sex. The behavioral geneticists believe that the frequency and kind of sexual activity as well as a preference for a variety of partners is the function of a gene that also determines either high or low risk behavior. Genes are not destiny even for behavioral geneticists who accept other influences in personality including biological, developmental, environmental and psychosocial events. A footnote is that during the fifties, the Kinsey report[187] had already said that it was likely that there was a genetic influence on the number of orgasms in males whose weekly median was one or two but who varied from none to twenty-nine a week.

Bill Clinton's borderline personality is related to genetic inheritance and here there is some data from his mother's book. She was a regular racetrack gambler and a steady imbiber whose book mentions her own drinking twenty-six times according to the count of a Clinton biographer.[188] Bill's maternal grandmother, Edith became addicted to morphine after she had a stroke, so that she had to enter a state hospital for detox and rehabilitation. Bill's maternal grandfather Eldridge, a bootlegger during Prohibition was "a heavy drinker" according to one of Bill's biographers.[189] He died of bleeding esophageal varices[190] (enlarged veins) that are caused by liver disease, often the result of alcoholism. Bill's father, a traveling salesman, had personal problems about responsibility and identity that led him to conceal his three previous marriages and two children from Bill's mother. This family pattern continued with Bill's half brother Roger becoming addicted to cocaine and serving prison time for drug sales.

Genetic influences in the family patterns of alcoholism are well documented and are similar to those in the families affected by pathological gambling and drug abuse. These genetic profiles are not necessarily the same as the ones thought to be present in narcissistic and borderline personalities, but they may reinforce each other in their effects on behavior. A heredity predisposing to substance dependence, pathological gambling and social dysfunction may be expressed in a variety of ways including Bill Clinton's narcissistic and borderline traits.

Clinton's powerful intelligence, Elvis physicality, and his overall high energy as a tireless campaigner derive to a considerable extent from his genetic heritage. An observation about Bill's energy level is that he seems to need only four hours of sleep a night like his father William Jefferson Blythe, so maybe a poorly understood genetic factor is operating here. Bill was reading at three, and he has a photographic memory, both markers for intelligence which psychologists agree is strongly influenced by heredity. Bill's high school band director, Virgil Spurlin, is quoted by Allen and Portis on Bill's intelligence and his musical ability, "I haven't seen anything quite like him in my teaching experience."[191] Musical ability is another kind of intelligence that also has hereditary influences.

Developmental influences on Bill's brain play a role in his clumsiness that was noted by during childhood and adolescence and later during college. Clumsiness is recognized as a problem in child development and is the subject of a book by Daniel Arnheim, *The Clumsy Child*, which says, "Physical awkwardness can...be caused by...stress. It is often difficult to ascertain whether or not the clumsiness stems from some neurological dysfunction or whether it is a reflection of emotion and self-concept."[192]

Bill was so clumsy as a child that he couldn't catch a ball and he was thought too awkward for piano lessons. In his seventh grade shop class, Bill couldn't learn to square a wooden block while the other boys went on to build bread-boxes and tables, Maraniss says.[193] During college ROTC, he couldn't learn to march. At Oxford, he often tackled the wrong players in recreational rugby games. Nonetheless, he played the saxophone with distinction as a teen in the band and became a golfer. Bill's clumsiness diminished and disappeared as an adult suggesting that stress and a low self-esteem were the primary factors in his childhood clumsiness rather then a neurological condition. Bill certainly was stressed as a child in a dysfunctional home and he had low self esteem as described in the section on Bill's Castration Anxiety and Masturbation Guilt.

Bill's mental and physical constitution is from his unique DNA and from the prenatal and postnatal influences on his developing brain. His heredity affects his behavior directly and through its influence on his psychology.

## BILL'S ORAL AND ANAL DEVELOPMENT

Bill's infancy is not as well described as his childhood, but what is known is consistent with his adult character. His grandmother's feeding compulsion is mentioned by his mother, "Bill jokes that he can attribute his weight problem to the fact that he'd still be sitting in his high chair on Hervey Street if he hadn't cleaned his plate."[194]   Bill was overweight as a child and a teen according to the biography of Allen and Portis. Bill's addiction to junk food is well known, but by 1995, he was in detox eating soy burgers under the direction of a new White House physician, cardiologist Dean Ornish who emphasizes weight control and a low fat, vegetarian diet.

Bill's self confidence and communicative charisma begin with his mother and grandmother, who competed with each other to fill his oral needs. Bill's need to help and his need to give to people is called oral optimism, a variant of hopefulness and faith according to Erik Erickson, the Freudian developmental psychologist. The opposite is oral pessimism, emptiness and taking. Freud explains, "People who know they are preferred or favored by their mother give evidence in their lives of a peculiar self-reliance and an unshakable optimism which often seem like heroic attributes and bring actual success to their possessors."[195]

Bill Clinton is orally fixated, a visible optimist whose emotional faith is palpable along with compulsive eating, a near addictive dependence on jogging, and a repetitive need for new sexual partners.  A hidden or nether side of Bill's orality is his "emptiness" and lack of a "self" mentioned in the Slick Willie section. The powerful control by Bill's grandmother and mother was experienced as a deprivation of autonomy as the oral stage overlaps with the next phase, anality.

Anal eroticism is a stage in the infant's development of personality according to an orderly psychosexual scheme: the mouth first, then the anus and finally, the genitals. It is called psychosexual because although two of the three zones are nonsexual, they are all erogenous, that is they generate pleasure, sensual and sexual during the process of maturation.

During the anal phase in the second year, bowel and bladder mastery are the goals of parental training and the toddler's reaction influences future habits of work. Virginia calls his grandmother's schedule of Bill's bowel training "unrelenting" and says the same about his eating, napping, playing and burping schedules. Using derision more then irony, Virginia compares grandmother Edith to God.

The biography by Allen and Portis says that "Bill's grandparents had a lot to do with my early commitment to learning. They taught him 'to count and read. I was reading little books when I was three. They didn't have much formal education but they really helped imbed in me a real sense of educational achievement...'"[196]

Bill's strict toilet training resulted in orderliness and even compulsivity about study and work. His mother says, "He kept himself incredibly busy during his high school career." The pattern continued as a college student and later as Governor and then as President. His struggle as a two year old against strict and perhaps premature toilet training was followed by his assent. Like a tiny convert, he then became a control freak himself. This characteristic was expressed later on by Bill as the good child with his adolescent conformity, and his adult obsessiveness. This anality may have influenced his choice of the law as a career and then politics, both professions that are ultimately responsible for social control.

Not everything about the struggle for toilet training is hidden. Chronic lateness, mentioned by nearly all Clinton's biographers is often a sign of rebellion against strict toilet training. Virginia explains, "After being bound to my mother's strict regimen for so long, I don't doubt the man sometimes feels a need to dawdle."

Ambivalence is another aspect of conflicted toilet training that often emerges in adult life as indecision. First the infant controls the pleasure of expulsion of the feces and then the pleasure of the retention of feces. Holding on and letting go become part of a power struggle between child and mother so the child's ego builds a defense or coping mechanism involving compromise or ambivalence, a continuing pattern of indecision. The approaching Oedipal developments about the good father versus the bad father and the good mother versus the bad mother reinforce this paradoxical and conflicted behavior of holding on and letting go, retention versus expulsion.


## BILL'S EGO DEFENSES

Understanding Clinton's current behavior leads to a study of his ego mechanisms of defense that determine his actions, style, habits and his foibles. Like Hillary, his physical and emotional development, traumas, parental and adult influences, social milieu and genetics all converge in the formation of these defenses.

Understanding these ego mechanisms is necessary to explain Clinton's hesitancy, indecision and passivity in the face of opposition, desire to please, deceptiveness, sexual profligacy, food and exercise dependence, cowardice, risk taking, interest in study and music, fluidity in reinventing himself as well as his religious beliefs, intellectuality, charisma, ambition, perfectionism, need to help, misplaced anger, lateness, energy, courage and achievements. During the Monica crisis in 1999 George Stephanopoulos, the former Clinton advisor, asks, "How could a president so intelligent, so compassionate, so public-spirited, and so conscious of his place in history act in such a stupid, selfish, and self-destructive manner?" in an of echo Bob Woodward's list of Clinton's paradoxes. Of course we are not going to explain everything, but some of these questions can be answered by the way his ego defenses protect him against the castration threats, guilt, separation anxiety and sadomasochism which swirl around in his id, ego and superego.

*Repression* is the banishing or expulsion of events, feelings and ideas from the conscious into the unconscious, where they remain excluded from awareness. This is a response to signals of anxiety originating from threats of separation and castration. Bill Clinton may remember the move at four from his grandmother's house to his mother's new home with stepfather Roger, but likely the emotions of this separation were repressed.

Repression also affects the style of his response to later dangers of castration and separation like the draft during the Vietnam War. He repressed or "forgot" this experience, so he had trouble recalling the details of what had actually happened. Here again the repression is caused by the associated emotions not the experience itself.

*Denial* is a defense which affects the perception of reality so that what happens is not seen, heard or acknowledged. This lack of awareness of a painful reality is common among the children of alcoholics who don't recognize the alcohol-affected behavior in the home. Clinton mostly denied the experiences of Stepfather Roger's continuing abuse of his mother. More striking is the belief of some biographers that Bill was also abused, and this was denied too. It was Clinton's denial of the criticisms by the voters and the press during his first term as Arkansas governor that led to his defeat at the polls after two years. There is more about Bill's use of denial later on in the section on Monica.

*Reaction Formation* is another common defense which happens when an unacceptable impulse is turned into its opposite so that anger and rage become charm, ingratiation and manipulativeness. This behavior was learned from his mother and his grandmother and reinforced by his stepfather. Of course they were each skilled at maneuvering and captivating and dissimulating, we're told by Bill's mother, but they were often openly angry at each other, so Bill's affable adaptation is his own.

*Somatization* is the defense which channels conflicts to the physical realm away from the emotions resulting in Bill's gastrointestinal reflux, obesity, hearing loss, knee dysfunction, low back pain, and allergies. They have a biological and often a genetic basis as well as emotional meanings. One example is Clinton's gastrointestinal reflux, often called heartburn which is the periodic regurgitation of stomach contents for which he takes medication mentioned in the report of his 1996 physical examination.   Another example is the origin of Clinton's obesity from his oral fixation, the overindulgence of the infant who continues to use this pattern as a defense against a fear of oral deprivation, that is emotional starvation. Love is food in families and the overfeeding of little Bill by Grandmother Edith reinforces this pattern. Clinton's excessive food intake is an Elvis-like addiction that reduces his stress from guilt, depression and anxiety. Gastrointestinal reflux is another response to this same oral overindulgence.

*Acting Out* is exemplified by the bimbo eruptions (maybe they should be called Bubba eruptions) during his governorship and presidency. The expression of the impulse is more pleasurable and less painful then its control despite the consequences. The Bubba eruptions which chose Paula Jones in Arkansas and Monica Lewinsky in the White House were the results of poor impulse control as well as Bill's penchant for risk taking. Gennifer Flowers wrote in 1998 that she had to dissuade Bill from sex with her in a bathroom in the Governor's mansion during a reception with Hillary nearby.[197]

Clinton's frequent rages are another kind of acting out. As Governor, his fury was often directed at his chief of staff, Betsey Wright and Maraniss recalls he slapped her "like a brother hitting his sister."[198]   Woodward talks about Clinton's anger as outbursts and blowups and journalist Jeffrey Birnbaum speaks of "Clinton's fiery temper."[199]   These tantrums are classified by George Stephanopoulos in order of their seriousness as the morning roar, the nightcap, the slow boil, the show and the last gasp with the silent scream as the most virulent. Narcissism, to be explained in a later section, also contributes to Bill's acting out.

Acting out includes Clinton's alleged rape of Juanita Broaddrick with her lip injury and his widely reported and denied knock down punch directed at Dick Morris.

*Passive-Aggressive Behavior* is a defense in which frustration is expressed through inappropriate passivity or by its opposite, inappropriate aggression. Bill Clinton often failed to exercise leadership early in his presidency according to Bob Woodward who said, "Clinton did not project a sense of command," or even that "...he diminished the weight of his office." His periodic retreat from activity into Presidential passivity is described as Bill speaks of his fears as the captain of an old ship with oars when, " ... the people...can refuse to row...I can steer it, but a storm can come up and sink it..."[200] As Clinton's castration anxiety becomes intense in a confrontation with Congress and the media, he retreats from activity into passivity because of his unconscious fear of the loss of the penis.

Passive-aggressive behavior may also involve Clinton's inappropriate aggression as a defense against his passivity when his anxiety signals. During the Clinton presidency, bombing Belgrade and Yugoslavia, burning the Branch Davidians at Waco, raining revenge missiles on a pharmaceutical factory in the Sudan and Osama bin Laden's barracks in Afghanistan, and even the war on drugs are examples of the choice of aggression rather then attempts at nonviolent solutions. Policy considerations aside, Cabinet officers and advisors take their cues from passive-aggressive Bill.

*Ambivalence* is a defense taking the form of indecision, reversal of policies and uncertainty. These mark Bill Clinton's Presidency according to Bob Woodward, who wrote about economic policy during his first two years in the White House. James Carville asks, "Where is hallowed ground? Where does he stand?" An associate, Paul Begala says that the most perplexing question about Clinton is his "...two sides... a Southern populist, religious...connected to the average hard working middle class and a Northern, elitist, Yale Law School side..."[201]

Ambivalence was also a part of the Clinton trademark when he governed Arkansas. He waited until the last minute to veto a tax bill affecting education, so he had to slide it under the locked door of the House clerk's office and then he had to retrieve it later that night with a coat hanger. He had changed his mind again after a phone call to a college president[202] according to John Brummett, a Clinton biographer in *Highwire*. Ambivalence as a defense has its origin in the anal phase of development with infant Bill's conflict about expulsion versus withholding.

Ambivalence remained central at the end of his second term as Clinton avoided acting on the Missile Defense System which he authorized but left the decisions to build and deploy it in Alaska for the years after his term had ended, according to a *New York Times* report by Myers and Stemmata.[203]

*Intellectualization* is a defense mechanism that refers to the use of ideas and language as a substitute for emotions. An excess of thinking is used to control the unacceptable impulses that signal the danger of castration and separation. In *The Agenda* Woodward says, "Clinton spoke so often, said so much on so many subjects, that he further confused people about him and about his goals as President."[204]

*Sublimation* is a defense, which replaces unacceptable unconscious lustful and violent impulses by desirable goals, often their opposite. Serving the need of others and religious belief are solutions for some of the conflicts of id, ego, super-ego and reality. Bill's charisma is an aspect of sublimation. Arkansas biographer Brummett describes Clinton as a "...person demonstrating compassion, emotionalism, and an uncanny ability to connect and empathize with all kinds of people..."[205]

*Hysterical spells* are another defense, which affect Bill and also his family of White House advisors. "Chaos, absolute chaos," was Bob Woodward's characterization of Clinton's White House speaking on "Sixty Minutes."[206] Journalist Jeffrey Birnbaum says, "The (Clinton) White House is a madhouse almost all the time," pointing out that this was different from previous presidents.[207] Chaos was also the word applied to Clinton's campaign for Congress in 1974 by Hillary who began to turn things right side up when she arrived in Arkansas.

Well-ordered Bill doesn't have any visible hysterical spells so they are not seen directly although they are kin to his temper tantrums described earlier under the Acting Out defense. The disorder in Bill's White House is analogous to the patient who screams, faints and flails aimlessly for a while but on recovery is calm and may not recall the episode The physical events of the hysterical attack are often accompanied by a flight of ideas like a dream that defies conventional logic. Not all chaos is a hysterical spell; sometimes there is the planned confusion of the Marx Brothers in *A Night at the Opera*, Abbott and Costello and *Animal House*.

## BILL AS COWARD

Is Clinton a coward? Clinton's unwillingness to serve during the Vietnam War, called draft dodging by some, was a part of his concern about violence and death in a war he saw as unjust. Of course some baby boomers who supported the Vietnam War like Independent Counsel Ken Starr, 1996 Presidential candidate Phil Gram, Speaker Newt Gingrich and Vice President Dick Cheney, didn't serve either while others like Vice President Al Gore did. Fear of dying and of killing others motivated the men who sought draft exemption as well as those who went to Canada and to prison. Some of these men of Clinton's generation who didn't serve were conscientious objectors, pacifists or antiwar draft resisters while others were primarily pursuing career goals. Social class, family tradition, ideology, religion, politics and a raging national debate also had significant roles about who served in Vietnam. Still every personal and political position has a psychological face, so Bill's stance and that of the others involved their individual response to unconscious castration fears.

Clinton's avoidance of teen-age combative sports was an earlier manifestation of his fear of violence, fostered by his mother as a nurse who treated athletic injuries at the hospital. Bill was uncoordinated and clumsy, so he had another reason to avoid sports. He made a pacific choice for band as his extracurricular activity in high school and was successful on the saxophone. Still, Clinton was competitive, a winning contestant for high school class offices and many awards.

The pop psychologists often blame Clinton's loss of his father and the strong women who raised him for his failures of leadership, ambivalence, indecisiveness and fear. This theory ignores the Hamlet-like indecision of other presidents with powerful fathers like Woodrow Wilson, whose failure to take the initiative about the Treaty of Versailles was both a political and a psychological disaster according to the study by Freud and Bullitt. Presidents with dominant fathers also had major flaws in their decision-making and leadership like JFK at the Bay of Pigs and Nixon at Watergate. The other side of this coin is FDR, a remarkable leader with a dominant mother.

## BILL AS NARCISSUS

The role of narcissism in personality development is explained in Hillary and Narcissism. Hillary has a normal share of narcissism but Bill has a narcissistic personality disorder. A narcissistic disorder includes strong feelings of grandiosity and entitlement, self-centeredness, a need to control others, difficulties in love relationships and a diffusion of identity. Bill, who has these characteristics, also has both conscious and unconscious ego mechanisms of defense that hide many of them from himself and others. The label for Bill as a borderline personality in Slick Willie and the Genes overlaps with narcissistic personality, so there is no contradiction here.

Bill's narcissistic personality is the result of a narcissistic wound. Bill's narcissistic wound is expressed in his passive-aggression, his deceptiveness, manipulation and the bimbo eruptions, but his normal narcissism reflects his flexibility, initiative, ambition, self-confidence, empathy and charisma.

The contradictions of narcissism can be explained by the idea of Bill as a changeling. A changeling is a child that folklore tells us has two personas; one is good and beautiful, and the other is evil and ugly. Bill's childhood story tells us about his two aspects, one a fat, clumsy five year old who was a sissy and the other an attractive, active, popular and bright boy. Bill's companions from kindergarten recall both boys. So does President Bill when he describes himself to an interviewer as "a loner" as a child.

Bill's contradictions are at the center of his paradoxical personality; no one chooses the changeling role; the changeling appears again when Bill was an adolescent. His mother Virginia says, " He kept incredibly busy...Bill's crowd enjoyed one another as members of a group. I don't mean that Bill didn't have dates. He did."[208]  But Dixie Terrell Kline, his high school classmate writing in *The New Yorker*, says Bill had no dates and was not a ladies' man in high school although he was "bright, well liked, respected...but too involved with music and the school band to go out with girls."[209]  Are these two views consistent? Of course they are as they describe an adolescent who was inhibited sexually but creative musically and politically. Also he was stuck in his worrisome but satisfying Oedipal role taking care of his mother and brother Roger, who was five when Bill was fifteen as they were threatened by the brutal and alcoholic stepfather.

Bill's sexuality is the Mona Lisa of his narcissism with its in-your-face entitlement, high-risk pursuits and kinky venues. So there is a special interest as Virginia explains, "Neither of my sons got the standard parental lecture about sex...I could never summon up the courage...I couldn't make myself tell them even once...If I'd had daughters, I think it would have been easier...I'd have told them sex could be a sweet and beautiful thing - but precautions had to be taken." There is nothing unusual in this behavior by a more-or-less single mom in the Fifties but it amplifies the meaning of some of Bill's later sexual behavior. Virginia's explanation is prescient when she says, "...the lecture doesn't count as much as the values you've instilled during all the preceding years."[210]

Bill's high risk extramarital sexuality is an expression of narcissism reminiscent of the behavior of his father Bill Blythe and his stepfather's affairs as well as Virginia's flirtations. Local stories about a Virginia as "a rounder"[211] are noted by Meredith Oakley, a Clinton biographer while David Brock says her reputation was that she "slept around." [212]  Dolly Kyle Browning's novel about her love affair with Bill mentions that her father had an affair with Bill's mother.[213]

Bill's narcissistic wound in infancy creates an adult with an exaggerated sense of entitlement. This is the same Bill who desperately needs approval as he chases after skeptical editorial writers, cynical voters, recalcitrant legislators, and attractive women according to biographer Oakley. This is the Bill who seeks affirmation as he takes self-destructive risks in his behavior with women like Juanita Broaddrick, Gennifer Flowers, Paula Jones, Kathleen Willey and Monica Lewinsky. (Bill's most self-destructive relationships were with women who resembled his mother Virginia with her bright makeup and big hair.)

The cause of Bill's original narcissistic injury include episodes of separation, the first when his father died months before he was born and the second at about two years of age when his mother left him for two years with his grandparents. The others that occurred later are also the markers of Bill's narcissistic injury. Narcissistic injury is also marked by his childhood alienation as a fat and clumsy loner.

Deep within Bill's unconscious is the influence of his mother's own unsatisfied narcissistic needs, which Bill saw, reflected in Virginia's "shrine" to Bill on the living room wall. This space was covered with "...Bill's colorful band medals...(and) portraits of Bill..."[214]  In psychoanalytic jargon, Bill was a self-object for Virginia.

A self-object is the use of a child to fulfill the unconscious narcissistic needs of a parent. Sometimes they are "gifted" children. These children respond to the knowledge that they are props for the shaky self-esteem of a parent. They are children who are not loved as a separate person but as a part of a parent's ego.

Virginia's narcissism envelops little Bill to the extent that it is a painful struggle for him to separate himself as a person from the qualities that he developed to satisfy Mother Virginia's narcissism.

"The original narcissistic wound never has a chance to heal. Such a child has never felt loved for himself," says psychoanalyst Sue Erickson-Bloland who studied Bill's life.[215]

Another high-risk behavior that influenced Bill was his family's preoccupation with gambling. Bill was not a gambler, but stepfather Roger was, and his losses forced him to sell his car dealership in Hope when Bill was six. This loss led to the family's move to Hot Springs, where Roger took a job at the Buick dealership owned by his brother, Ray Clinton. Mother Virginia was a gambler too, who bet daily at the local racetrack. Gambling is excitement displaced from infantile conflicts about masturbation according to psychoanalytic theory.

Is this the whole story? No, because most personality theorists believe there are constitutional, that is hereditary biochemical factors along with the family style issues that contribute to narcissistic injury and the resulting narcissistic personality. (See the Slick Willie and the Genes for a discussion of these constitutional factors.)

Narcissism, which is said to be the leading cultural disorder of the late twentieth century, remains a controversial subject. A recent debate is whether narcissism is socially or individually determined. *Time Magazine* recognized this when it called psychoanalyst Heinz Kohut, "the preacher of narcissism...[who] replaced Freud's tragic vision with an optimistic creed...that man is born good and evil is produced by the culture." Kohut's emphasis on narcissism in a system called Self Psychology has shifted attention away from Freud's oral, anal and Oedipal developmental phases, but despite this "whiff of heresy," Kohut remained a Freudian.[216]

## BILL'S CONSCIENCE AND BILL'S GUILT

What about Bill's conscience or superego? The development of Bill Clinton's conscience begins with castration anxiety, the fear of the loss of the penis, as he learns that he can't kill his stepfather and possess his mother. His infantile world is one of castration fears from threats about masturbation and the vision of a primal scene, which interprets the female genitalia as having lost a penis. The broken leg when his kindergarten classmates tripped him is an icon for castration anxiety but fear alone isn't a conscience.

The guilt-producing part of the mind, Bill's superego, came into existence with grandma's flash cards at three when he was already able to read. She trained him in guilt by using the power of reward and punishment for the recognition of the alphabet on the flash card. His mother's book tells us that this family's system of control and authority was driven by guilt, and Bill learned quickly and well. This was the same training that led to the demand for Virginia's conformity earlier by Edith, Bill's grandmother so we have a family pattern of strict superego development. Virginia explains, "Mother had always been very strict, very protective...trying to control my life."[217]

Bill's public promises not kept; his political manipulativeness and his extra-marital affairs argue against an effective conscience or a full quota of guilt. After all, he resolved his castration anxiety by besting the unstable alcoholic stepfather in the contest for his mother's love although there never really was any question of her loyalties. Bill felt guilt about his idealized real father's death, which happened before Bill was born, so it was both, harder to hate him and to resolve that hate by identification with him. His stepfather, whose last name he used when he began school, was weakened as a person and as a symbol by his alcohol addiction while his powerful Uncle Ray Clinton was a more distant part of the family.

The wound that determines his narcissistic personality deforms Bill's superego or conscience. The resulting superego deficit encourages impulsive action about the choice of sexual partners in high-risk situations. Not all the bad choices are about impulsive sex; some are about Big Macs when the problem is food addiction.

But it was also Bill's superego that determined his achievement in school classes and in saxophone practice for band, and in his high school political leadership. This conscience was elaborated during his teens I into an ego-ideal with its models, John Kennedy and Arkansas Senator William Fulbright. Bill took the initiative to please his mother and his teachers, and so he avoided guilt, the internal pain of self-punishment from his conscience. Bill's conscience internalized his mother's behavior and aspirations. Mother Virginia wanted to be at the top, so we see her photo in her book at the apex of a pyramid of teenage bathing beauties. Later as a nurse and single mother, she trained to become an anesthetist, a solo practitioner in a specialty that is dominated by male doctors.

The conscience or superego includes the moral and religious system with its reward and punishment in heaven and hell. Interestingly in this culturally Baptist family, Bill is the only one who was a churchgoer. Guilt is the trigger of the conscience, an internal sense of right and wrong. Much of this is unconscious although its expression reflects personal, family and religious beliefs. Bill Clinton's religion is a sublimation of infantile incestuous and murderous wishes as a response to a fear of the punishment of castration.

90

The superego requires certain activities while others are forbidden. A desire to be liked by everyone during his school years is prominent in the Clinton story and it was compulsive during his political career as agreeable legislators were key to a Governor's and a President's success. David Gallen, a Clinton biographer, notes that Bill needs constant reassurance," quoting a staffer in the Governor's office.[218] Another expression of this psychic energy is FOB, the Friends of Bill mystique, an authorized clique of admirers.

Bill's pursuit of success is the rule of his internalized superego or conscience. The superego represents the parents, and Bill Clinton's superego is his mother's behavior speaking to him. She describes herself as "street smart...tough...never ruthless..."[219] so this becomes his style, mostly. This is not exactly the Golden Rule, which Virginia said Bill learned from his nannies. Perhaps Virginia thought she couldn't teach it to Bill herself because she lived according to the talion law of the Old Testament, "a fracture for a fracture, an eye for an eye and a tooth for a tooth."

Virginia's struggle in the competitive medical world of Hot Springs echoes Virginia's use of Leviticus rather then the Golden Rule. Virginia had to overcome a monopoly by two nurse anesthetists when she first came to Hot Springs. She established herself as a professional yet for thirty years she fought "...against the men who because they were M.D.'s and I was a lowly nurse anesthetist expected to walk into town and have me work for them...I began to retaliate...the weapon of choice was innuendo."[220] Eventually new hospital standards required M.D. control of anesthesia, and two malpractice cases against Virginia had been filed. Meanwhile the atmosphere of the Hot Springs medical community was poisoned, and Virginia admitted "...that it was a poison I had helped to inject." Her street smarts and her "tooth and nail" struggle were a part of Bill's legacy. They passed from Mother Virginia's mind and life into Bill's superego. Bill used this *lex talonis* as he came to favor the death penalty, bombed Iraq and Yugoslavia, struck the Sudan and Afghanistan with missiles, and required workfare for welfare mothers.

Of course, the structure of the conscience and its power are separate from its contents, so a "bad" goal may be pursued just as avidly as a "good" goal. Bill does feel guilt, but it may not be in the same value system as that of the observer. Beauty is in the eye of the beholder.

The compulsive performance of success-driven Bill is based on his superego, which cannot be measured because it is buried in the unconscious along with the id. One of the unsolved paradoxes of psychoanalytic theory is the close linkage of the libido of the amoral id and the conscience or superego. In fact the id energizes the superego and the ego, our conscious self, is at the mercy of this balance. Freud said, the superego is always in close touch with the id..."[221]

Stay here with me as we slip and slide through the Freudian jungle of jargon.

## BILL'S SOUTHERN MIND

The South as the mythic and cultural context of Bill Clinton's psychology demands special attention. Arkansas was a slave state and a member of the Confederacy that was defeated in the Civil War and it remained monocultural: rural, poor, Protestant and untouched by the European immigration after the Civil War. The individual psychology of white Southerner in the modern era is affected by the ways in which the mythology of the South is different from the rest of the United States and also from the African Americans who often left the South for the Northern cities.

Bill Clinton's ethos or collective unconscious was the poverty of the South, Protestant fundamentalism, the military and rural life. Of course Bill was not poor, avoided the military, never was a fundamentalist, and grew up in the second largest city in his state, Hot Springs, but the powers of myth reside in the unconscious.

Beneath the Southern brag and boast of the good ol' boys and their unsullied ladies is a fear that one is really white trash, that irreparably inferior. Why? The South lost the Civil War and afterwards was punished by a hundred years of regional poverty compared to the industrial, banking and railroad wealth of the North. The nexus of the South was country life, Bible Belt religion, violence, guns, the military and patriotism, again in a formula that differed from the rest of the country. The preeminent Southern historian, C. Vann Woodward says, "...the Southern heritage is distinctive. For Southern history, unlike American, includes large components of frustration, failure and defeat. It includes not only an overwhelming military defeat but long decades of defeat in the provinces of economic, social and political life."[222]

The burden of the white Southerners, at least those not descended from planters or aristocrats, was the dread of being considered white trash, shiftless and worthless so well described by Dorothy Allison in *Bastard Out of Carolina* and by William Faulkner in his sagas of Yoknapatawpha County. But the core of the white trash image is the unspoken and unconscious belief that inside one is really a Black, a changeling who should be reclassified even lower in the white South's traditional hierarchy. This mythology explains some of the psychological force of the South's racism, the Klan, lynching, and segregationists like Arkansas' Orval Faubus.

The racism of the Northerner is just as destructive, but is not fueled by this mythology because Northerners lived separately from Blacks mostly in cities populated largely by the post-Civil War often Catholic immigration from Europe. New Orleans with its Cajun Catholic culture is the exception to the Anglo-Saxon Protestant South that received few immigrants after the Civil War until the 1970's and 80's when Cubans came to Miami and a few Vietnamese fisherman moved to the Gulf Coast.

All of Bill Clinton's grandparents were from poor farming families according to his biographers even though his maternal grandparents eventually owned a country store while his father Bill Blythe was a salesman and his mother was a health professional. The culture was fundamentalist although Bill's mother and stepfather spent little time in church and Bill's mother says that her values were in opposition to the conservative Pentecostal preacher who lived next door in Hot Springs.

This phenomenon is worth explaining because the Southern ethos and its myths are part of Bill Clinton's ego identity, that is the ideas and values of adolescence that form the content of the adult personality. Despite Clinton's handshake in the Rose Garden with JFK at seventeen, the tribal models for Clinton's inner self are the Southern presidents, Truman, LBJ, and Jimmy Carter.

The ability of Clinton to offer racial reconciliation and civil rights enforcement is inherent in his Southern ability to tap into his white trash-black identity. This link between the white and Black Southerners is explained in W. J. Cash's classic *Mind of the South*, which says that the South's emotionalism, hedonism and romantic imagination is connected with a "Negro entering into (the) white man" and vice versa.[223] It was Helena, Arkansas on the Mississippi River Delta that gave us the blues of legendary Robert Johnson and Big Bill Broozy and the country music of Johnny Cash.

In 1998 Toni Morrison announced that Bill Clinton was the first African American president citing his cultural identity to blackness, born to a single parent, poor and working class, saxophone-playing, a McDonald-and junk- food loving boy from Arkansas.[224] "Black Bill" was the pejorative some Arkansas whites used for Governor Clinton. These perspectives go beyond Clinton's conscious moral and legal beliefs. In an interview by Dewayne Wickham in Harlem, ex-president Bill says, "I have always felt very much at home in the the African American community...the churches or the restaurants or walking the streets." The voters of all races are influenced by Clinton's racial attitudes about integration and affirmative action, which are received as either positive or negative according to their own value systems.

An unexpected confirmation of Bill's biracial identity came with his announcement midway through his second term that he was part Indian because his maternal grandmother was a quarter Cherokee. He mentioned this background during a meeting of his commission on race perhaps to deflect the criticism that it was limited to a black-white dialog. An ego defense of denial kept this factoid from the biographers and journalists until in 1998 Bill called up a biological identity with Americans of color. Later ex-president Clinton recalled during an interview for Dewayne Wickham's book a "Spanish...grandmother" although else-where his maternal grandmother Edith Cassidy was from a poor farming family in Bodcaw, Arkansas.[225]

## BILL'S DEATH INSTINCT

Does a death instinct operate in Bill Clinton? Freud formulated his ideas about the death instinct, which he called Thanatos, after witnessing the human and psychological destructiveness of the First World War. Nowadays most American psychoanalysts don't believe there is a death instinct and consign it to the realms of philosophy and biology rather then psychology but that instinct can help in understanding Clinton. The death instinct was renamed the Death Fear by psychoanalyst Otto Rank, and so it was removed from the controversy about the biology of the instincts to the psychology of fear.

Thanatos is an expression of human self-destruction, a return to the inorganic that is paired with Eros, the life instinct, sexuality and the preservation of the species. The Nirvana Principle is a metaphor for Thanatos, the need of life to return to its source. The libido's aggressive instincts are thought to have an origin in Thanatos. There is an echo of this in Hindu cosmology, where the main Gods are Brahma, the Creator, Vishnu the Preserver and Shiva the Destroyer. A blend of the instincts reach their goals from the unconscious indirectly through the flow of psychic energy usually called libido into love and sexuality, but sometimes also toward destructiveness and aggression. Casanova tells of a woman who allowed him to have his way with her while they watched an especially nasty execution in a public square through an open window.

Clinton supported the death penalty during the 1992 presidential campaign when as Governor of Arkansas he refused to halt the execution of a mentally defective inmate and underlined his action by a flight back from New Hampshire to Little Rock to announce this decision. Rickey Ray Rector was a convicted murderer whose intelligence was so diminished by a brain injury that he saved the dessert from his last meal to eat later on. Here was a personal as well as a national endorsement of capital punishment from Presidential Candidate Bill who earlier during his first term as Governor had refused to set execution dates.

Death penalty doesn't mean death instinct, but it does suggest that Clinton and many other citizens are receiving new aggressive libido from their fear of crime, hatred of the criminal and a desire for revenge by the death of the killer. Why? Pleasure from the destruction of others, sadism, often hides masochism, its opposite, pleasure in suffering. Both are involved in the response to executions, which allow identification with the killer, the executioner and the victim. Execution is a spectacle like the public hanging from another era that stimulates a communal emotional catharsis that is absent in a life sentence.

President Clinton is preoccupied with crime and punishment although the crime rate was falling before he entered office, a decline that continued. His Crime Bill in 1994 was opposed by fiscal conservatives because of its cost and by civil libertarians because of First Amendment problems and included controversial Federal three strike provisions. He continued with an anti-terrorism bill that again compromised constitutional safeguards and many said offered no real shield against terrorists. Automatic weapons control was supported by Clinton and the police chiefs in a confrontation with the National Rifle Association. Clinton's death instinct choose a political preoccupation with violence, death, crime, guns and a need to strike back.

It's a gross oversimplification to say that Thanatos jumps out of the ego of an adult and makes him do things. But it or something in his psychology energizes Clinton's preoccupation with death, crime and murder. At the end of his second term in 2000, Clinton spoke of his fears of terrorist attacks using miniaturized weapons like a cellular phone, computer viruses and a New Year's Eve bombing by Osama bin Laden during "...a somber and foreboding address at the U. S. Coast Guard Academy..."[226] It was also at the end of his second term that Clinton revealed that he "felt personally responsible" for the eighty deaths by gunshot and fire when an FBI assault ended the Branch Davidian siege at Waco, Texas in 1993. "I made a "'terrible mistake' in yielding to Justice Department pleas to storm the compound at Waco..." he said.[227] The self-destructive tendencies of the death instinct are often manifest by both fear and aggression.

These are the facts from the mainstream about Clinton and the death penalty and Clinton on crime and guns as viewed through a psychohistorical lens. Meanwhile the underground speaks of a Clinton conspiracy as "A Blood-Spattered Trail" from the Ozarks to the Potomac according to George Carpozi, a Clinton biographer.[228] The hate-Clinton movement speaks of a "Clinton Body Count ...A list of dead people connected with Bill Clinton." There are lists of eighteen, forty, forty-one, sixty-one or ninety deaths that "require further investigation." There is a "Clinton 'Death List' " of F.O.B.'s who have died under mysterious circumstances because they were on Clinton's "hit list." There are several sources of these theories, including Sam Smith's *Progressive Review* on the Web and *The Clinton Chronicles*, a video.

An aura of death and murder in Bill's unconscious resonates with the Clinton crazies who translate it to events like the death of Vincent Foster, drug wars and murders over the cocaine smuggled through the airport at Mena, Arkansas, the death of Kathleen Willey's husband, and even the suicide of Admiral Borda. The facts in Bill Clinton's life lead to his unconscious, where the mythos includes Thanatos or the death instinct. The American national mind with its own unconscious Thanatos shares in this Death Clintonia. This phenomenon is explained later in Clinton's Equivocal Decade with references to America's sexual repression, environmental destruction and political nihilism.

What about Bill Clinton and war? He avoided connection with war at first withdrawing from Somalia after the death of American troops, entering Haiti cautiously and acting as a peacemaker in Korea, Ireland and the Middle East. Nonetheless, Bill placed American forces in Kosovo, Bosnia, and Macedonia, and they stayed in the Persian Gulf. Other dangers and temptations remained so American missiles were fired at Sudan and Afghanistan in 1998 after terrorist bombings of U. S. embassies in Kenya and Tanzania. Both Iraq and Yugoslavia were bombed by the U. S. and the bombing of Iraq in the no-fly zone continued in 2000 and on into the Bush administration.

The bombing campaign in 1999 against Yugoslavia was conducted without ground troops despite the judgment of the hawks in Congress and in NATO like England's Tony Blair that ground forces would be needed to win. This military action started after the diplomatic failure to resolve the question of Kosovo and its Albanian population. There was a debate about whether the United States had already been too patient with Milosevic's failed pledges of nonviolence in Kosovo or whether the negotiations finally broke down at Rambouillet when we delivered an ultimatum that demanded the virtual military control of Yugoslavia. In any event, the Balkan politics and NATO policies that led to the bombing were filtered through Bill's mind with its psychological defenses based on his active death instinct.

Why were there no combat troops in the Balkans like those fielded by Old Soldier Bush in \ against Iraq? (Notwithstanding the belligerent tone of my question, I opposed both these wars.) Clinton's avoidance of military service because of his fear of death in the Vietnam War is an expression of castration anxiety and this is a personal factor in his fear of using ground troops. Of course the polls, consultants, Congress and military advisors played their roles. Clinton's aggression produced by his death instinct and his fear fueled by his castration anxiety were now in conflict. The result was a synergy analogous to the contraction of a muscle with its simultaneous relaxation and expansion of the fibers. So, there was a seventy-eight day air war during which both the peacemakers and the generals expressed frustration.

As the Balkan winter approached, an option of 150,000 ground troops was on the table. Everyone was worried but the debate occurred without the presence of Wesley Clark, NATO's American commanding general. "The Pentagon told him not to come," Jane Perlez says in the *New York Times*.[229] As I read this I wondered if General Clark's name was even mentioned at Bill Clinton's June 3, 1999 White House war council. Denial was joined by Ambivalence in Clinton's theater of diplomacy. Wesley Clark, who has written his own book about America's Balkan War, *Waging Modern War* says that Clinton was neutral about ground troops but Clinton's role can be better described as Ambivalence, a mechanism of defense. The White House Ambivalence created a deadlock: Secretary of Defense William Cohen and General Hugh Shelton, Chairman of the Joint Chiefs, who opposed ground forces, versus Wesley Clark and Javier Solona, the UN Secretary General, who favored them. A military strategy of caution and indecision was fashioned by Ambivalence and Denial in Clinton's Balkan War, more like Vietnam then Korea.

By the end of his second term, Clinton revived the plan for a missile shield in space often called Star Wars, which began during the Reagan administration. It wasn't effective as a defense weapon according to the tests although its development had cost billions. It was regarded by Russia as a hostile violation of the Antiballistic Missile treaty of 1972, and so it endangered the foundations of nuclear disarmament.


## BILL'S SADISM AND MASOCHISM

Bill as a masochist receiving pleasure from pain is less visible then the sadistic Bill who gets pleasure from inflicting pain. Still Bill was a marital masochist when he was seen with deep cuts on his neck (see Hillary's Sadism and Masochism) inflicted by Hillary and he was the target of keys and books thrown by Hillary in the Arkansas state limousine. Bill's unconscious pleasure in this pain arises from the dynamics of Mother Virginia's sadomasochism with Grandmother Edith and later with Stepfather Roger.

"...Sadistic...behavior may veil an unconscious masochistic aim," psychoanalyst Otto Fenichel explains.[230]  Bill's masochistic impulses are more covert then his sadism in his political life and his public sexual life.  Recall that Gennifer Flowers said that she wouldn't let Bill Clinton tie her up in a sex game with Bill playing sadist although he let her tie him up so he could play masochist.

Many of Bill's love affairs ended on an angry and threatening note. Both Dolly Browning and Gennifer Flowers felt intimidated and frightened by Bill after he became a candidate for President, and they say so in their books. During the media frenzy about her relationship with Bill in 1992, Gennifer said, "I could have been killed..."[231] Dolly tells us that when her tabloid exposure seemed imminent in 1992, Bill threatened to "destroy" her and she countered with "MAD," an angry acronym for Mutually Assured Destruction.[232]  Affairs often end in recriminations, but this choice of weapons suggests an influence from the fear and the violent threats that Bill heard between his mother and stepfather as he was growing up.  Bill's mental environment included his stepfather's brutality and his mother as the victim of his stepfather's sadism.

Gennifer and Dolly's fears of being killed or destroyed point to a sadistic current in Bill's personality. Sally Perdue, a former Miss Arkansas, talked about her affair with Bill on the Sally Jesse Raphael Show and later she found a shotgun cartridge on the driver's seat of her Jeep and her car window was shattered. Paula Jones was characterized as "trailer park trash" by James Carville, a Clinton spokesman. Kathleen Willey said her life was threatened, her tires were slashed and her cat disappeared. They were all fearful of a Clinton inspired attack.

Monica and Bill seemed angry at each other as they talked through lawyers and press leaks before Bill's August 17, 1998 apology. Afterward the Starr documents reported that Monica told Linda Tripp that she was in "fear of my life." Monica's former duenna, Linda Tripp, who turned snitch, is said to have lived in an FBI safe house during the Starr investigation.

The political risks of Bill's casual sex made public by Kathleen Willey, Monica Lewinsky, and Paula Jones produced a major threat to Bill's Presidency. The pleasures of sex produced the pain of Ken Starr's prosecution, the huge presidential legal bills, impeachment and the effect on the Clinton legacy. The sex scandals may have cut the Democratic gains in the 1998 congressional elections and reduced the Gore vote in 2000. The reaction of presidential masochism is best expressed by the whine of Jack Stanton, the Clinton surrogate in *Primary Colors*, who says, "I can't catch a break, can I," as he learns that his casual encounter with a teenager has left her pregnant.[233]

But isn't Bill a lovable rogue, a Falstaff of gargantuan appetites? Yes, and that's one reason why his poll numbers kept going up. The soccer moms and America's dads put Elvis in the White House, and they didn't want to hear about his or their own unconscious sadomasochism.

The stories of JFK's mistresses are mostly hidden but the JFK biographies say nothing about his lovers being threatened. Still Judith Exner continues to sleep with a gun under her pillow according to Seymour Hersh in the recent Dark Side of Camelot. She was harassed and threatened by both the CIA and the FBI according to her book about her affair with JFK. Marilyn Monroe was depressed after her affair with JFK, and she continued to talk about how Jack would divorce Jackie and marry her as she approached her own suicide. We know one of Jack's White House lovers, Ellen Rometsch, who was rumored to be an East German spy, was sent back to Germany in 1963 and Jack paid her to insure her silence.

Kay Summersby was probably not totally forgiving about being dumped by Ike but she didn't feel danger and malevolence. After their wartime romance, Kay wrote a book about her relationship with Ike, whom she continued to love from afair. Lyndon Johnson's first long term affair ended when Alice Glass disagreed with his position on the Vietnam War although they continued to correspond.  His other long affair with Madeleine Brown from 1948 to 1969 ended when he failed to acknowledge their son, who was then eighteen although he had provided financial support for them. Her son sued LBJ's widow in 1987 for a share of his father's estate, but in 1992 Madeline told a reporter that she still loved LBJ.

To compare Clinton with the past is really impossible because the Nineties had different standards on presidential behavior and new rules for the media about privacy as well as a special prosecutor. It is these new norms that have led to the publicity about the affairs of the other post-war presidents.

Bill's behavior toward Hillary is sadistic too, and this sadism dovetails with Hillary's masochism. Again, this behavior isn't necessarily conscious but it's certainly visible.  Bill's casual infidelities as well as his long-term affairs cause Hillary pain and maybe a kind of perverse pleasure. (See Hillary's Sadism and Masochism and Hillary's Moral Masochism and the Monica Porno Flick).

Bill's sadomasochism is manifested by his unconscious switch of Hillary from her role as a sexually desirable woman, the Whore, to the sexually taboo woman, the Madonna. This switch is signaled by Gennifer's arrival in 1977 as well as the other affairs as explained in Bill's Good and Bad Women. The section on Bill's Narcissism explains another unconscious factor in Bill's quest for love affairs: Bill needs the adulation of the affair and the mistress to bolster his self-esteem because he has a hidden childhood inferiority as a loner, a clumsy, fat sissy who was rejected. This explanation fits well with Bill's Acting Out, an ego defense that is most visible as the bimbo or the Bubba eruption.  To make matters more complex, there is an affinity between Bill's sadomasochism and his death instinct if one believes that aggression originates in Thanatos.

How did Bill's sadomasochism get started?  It has already been noted that Bill may have been a victim of Stepfather Roger's physical abuse. In any case, the assaults on his mother Virginia from the time Bill was a child to age fourteen were like attacks on Bill. As a victim of actual or vicarious child abuse from his stepfather, Bill is stimulated by this acting out of sadomasochism. His identification is with both the aggressive sadistic stepfather and the masochistic mother, who divorced and then remarried the stepfather. Tracking sadomasochism to its origin suggests some oral sadism mixed in with Bill's predominant oral optimism and some anal sadism along with Bill's strong anal control.

Bill's sadomasochistic legacy is also an extension of Mother Virginia's conscious and unconscious behavior. Reading her autobiography for her sadism and masochism leads first to her teens and then to her marriage and finally to her professional struggles.

Mother Virginia's behavior was an attack on her Mother Edith that was sadistic beneath its Oedipal trappings. We learn of Virginia's teenage rebellion against Edith's repression when she first left home for nursing school. She was free at last to release her repressed sexuality and anger, the first as her love at first sight for Bill Blythe and the latter as her attack on the maternal authority of the nursing school.

Virginia drank alcohol in the dorm, sneaked out after being restricted on New Year's Eve, threw an electric fan at her roommate, wore excessive makeup and a lace handkerchief on her uniform, took an unauthorized trip home, and married while still in school, all against the rules. These were attacks on Edith's decorum and standards via Nurse Frye, the nursing school director, who was a Mother Edith surrogate. Virginia's pleasure included the "wrath" caused by her attack on authority. There was the possibility of her expulsion from school, but she escaped this. Her behavior led to reprimands and being suspended from school for thirty days. These were more then punishments; they were the pleasure of suffering from self-inflicted wounds, that is masochism.

Virginia dwells on how much Mother Edith disliked Roger, her second husband, whom Edith didn't want her to marry. Choosing Roger gave Virginia the pleasure of a sadistic attack on Mother Edith in addition to her own masochistic suffering from Roger's alcoholism, philandering, gambling and abusiveness. Mother Edith was right about Roger, but Virginia rationalizes her attitude saying, "In hindsight, I suppose you could make the case that Mother knew best - about Roger Clinton...but...I know you can't live other people's lives for them...and ...you can't relinquish responsibility for your life to anyone else."[234]

Virginia remained married to Roger except for a brief period despite his abusiveness for seventeen years until his death. She did divorce him after fifteen years of marriage when his abusiveness led to a confrontation with fourteen-year-old Bill and to an increasingly fearful five-year-old Roger Jr. Then, three months later, she felt sorry for Roger, a tearful ex-husband, who camped in a car outside her home, so she remarried him.

Mother Edith and Husband Roger continued to hate each other, and Virginia tells us that stubborn Mother Edith waited Roger out; she died at 66, two months after Roger died at 57. It is the sadomasochistic Virginia who delivers the final benediction on these two love-hate relationships when she hopes "...that Heaven for them meant that neither will ever have to shriek through the night again."[235]

Virginia as the physically abused wife with a philandering and alcoholic husband is a story from a textbook of masochism, but there was yet another side to this story. Virginia tells us that when she decided to divorce Roger, Mama Clinton, her mother-in-law called weeping and wailing, "Please don't do this to my baby..." and so Virginia was cast in a cruel if not sadistic role by at least some other members of this extended family.

Another drama laden with sadomasochism is Virginia's struggle with the

Hot Springs medical establishment to maintain her independent practice as a nurse anesthetist. She explains the sadomasochism about this struggle when she says, "There are... people today, some of them my supporters who say I brought my thirty year battle...on myself... my response was just me...pride, gender, and personality entered into the mix..." The atmosphere in the Hot Springs medical community "...was a poison I had helped to inject."[236] Many things happened, but Virginia's sadism and masochism are both at play here.

## MOTHER'S DAY FOR BILL

In 1996, Bill Clinton wrote a public Mother's Day tribute to Mother Virginia mentioning their separation when he was a toddler and she was away in New Orleans for training as a nurse-anesthetist. His words are almost identical to those in her book about their tearful parting. Both Virginia and Bill suffered from separation anxiety. Bill remembers the separation, but he repressed the powerful emotions of this experience which reemerge later in his ego defenses.

Bill's repression is underlined by his remembrance of his mother's death in 1994, "...after she got home (from Las Vegas), she called me. Hillary, Chelsea and I ...had a four-way conversation. Just a few hours later, she died in her sleep...And while I regretted not having the chance to say goodbye, I knew... we had said all we needed to say...There were no accounts to settle...no words or emotions left unsaid."[237] These words also points in the opposite direction toward an endless reservoir of unconscious and unresolved Oedipal emotions.

A few days before Virginia died of cancer, she was a guest at Barbra Streisand's New Year's Eve show in Las Vegas. They met at Bill's inauguration and became special friends and there were rumors of Bill's brief affair with Barbra. Virginia's visit to Las Vegas as she is dying reaffirms her choice of Barbra for Bill as an Oedipal prize. So Virginia is Oedipally united to Bill, and she delivers a final attack on Hillary.

Bill's Mother's Day card at a midpoint in his life and his Presidency says, " I miss her laugh...hugs...fire in her eyes...never-say-die attitude. There are still some Sunday evenings when I have the urge to pick up the phone to call her and suddenly realize that I can't do that anymore." Beneath this rational and loving appreciation of his mother, there are the unconscious forces of a mourning reaction. Clinton the child-man is depressed over his loss, guilty about his survival, and angry with his mother for leaving. These emotions after his mother's death mirror his childhood separation reactions of depression, guilt and anger. Virginia's sudden death was a major stress for Bill in the first two years of his presidency according to Bob Woodward in *The Agenda*.

## MONICA TALKS ABOUT BILL

A different kind of look into Bill's mind appears in the tapes of Monica Lewinsky's phone calls to Linda Tripp made during the last three months of 1997. These calls were recorded by Linda without Monica's knowledge and given to Special Prosecutor Kenneth Starr and are among the evidence released by the House Judiciary Committee on thirty seven tapes that have a playing time of twenty two hours. These tapes were played during a marathon broadcast which ran from a Friday to a Sunday on San Francisco's KSFO during November, 1998.

These tapes are a longer and more emotional version of Monica's testimony before the grand jury. Through Monica's love, anger and depression she tells about Bill and their failed relationship. No one altered this oral diary, unlike Monica's book and the others written by Bill's friends all of which went through self-censorship and an editorial process. Monica talked to Linda several times a day for over a year, but is on tape from October to December 1997 after she and Bill had been lovers for eighteen months from November 1995, to May 1997.

Linda was told to make the tapes by Lucienne Goldberg, who said she should do so to protect herself from being "destroyed," that is, called a liar after she told the story of Bill's affair with Monica. Linda, a "Republican in my value system,"[238] leaked the Monica tapes to Ken Starr and the Paula Jones' attorneys. Literary agent Goldberg said Linda could get a book contract for the story of the President's affair with Monica.

Bill's lovers from earlier decades, Gennifer and Dolly, who told their stories in books, had longer relationships with Bill, twelve and thirty-three years respectively, but their fantasies, activities and visits with Bill were not confirmed by physical evidence, logs, witnesses, interrogations or verified tapes, although some Gennifer-Bill telephone recordings were made public in 1992.

After their affair was over, Monica remained in contact with Bill and sought a job in New York, where her mother lived. She couldn't find a job that she wanted despite the help of UN Ambassador Bill Richardson and Bill's friend, corporate attorney Vernon Jordan, and some of the phone conversations are about her job search. Finally the demand of Paula Jones' attorneys for a deposition led to her affidavit denying a sexual relationship with Bill. After being threatened with a perjury charge by the Special Prosecutor, she negotiated immunity and then testified before a grand jury in August 1998. She met with representatives of both the House and Senate during the impeachment hearings in 1999. Afterward she and Andrew Morton wrote *Monica's Story* and she did a television interview with Barbara Walters.

The hours of rambling phone dialogue between Monica and Linda are evocative of Handsome Bill as Monica longs for a call from him, wants him to get her a job, plots to conceal their relationship from deposition, and is lovelorn, suspicious, angry and tearful. This serious girl talk is mostly about Monica in jokey and chatty tones with threads about love, friends, hair, food, weight, moms, clothes and travel. Monica's posture was naive and questioning while Linda was tutorial about jobs and relationships. Monica's need for attention interrupted Linda's television time, so the TV is heard in the background. One hears fragments of Linda's comments to her cat and dog, and sometimes she talks to visitors including her adult children. At times the calls interfered with Linda's meals, so the talk went on as she ate. They gossip about friends and coworkers whose names are sometimes deleted. Expletives are censored. Monica's endurance on the phone often exceeds Linda's bedtime, so Linda pleads for sleep and signs off.

Monica says Bill is "hiding" and wonders if "he stopped liking me" or if he has a new relationship. She is obsessive about Bill as she speculates wildly, "maybe he's on drugs" when he doesn't call back. At other times Monica feels sabotaged by the White House staff as she sends notes and gifts to arrange an appointment with Bill. Anger and depression are heard as Monica says, ""[Bill] yelled at me... he scared me." Appointments with Bill are made and broken. The emphasis shifts over time from her return to a job at the White House to working in the private sector in New York to get away from Washington. Another reality intrudes at times when Linda says of Bill, "he's a guy" and Monica agrees. Linda's judgment is that "he needs supervision," and they recall the role of Betsey Wright, who screened the women coming to Governor Bill's office in Arkansas.

The relationship between Monica and Bill can be seen in terms of the stereotypes. Monica is a material girl of the Madonna legend seeking fun and connections, love and sex, success and fame, a Beverly Hills vixen with big hair, a big chest and a short skirt among the White House suits and secretaries. She is poised, smart, funny, and self-assured according to Dominick Dunne writing in *Vanity Fair*.[239] Monica jokes about asking Bill for a position as the President's special assistant for blowjobs, and she wants them to run away together. While in mourning for the lost Bill, she dates Thomas Longstreth, a fellow Pentagon employee, and becomes pregnant and has an abortion. She has an affair with "a nutrition guy" at a fat farm described in the tabloid press, and she notices that Vernon Jordan is "quite the ladies' man."

The Bill of the tapes fits the errant husband formula, a horny fifty year old that seeks sexual conquests with charm and explanations about his need for love. Bill tells Monica, as he had told Gennifer and Dolly, about his loveless marriage to a cold, bad tempered wife.

What can be learned about Bill Clinton's inner life from the Monica-Linda tapes that isn't already known? Bill's passivity, deceptiveness and charisma receive new dimensions from the words of Monica, the Wounded Stalker, and Linda, the Righteous Snitch. Monica and Linda are both stressed during their intersection, and their insights reflect this anxiety. Bill emerges from this dialogue as more passive in his relationship with Monica than in his earlier love affairs with Dolly and Gennifer or in his courtship of Hillary for that matter. He met Hillary in his twenties and Gennifer in his thirties. He met Dolly in his teens when he was inhibited with girls, but later in his twenties and thirties he was more active in their affair.

Does Bill's passivity in his affair with Monica mean passivity in his life or for that matter does activity in affairs of the heart mean an aggressive career? Of course not, but love is life. Examples muster themselves. Monogamous Truman was at least as active in love as adulterous Roosevelt. Both were active Presidents. LBJ was an active President while Bush I was a more passive president though both had affairs.

Bill's deceptions and ambivalence speak in the tapes and in Monica's book. His fluctuations of mind and heart during their affair deceive Monica and probably Bill himself according to the Monica-Linda duet. These fluctuations are illustrative of his narcissism and superego deficits that affect both his political and sexual behavior. Bill believes everything he says at the time he says it according to biographer David Maraniss. Narcissists need instant gratification and one of the ways to get that gratification is to offer it to your lovers, friends and the voters.

*Monica's Story* covers the same territory as the tapes and the Starr report, but now Monica speaks alone. The book focuses on her background of weight problems, a sense of entitlement, immaturity, perfectionism, and low self-esteem that led to her enticement of and enthrallment by Bill and then their breakup. In the book we hear about the errors and bias of the Starr report and how Linda Tripp manipulated Monica's words on the tapes.

We do learn new things: Monica had an orgasm the first time she gave Bill a blow job; they were soul mates; Bill sang "Try a Little Tenderness" to her; they discussed their childhood weight problems; he said she was full of piss and vinegar like his mother; she told Bill he was like her mother, an ostrich with his head in the sand who avoids confrontation; Bill and Monica both lied; Monica and Bill both cried; he was furious with her for fifty-six minutes on the phone, and she was often angry with him too; Monica, her mother and her father were all suicidal at one time or another.

Monica tells about Bill's charisma, but it's easier to characterize it then to explain it. His sex appeal for both women and men can be in part attributed to the psychobiology of Bill's genetics but this attribution discounts his performance. Monica says Bill "He had a glow about him that was magnetic. He exudes sexual energy. I thought to myself: 'Now I see what all the girls are talking about.[240] If impeachment means they're going to turn Bill into a peach, singer Sinead O'Connor asks, "Can I eat him?" Billy Graham, the evangelist says Bill has "a tremendous personality" that makes the women "go wild."[241]

The reaction of other men is similar. Bob Woodward, who talked in San Francisco in 1999, recalled an interview with Bill for his book *Shadow* when Bill's eyes "drilled him" and he was "seduced." Republican David Gergen's book calls Bill "seductive." A man whose only meeting with President Bill was a chance encounter in a country restaurant told me about the raw emotional power of Bill's intensive listening while this minister expressed his own political opinions.  Bill wasn't talking; he was listening and hearing.

Arthur Miller uses the language of the theater to explain the charisma saying, "Clinton was relaxed on camera in a way any actor would envy. Relaxation is the soul of the art because it arouses receptivity in an audience...What Clinton projects is a sort of love...he loves to act and he is most alive when he's on...there is no dividing line between his performance and himself - he is his performance."[242]


## BILL AS IMPOTENT

Bill had  "hundreds of affairs" before "turning forty" but then he began a "concerted effort to be faithful," he told Monica which she reported to the Starr grand jury. This information suggests to a psychohistorian that Bill began to have episodes of impotence, called erectile dysfunction in the medical nomenclature, after he turned forty in 1986. It was about this time that Governor Bill, "... surrendered his lifelong dream..." when he announced tearfully in July, 1987 that he wasn't going to run for president because Betsey Wright, his chief of staff said that he was vulnerable because of the rumors of his womanizing.[243]

Premature ejaculation is the most common kind of erectile dysfunction but there are others such as the loss of an erection or an inability to get it up at all. Such events give Bill a reason to avoid sexual intercourse and to substitute masturbation and oral sex. That reason is fear of failure.

Another saga about an impotent American is Hemingway's *The Sun Also Rises* where we meet Jake Barnes who suffered a mysterious and symbolic "wound" in the First World War. Jake's malaise is a badge of his membership in a Lost Generation like Bill, who belongs to the burdened post Vietnam era.  We never learn whether Jake has shell shock, World War I's post traumatic stress disorder, a genital injury, or spinal cord damage. Another hero whose sex life is restricted to masturbation fantasies is Leopold Bloom in Joyce's *Ulysses*, who became impotent in midlife after the death of his infant son.

The juxtaposition of hypersexuality with the loss of sexuality is expressed in the paradox of Priapus. This is a Greco-Roman god with an enormous deformed penis in a permanent erection who never actually reaches orgasm and ejaculation although he is a symbol of fertility.

Did Bill's failed erections and his fears and inhibitions about sex begin in his midlife crisis? This theory leads to Bill's unconscious and its vicissitudes beginning in his forties. Bill's potency disturbance at forty was a punishment imposed by the superego or conscience that he rationalized as moral improvement. This was part of a midlife crisis that revived his child hood masturbation guilt with its castration anxiety and separation fears. Bill's separation anxiety echoes as he says to Monica, "Why do they have to take you away from me? I trust you so much..." Bill's description of his "empty life" and his memories of inadequacy as a "fat kid" were relayed by Monica during her taped telephone conversations with Linda Tripp. Bill's ambivalence, an unresolved complex from his early development, becomes more powerful as he begins an affair with Monica and then he withdraws "to avoid temptation."

Bill's erectile dysfunction is psychological in origin because his penis functions normally in masturbation, oral sex and sometimes in foreplay, too. Overall about half the cases of erectile dysfunction are psychological like Bill's, while the other half are caused by organic problems. Most erectile dysfunction is occasional, but serious sexual potency problems are estimated by the National Institute of Health to affect five percent of American men at age forty rising to fifteen to twenty-five percent by age sixty-five.

The Starr Referral says, "...the President inserted a cigar into (Monica's) vagina and then put the cigar in his mouth and said, 'It tastes good.' " Explicit Bill tells us of the pleasure of tasting Monica's vagina which includes a bisexual fantasy about the flavor of a penis. Bill's playful comment on tasting of the phallic cigar exposes a bisexual fantasy that flits from the masturbatory to the homosexual and then to the street challenge, "Go fuck yourself." There is a statement about Bill's felt need for a better penis, more dependable, harder and larger. Freud said that sometimes a cigar is just a cigar, but this isn't one of them.

Monica tells us via the Starr report, "...that her physical relationship with the President included oral sex but not sexual intercourse...he touched her genitals...bringing her to orgasm on two occasions...initially the President would not let her perform oral sex to completion...(but) during their last two...encounters, both in 1997, he did ejaculate." The report said that on March 31, 1996, the President " '...focused on me pretty exclusively...' kissing her bare breasts and fondling her genitals..."

Bill's preference for foreplay rather then sexual intercourse with Monica is the routine as he, "...'unzipped his pants and sort of exposed himself,' " when they met in the Oval office. Altogether they had oral sex nine times and phone sex fifteen times according to the Starr report. Monica wanted sexual intercourse with Bill, but it never happened although once there was "...brief genital to geni-

106

tal contact."

Bill, the horny hunk with a potency problem, might just as well have said, "Not tonight dear, I have a headache," as he complained about his "sore back." Monica says, "We tried...but ...he couldn't bend because of his knee, it really didn't work..."

Maureen Dowd has it right although she doesn't intuit the reason for Bill's fears. "It is Ms. Lewinsky who comes across as the red-blooded predator, wailing to her girl friends that the President wouldn't go all the way. It is Mr. Clinton who behaves more like a teen-age girl trying to protect her virginity, insisting on holding back, reluctant to even remove any clothes, even pushing Ms. Lewinsky away and pushing up her slipping bra strap...emotionally upset about it...(saying) I'm trying to be good..."[244]

## BILL AS PERVERT

A perversion, Freud says is sexual behavior with an infantile rather then an adult goal although it is now also called a paraphilia, a more neutral term. Some of these activities are a part of the normal foreplay that leads to intercourse but for a pervert they are his only avenue to a sexual climax. The pervert is expressing his sexuality according to an infantile pattern. According to this theory, Bill regressed after the age of forty to behavior reminiscent of the oral stage of development by avoiding sexual intercourse in favor of fellatio, masturbation and phone sex. Of course, these perversions are defenses against infantile oral impulses rather then the impulses themselves. Perhaps there is some truth in a tabloid, *The Star*, which says that Bill hasn't had sex with Hillary since 1984,[245] or Hillary's outburst reported by biographer Anderson that Bill only has sex with her twice a year.[246]

Case studies are filled with men whose orgasm requires special conditions: exhibitionists who show their penis to women at bus stops, voyeurs who peek at undressed women through specially constructed peep holes, fetishists who fondle women's underwear, and the pedophiles who seek child pornography or sex with children. These can be lifelong perversions, or they can be temporary and sporadic at those times when defenses fail and infantile castration fears and sado-masochism emerge from the unconscious.

Bill's orgasms by phone sex and fellatio are an expression of oral dependency in a man whose Oedipus complex is unresolved, so he avoids sexual intercourse in his new relationship during his prolonged midlife passage, the male menopause. Consult Hillary's and Bill's Change of Life for details about this phase.

Bill's choice of oral sex indicates unresolved problems originating in the unconscious. Oral sex avoids pregnancy as well as the love, responsibility, bonding and the psychobiology of sexual intercourse. Oral sex involves recreation not reproduction in the fantasies of the participants. Rock star Marilyn Manson says in *Rolling Stone*, "...blow jobs are right there with handshakes and autographs as part of the job. It's like kissing babies."[247]   Among fifteen to nineteen year-olds, fifty five per cent engage in oral sex according to a Kaiser Foundation poll reported by *Seventeen Magazine*.[248]   Monica called it "fooling around" in her conversations with Linda Tripp. Oral sex is clothed sex, and phone sex is even simpler since masturbation doesn't even require getting dressed up. The desire for fellatio, which mirrors the nursing experience both for its giver and its receiver, is "...to some extent, a displacement of the infantile desire for the mother's breast, " according to psychoanalyst Richard Sterba.[249]   Sexual fluids and semen are like milk in this unconscious scenario so both cunnilingus and fellatio have an analogy to offering and accepting the breast.

Why did Bill initially refuse to climax during oral sex with Monica. She urges him to come but he doesn't trust her fully during their first seven encounters, but finally during the last two episodes, he ejaculates. This mistrust originates from Bill's fantasy of a hungry devouring mother, a mirror of Bill's own infantile desire to consume both the milk and the breast. Bill's unconscious also includes fantasies of oral impregnation so his inhibition about orgasm with oral sex is a fear of oral pregnancy, an idea originating with infantile development. This fantasy begs the question of who in Bill's unconscious is the impregnator and who is impregnated. The answer is that the infantile mind is bisexual, so he has both male and female fantasies.  Bill plants the magic seeds in mommy that start a baby like his brother Roger, but he is also the recipient of seeds from Daddy so he grows a baby too. After Bill finally does climax during oral sex, his fear of an oral pregnancy and his fear of being devoured may be so threatening that he breaks off the affair with Monica.

The Bill who withheld semen from Monica during fellatio was a Bill who was in control. This unconscious need for control comes from his anal fixation. Despite his oral optimism, Bill is an anal compulsive campaigner, speaker and leader who shares or gives up power reluctantly.  Once Monica recalls that Bill stopped oral sex part way through to climax and then she notices that he masturbated into the sink. In control again!

Anal and oral impulses unite sexually in Monica's and Bill's anilingus mentioned in the Starr report, which neglects to tell us whose tongue and whose anus it was. Maybe it was both.

Cunnilingus with Monica becomes an issue when she says, "The President 'was talking about performing oral sex on me' but she stopped him because she was menstruating..." Monica was in control now. Was she really menstruating or just teasing? Anyway isn't the yuck in the tongue of the beholder? Monica didn't take up Bill's offer later on either. However, Gennifer did enthusiastically in Arkansas, and she says, "I had never known a man so eager to use his mouth for pleasure and so skilled at it."[250]  Infant Bill wanted cunnilingus with Mother Monica, but she continued as the baby sucking on Mommy Bill's nipple-penis.

Bill's oral sexuality is center stage with Paula and Gennifer too who says, "...Oral sex seemed like the natural thing to do, I was a little surprised, though, when he came in my mouth the first time we did it." The Paula Jones case which led to the investigation of Monica started in Little Rock when Paula says she was taken to a hotel room by a State trooper in 1991 to meet Bill Clinton, who briefly admired her and then dropped his pants and asked her to kiss his erect penis. Paula insisted Bill's penis was distinctive in appearance, "crooked," which led to unconfirmed speculation that Bill had Peyronie's Disease, a midlife condition that causes a curved and deformed organ and often makes sexual intercourse painful or impossible.

Although Bill had argued that oral sex isn't adultery in the Biblical sense, there is no question that Bill knew his behavior with Monica was "inappropriate" according to his Bible-based Baptist religion and so he felt guilt. His conscience or superego was the same in 1996 at fifty when he began the oral sex affair with Monica as it had been in 1977 at thirty-one when he started his genital affair with Gennifer. But in his midlife forties, Bill's sexuality was affected by erectile dysfunction and maybe the "wound" of Peronie's Disease. Now in midlife, Bill's sadomasochistic "enjoyment" of his compulsive sexuality shifted from sexual intercourse to oral and masturbatory sex. This change was necessitated by the erectile difficulties that were rationalized by a change in the values or content of his superego or conscience. See Bill's Superego for an overview on his conscience.

Bill's monologues denying a sexual relationship with Monica followed by his many apologies lead one to consider his favorite book, *The Mediations* by the Roman philosopher and emperor, Marcus Aurelius. He writes, "If you are distressed by something outside yourself, it is not the thing which troubles you but what you think about it and this is within your power to obliterate at once." Bill's mother Virginia often acted with this kind of Aurelian denial, and Hillary's family legacy also makes denial prominent. Bill and Hillary trained Chelsea in denial by role playing when she was six in Arkansas as they simulated angry criticisms about Governor Clinton by rival candidates like Orval Faubus after which Chelsea herself played the roles of candidate Bill and his opponent.

How did Bill go from a pleasure loving Bubba to a worried prim middle age, from saying, "I'll always feel sixteen" to "trying to be good"? Bill was already a changeling who had gone from a repressed adolescent with no dates except for a prom with Dolly Browning when he was too fearful to have sex, to a man who became a Casanova in his twenties and thirties. The turnabouts of Bill as a changeling/narcissist without a central identity are hard to distinguish from his personal growth. The section on Bill as Narcissus discusses this complex and controversial matter further.

When Monica called Bill "handsome," he replied, "When I look in the mirror, I sees [sic] a fat kid who couldn't throw a ball straight." The low self esteem of Bill's childhood returned during his menopause with fears about sexual potency and his likely erectile dysfunction. His change of life started at about forty in 1986, but ten years later it was still ongoing.

"I have an empty life except for my work," Bill told Monica. These are the spoken words of the midlife crisis with its hormonal changes, fear of aging, loss of virility, depression and existential anxiety. Stress and particularly losses play a role in the onset of the midlife crisis and we know of one of Bill's major traumas was the death of his mother Virginia in 1994. Other stressful experiences remain to be reported in Bill's memoirs.

The Lewinsky disaster should be viewed as an episode in Bill's Sadomasochism described earlier. The influence of his sadomasochism is stronger at fifty than it was at forty so this unconscious primitive preoedipal force along with the castration fears fuels his continuing midlife angst. This is Bill's repetitive sadomasochistic sexual epic: a sexual affair, its discovery by his political enemies, a denial and then the pain of exposure followed by public censure. This sequence happened with Gennifer Flowers and Paula Jones, then in the Kathleen Willey episode, the Lewinsky affair and the Juanita Broaddrick rape story, Post-presidency the tabloid stories continue about affairs with Denise Rich, Patricia Duff, Lisa Beltzberg and Saffron Burrows.

When does a taking risk about sex in the White House become sadomasochism? It was just a part of being the POTUS (president of the United States) if you were Kennedy or LBJ when there was national denial about presidential adultery. JFK 's nude White House pool parties with the two nymphs Fiddle and Faddle were guarded by the Secret Service. But in the Nineties, extramarital sex in the White House is a sadomasochistic performance with Starr and the media snooping for a prurient audience as Betty and John Q. Public peek through the curtain.

Bill's sadomasochism in his love affairs involve his phone and oral sex with Monica and then his public punishment as Elvis, the bad boy superstar. He has corrected the image of the awkward sissy, an over achiever who didn't have dates. Of course, Bill is in pain after his sadistic pleasure in hurting the public and his wife but then there is a healing with masochistic pleasure as he suffers for what he did. This is a largely unconscious process for Bill and for the public but it's real enough to have cost the taxpayers millions for the Special Prosecutor and the impeachment process. The increase in the ratings of the media was worth millions from advertisers who sponsored the crowds attending the print and electronic circuses. Meanwhile the attorneys received huge sums from Bill and the witnesses. Slick Willie, like Tricky Dick, is a sadomasochistic president with secret affairs, cover-ups, denials and explanations.

At some point in my study of Bill and Monica's sex life, I became aware that I needed a real life perspective. I knew that porno guides to oral sex on the internet, the counting of oral orgasms by scientists in the Kinsey tradition, the sculptures of oral sex in the Hindu temples of Khajuraho and psychoanalytic theories are not the whole answer. A local paper reported about a male stripper at a teen Girl's Night Out in a San Francisco suburb who ended his performance by letting one of the fifteen year olds perform oral sex on him, a misdemeanor.  Fellatio was the way novelist Joyce Maynard, then eighteen consummated her affair with fifty-three year old J. D. Sallinger according to her recent memoir.

In *Ulysses*, Molly Bloom contemplates, "...listen theres real beauty and poetry for you I often felt I wanted to kiss him all over also his lovely young cock there so simple I wouldn't mind taking him in my mouth if nobody was looking as if it was asking you to suck it so clean and white he looks with his boyish face I would too in 1/2 a minute even if some of it went down what its only like gruel or the dew..."[252]

Before I really had a chance for further rumination, I was at lunch with fellow senior citizens at a local university where we take classes.

After the Starr report came out, there were a few comments about Clinton and then I asked, "Why do people want oral sex?"

" There won't be a pregnancy," a serious dark haired woman pointed out.

"It's a power trip for Bill " said a man with a cane.

A gray haired women with a single chin whisker smiled as she said, "It doesn't do much for a women."

"If you're in a hurry, you don't have to take off your clothes," commented a woman in a rose jump suit whose lined face resembled a washboard.

"In cars," was the last word about oral sex from a man who takes the grandfather role in TV commercials.

It was an intense and all too brief focus group.


## BILL'S IMPEACHMENT AS PSYCHOLOGY

Bill Clinton was the first elected president in our two hundred year history to be impeached although Andrew Johnson, the vice president who succeeded to the presidency after Lincoln's assassination, was also impeached. Earlier Andrew

Jackson was censured by Congressional resolution and there were calls for FDR's impeachment during the Thirties. Richard Nixon was threatened with impeachment before he resigned.

The constitution says the standard for impeachment of a president is "high crimes and misdemeanors." A majority of the House of Representatives must vote to impeach a President and after a trial by the Senate, a two-thirds majority of the Senate is needed to remove the President from office. Impeachment has a complex history since 1386 in England and then in America but a notable empirical definition in 1970 by President Gerald R. Ford, then a Congressman, states, "An impeachable offense is whatever a majority of the House of Representatives consider it to be at a given moment of history." Impeachment, like the law itself is a psychodrama where emotions are major players.

Two psychological questions stand out in the impeachment maelstrom.

First, how did Bill Clinton's unconscious lead to impeachable behavior, his lies under oath, and the related charges? The answer leads immediately to Bill's sexual invitation to Paula Jones to "kiss it" and her response by lawsuit; to the Lewinsky affair; and to Bill's untruthful answers about sex to the Jones' attorneys. The motivation lies in Bill's unconscious where his sadomasochism, his risk-taking, his narcissism and his flawed conscience or superego reside. (See the earlier sections on these topics.) It is these forces that resulted in Bill's sex with Monica and the lies that led to pain for sadomasochist Bill and for many others. Bill's defenses and his superego weren't working very well.

A precarious balance existed between Bill's id, his ego and superego. But it didn't lead to impeachment during his twelve years as governor of Arkansas or during his first term in the White House. Whether this is luck or caution, it calls for a psychological explanation. After sixteen years, Bill's internal psychological balance had changed. This shift coincided with his change of life in his forties but more precisely with the time of the death of his mother in January 1994. The threats of the Whitewater inquiry from the press and the pressure from legislators continued and Bill was "exhausted."[253] Bob Dole, the Republican leader attacked Bill about Whitewater on the day his mother died and again on the day of her funeral. It was then that Bill requested Attorney General Reno to appoint an Independent Counsel, first Robert Fiske for eight months and then Ken Starr whose investigations eventually led to his impeachment. (See Bill and Hillary's Change of Life for details.)

Second, what was the national psychology behind the impeachment? The answer is the murder and the devouring of the father by the primal horde, Freud's explanation of social development in prehistoric times.

Freud writes about this event,

"The father of the primal horde, since he was an unlimited despot, had seized all the women for himself; his sons, being dangerous to him as rivals, had been killed or driven away. One day, however, the sons came together and united to overwhelm, kill and devour their father, who had been their enemy but also their ideal. After the deed they were unable to take over their heritage since they stood in one another's way. Under the influence of failure and regret they learned to come to an agreement among themselves, they banded into a clan of brothers...and they jointly undertook to forgo the possession of the women on whose account they had killed their father. They were then driven to finding strange women..."[254]

Freud explains how this behavior led to a system of marriage that prevented incest by requiring a wife from outside the man's own clan and also to the beginning of guilt and conscience and then on to morality, religion and finally to government. These dire events were memorialized by the universal reverence of the tribe for a totem animal representing the murdered father, a totem animal that could not be hunted for food, but once a year was it was killed and eaten in a religious ceremony.

The time line of the impeachment's main emotional torrent ran from the House resolution for an impeachment inquiry in November 1997 to Clinton's acquittal by the Senate in February 1999. The rush toward impeachment had a life of its own as it engulfed both the Republican mainstream and the hate-Clinton fringe with its Arkansas Project bankrolled by multimillionaire newspaper publisher Richard Mellon Scaife[255]  After Clinton's acquittal by the Senate, threats to indict and prosecute him for perjury lingered until the last day of his presidency, when he settled with the Independent Counsel. He had been fined $90,000 by a Federal court for false statements. His Arkansas law license was suspended for five years, and he paid a $25,000 fine.  There was a dustup about gifts he took from the White House and other gifts given to President Bill and First Lady Hillary on the eve of their departure from the White House. These were the tail of a spent impeachment comet along with the controversy about whether the ex-President's office should be in pricey midtown Manhattan or in low-rent Harlem and the investigation of his pardon of a fugitive billionaire businessman, Marc Rich.

Freud mentions a maternal Goddess-centered culture that may have preceded the primal horde events or maybe followed them although he writes a patriarchal story of the origin of civilization. The murder of the primal father in prehistory was not a single event but rather a repetitive one as it exerted its crucial influence on the evolution of the prehistoric hordes. The primal horde lived without a shared culture until becoming a group with a newfound guilt over the father-murder and then a conscience eventually leading to societies with morality, religion and governments. These psychological developments were a part of practical ones that helped keep peace within the hordes and then in larger groups. Freud assigns the transmission of these psychohistorical influences across fifty thousand or a hundred thousand years to the continuity of the human unconscious, an idea that is as controversial as the father murder-primal horde theory itself.

The murdered primal father was tyrannical, admired, violent and jealous; a man who kept all the women for himself while the impeachment attacked a powerful president who was widely admired even among his enemies as an astute politician and a charismatic vote getter. Bill was attractive to women, unforgiving to his political enemies and jealous of his prerogatives, which ranged from revising the Democratic Party to crafting a new North American trade system. He was violent in his temper outbursts, striking pollster Dick Morris[256] and exploding in a death threat against a blundering staffer[257] according to Bob Woodward. (Also see Acting Out among Bill'sEgo Defenses) Bill's former lovers often said they feared for their lives after their relationship with him ended.

No precise symbol for the cannibal feast of the sons on Primal Father Clinton's flesh emerges, but the journalists' (called "scorpions" in Joe Klein's *Primary Colors*) endless chewing of the impeachment bones may qualify. The timelessness of the unconscious is seen in a fifty-two year old son, Ken Starr and a seventy-five year-old son, Republican Congressman Henry Hyde savoring Primal Father Bill Clinton's fifty-two year-old meaty remains. Pressing the analogy toward its limits, the sons who were now a clan of brothers rejected Primal Father Bill's women, Hillary, Monica, Gennifer Flowers, and the others.

The group psychology of impeachment results from an American unconscious which contains the murder and cannibalism of the primal father by a horde of sons. The precipitating event began in President Bill's unconscious mind resulting in the sexual crimes and misdemeanors.

# PART FOUR

## HILLARY AND BILL IN LEGEND AND STORY

"...The Oedipus complex is not normal in the way the nose is normal. Rather it is like the thymus gland - i.e. it is normal at a certain period but abnormal if it persists unchanged beyond that period. Everybody has it between four and six; later in normal people it seems to vanish...The adult neurotic has retained his Oedipus complex. He knows nothing about it, but nevertheless we can show it to be operative, and this is what we mean when we say it is 'unconscious.' " *The Collected Papers of Otto Fenichel*, W.W. Norton, 1953, p. 205.

"Mein sohn ist kein menchenkenner" translated as "My son does not know people." An opinion attributed to Freud's mother by hearsay according to Manfred Wolf in a lecture at the University of San Francisco on September 30, 2002.

"I've always felt the past is irrelevant." Virginia Kelley (Bill's mother) in *Leading With My Heart*, Simon and Schuster, 1994, p. 66.

"Man's character is his fate." Heraclitus in *Familiar Quotations*, John Bartlett, Little Brown, 1992, p. 62.

"...I don't know why I'm doing it. It's trying to kill to keep yourself alive...I'm crazy as a coot and being as cruel to as I can be." Harry in "The Snows of Kilimanjaro" in *The Complete Short Stories of Ernest Hemingway*, Scribner, 1987, p. 43.

## BILL AND HILLARY IN GROUP PROCESS WITH DICK, DOLLY, GENNIFER AND ROBERT

Interpersonal psychoanalysis is the work of Harry Stack Sullivan, the American born psychoanalyst who in the 1930's led Freudians to a view of the mind as an appendage of its relationships with people. Freud's paraphernalia of id, ego, superego and the psychosexual stages remained, but Sullivan explained that the mind of the infant develops in response to its relationship to significant people and their mental representations. He called these life long influences that form the mind, dynamisms. "We are our experiences," is the slogan of Sullivanian psychoanalysis, which looks to the interpersonal for a measure of mental health.[258] There is a connection between interpersonal psychoanalysis from the Thirties and the more recent object relations theory[259] as alternatives to the older instinct model of maturation.

Bill and Hillary must be examined by this interpersonal yardstick. The resources include the political books about Bill by friends like Robert Reich and Dick Morris, who knew both Bill and Hillary for many years. It was Hillary who often called Morris to help Bill with election campaigns. Reich knew Hillary even before he met Bill in 1968 on the boat going to England for their Rhodes scholarships at Oxford. These books are positive about the Clintons but they also offer useful critiques.

Reich who served as Secretary of Labor during Bill's first term, left in 1996 to resume teaching, spend more time with his family and recover from the burnout of being *Locked in the Cabinet*, the title of his book. He says Clinton wanted him to stay for his second term. He is four feet ten inches because his growth was affected by a hereditary condition, Fairbanks disease. Reich is an attorney; a professor of public policy; a journalist and an activist for workers' rights. He was on the left in Clinton first term along with Hillary and Harold Ickes during the internecine warfare with Clinton's right of center cabal, Treasury Secretary Lloyd Bentsen, the Federal Reserve's Alan Greenspan, and Dick Morris.

Morris, who is often called a spin-doctor, was a consultant who helped Bill with polling voters and formulating campaigns and issues beginning in 1980 when Bill lost the Arkansas governorship after serving his first term. Morris, who continued to work for Clinton in Arkansas and Washington, resigned as a consultant during the 1996 Democratic convention when his relationship with a prostitute became public.

Another kind of book is also helpful, the kiss-and-tell. Gennifer Flowers tells the story of her twelve-year affair with Bill which ended in 1992, while Dolly Kyle Browning wrote a novel about their relationship that lasted from 1959 to 1992. Bill denied the affair with Flowers during the 1992 campaign, but in 1998 Bill acknowledged it, offering an abbreviated version in his deposition in the Paula Jones lawsuit. Attorney Dolly Browning's love affair first received public attention when she was also deposed in the Jones case. The details of these books cannot be verified, but they are from Bill's widely known Kennedy-pattern womanizing. Jack Palladino, a private detective tells The New Yorker that he "was hired by Clinton's 1992 campaign to check out the credibility of Gennifer Flowers and that of twenty-six or so other women" who could say they slept with Bill Clinton.

What is learned from these four tales of Hillary and Bill? Of course, the authors' credibility is the first question in the mind of the reader. These books, like many others, are self-serving milestones for these four career minded authors, Bill and Hillary's peers. Their relationship to Bill Clinton  gives them a unique audience so their words are shaped carefully. But in a real sense the authors are all frustrated by the Clinton Presidency. The two women say that Clinton's election meant they lost their connection to him as a lover. Morris left the White House in disgrace although he hoped to come back, while Reich failed to achieve many of his goals for social change, and so he laments his lost main chance. The books are each protestations of sincerity, passionate statements of the authors' achievements, their ties to Bill and their future hopes. Each presents the mind of Bill and Hillary with a perspective that can't be obtained in any other way. The men, Morris and Reich are FOB (Friends of Bill) and FOH while the women; Flowers and Browning are FOB but not FOH although they certainly don't ignore Hillary.

During his twenty year relationship with Bill, Dick Morris worked to increase Bill's popularity and electability by taking polls about Bill's campaigns and policies in Arkansas and then nationally when Bill ran for president in 1992 and 1996. Morris' idea of a continuous campaign requires polling for each policy decision, speech, legislative session and election. Bill was constantly concerned with his image among voters and looked to Morris for answers. He wanted approval about everything from policy issues to whether a swimming pool should be built in the governor's mansion and where he should vacation.

Morris didn't develop polling but he used the polls to triangulate a third position between the opposite views of the two political parties for Clinton. It was this use of triangulation for policy decisions such as welfare reform that was characterized by George Stephanopoulos as stealing popular positions from the Republican platform to gain voter approval. Morris' triangulation certainly fits

Bill's style of avoiding confrontation and his desire to be liked and to win everyone's approval.

The Bill Clinton who needs affirmation was five when his stepfather Roger fired a gun during an alcohol-fueled argument with his mother. Bill recalls, "That bullet...could have killed me." In the same interview by Nancy Collins, he describes how he was a "loner" in childhood because of a dysfunctional home. By fourth grade, Bill is remembered by a friend as the smartest kid in class and "running the school," but another classmate says Bill felt "fat and rejected." The two Bills coexist: a glass that is half full and a glass that is half empty.

Morris' continuous polling represents Bill's unconscious need to enter into a popularity community from which he felt excluded. Another impetus for the questioning was to get the answers that he lacked about the earlier family turmoil: Virginia vs. grandmother Edith when Bill was a toddler, Virginia vs. stepfather Roger during Bill's childhood, Virginia the racy iconoclast vs. the local bluenoses and Virginia vs. Bill when he decided to marry Hillary. Bill's politics of approval leads him away from the politics of leadership as practiced by recent presidential candidates like Pat Buchanan from the Republican Right and Paul Wellstone and Jesse Jackson on the Democratic Left.

Clinton used Morris to edit speeches and develop policies in accordance with polls, but he also fought against control by Morris. Bill struggled to maintain his independence against this powerful genie that he had called up in a Faustian bargain. It is as though Bill's latent opportunism is unleashed by Morris with unforeseen consequences that Bill's ego can't control. When Bill feels anxious, he calls for Morris, who arrives on the scene before or after electoral crises; at times only Hillary is strong enough to call Morris to the rescue as she did in Arkansas in 1980 when Bill lost the race for governor after his first term and in Washington in 1994 when the Republicans took over control of the Congress. Morris' consultations were often hidden from the public and sometimes even Clinton's own advisors were not told about them. Clinton's guilt about his loss of self-confidence that leads him to call for help from Morris is like his shame about masturbation.

The president's shame is the focus of an appropriately named movie, *Wag the Dog*, in which a Morris character is an anti-hero who is concealed in a White House basement. The embarrassed president is almost entirely absent from the film. This is a black comedy about a clandestine and anonymous consultant who creates a pretend-war on Albania as a pageant to seize the headlines after the President makes a newsworthy pass at a preteen Firefly girl. So life imitates art as the rocketing of terrorist bases in the Sudan and Afghanistan and the bombing of Baghdad and Belgrade take the headlines away from the Monica Lewinsky scandal and post-impeachment malaise.

In the contest for control between Bill and Dick, Bill's easy anger surges and in 1990 he is reported as hitting Dick.[260]   Clinton apologizes immediately although both deny the story. Dick left him but not for long. This story highlights Clinton's rage and his obsessiveness about voter and media approval. Bill's narcissism emerges as he asks Morris where he will rank among America's presidents. Morris' operations are a balm to Bill's narcissistic wound just as Morris' own injured narcissism is salved by being the Presidential advisor.

Two of Bill's lovers, Dolly and Gennifer, chronicle long, intermittent and satisfying love affairs in their books.  Dolly's story begins when she is eleven and meets thirteen-year-old Bill at a golf course. She is smitten for the next thirty-three years, which end in 1992, as Bill becomes a candidate for President. During their affair Bill is ambivalent and distant at times despite his sexiness and ardor in bed. Her story describes the inhibitions of a man with unresolved castration and separation fears. They begin with Bill's refusal to make love the night of the Senior Prom to Pretty Girl, his name for Dolly because of his feeling of sexual inadequacy and they go on to his failure to give her the attention and time that she thought she deserved. Then she excuses him by saying that he was "afraid to let me touch..." and this is because he was "pure." She repeats this conceit in a higher octave when she says to him, "...you can't or won't receive what I have to give."

It's down and dirty time as we hear from Gennifer that Bill wasn't especially well endowed although he was a successful lover. The echo from Monica is of a Bill who is "a little on the slender side" as she mourns his loss on the telephone to Linda Tripp. Paula Jones says in a affidavit quoted by Haynes Johnson that Bill's penis was "...rather short and thin...five and one half inches...having a circumference of the approximate size of a quarter...the shaft... was bent or 'crooked'..."[261]

Is this a case of "Women are from Venus and Men are from Mars"? Of course, and that is a reason the women offer a unique and important perspective about Bill's mind. Wouldn't stories by Lyndon Johnson or FDR's mistresses offer unique insights into these presidents? Yes, but it's worth a reminder that although not everything in a leader's life is politically significant, all the experiences are important for biography and especially for psychobiography.


## HILLARY AND BILL IN THE SADOMASOCHISTIC MARRIAGE

The Clinton marriage, which was already a puzzle, became an enigma with the Monica Lewinsky firestorm, and Bill's apology to Hillary and the nation on August 17, 1998.

There are two common speculations about Hillary and Bill's marriage. One opinion is that it is a love match in which Hillary remains devoted and makes periodic denials about Bill's philandering, and Bill is dependent on Hillary for support and guidance despite his infidelities. The other view is that it is an arrangement or understanding about sharing political power and tolerating extramarital activities. This scenario says that Bill's numerous infidelities are ignored; Hillary has a lesbian love life and she had an affair with Vincent Foster. The two theories aren't really contradictory although they imply that a love marriage couldn't include political power sharing and a permissiveness about extramarital liaisons while a power marriage couldn't involve real love.

The first answer about this dichotomy was in 1992 during the Gennifer Flowers flap when Bill said on national television that he and Hillary were in love and it was a marriage, not an arrangement or an understanding. In 1999 Hillary said, "We have love." Despite the proliferation of comments on their marriage, we lack a satisfying explanation.

The Bill and Hillary story begins with their first meeting in the Yale Law School library in a fabled and maybe even true story of how Hillary introduced herself to Bill, who was so smitten he couldn't remember his own name. In psychohistory, fables are usually more useful than "the facts" in reading emotions. Bill, a freshman, and Hillary, a sophomore, were eyeing each other across the length of the Yale Law Library in November 1970. Bill was a shaggy, story telling Southerner while Hillary was a star having been pictured in *Life*[262] as a leader of the counterculture and the antiwar movement. A classmate describes her as a member of the "look like shit" school of feminism.[263] Hillary was an activist at Yale, where she was an articulate student with top grades. She and Bill met briefly earlier through Robert Reich in the cafeteria and had been in eye contact. Bill had trailed Hillary out of classes. In the library, Bill was being unsuccessfully recruited for the Yale Law Journal by another student in a conversation that didn't really engage Bill. As his eyes met the studying Hillary again, she got up from her books and notes and walked the length of the room and said to Bill, "If you're going to keep staring at me and I'm going to keep staring back, we should at least introduce ourselves, I'm Hillary Rodham."

Fables abound so the story of their first meeting in Oppenheimer's book is attributed to Hillary, who says they met in a registration line. Bill asked her where she was from, and as she replied, "...his leg was rubbing against mine."[264]

Their friends noticed the chemistry and Hillary explained Bill's appeal saying, "I've actually found a guy who is not afraid of me. Not one bit."[265]

Bill's housemate recalled Hillary's Midwestern directness as the "...counterpoint to Bill's southern charm."[266] By most accounts, Hillary took the initiative in their courtship.

Love operates in both the unconscious and the conscious mind, and they aren't separate like playing cards. In Hillary's mind, Bill was the opposite of her Daddy Hugh as warm, not a curmudgeon; complimentary, not critical; gregarious, not isolated; easy going and passive, not rigid and aggressive. In fact, Bill's traits were more like a Good Mother (maybe a maternal Grandmother Della or Aunt Isabelle, not the stern and bitter Mother Dorothy) and this view could have weighed in Hillary's thoughts. In Hillary's mind, the process was not a counting of qualities but a balance between the sexual energy of the id and the critical superego. In Bill's mind, Hillary was an exciting Yankee intellectual who offered an escape from Mother Virginia's control in Bill's unconscious dilemma about the Whore versus the Madonna described in Bill's Good and Bad Women.

The question is what keeps the marriage together. Of course, President Bill and First Lady Hillary are power people but so are the Governors, CEO's and university Presidents, some of whom have power-oriented spouses too. During the Monica crisis, columnist Stephanie Salter wrote, "It's the love, stupid" as she looked at a photo of Hillary and Bill about to kiss.[267] Meanwhile Maureen Dowd, who talked about a power marriage, says that the reason Hillary doesn't walk or talk is that she likes "the look of the world from 1600 Pennsylvania Avenue."[268]

People aren't packaged as tightly as the pundits' explanations so maybe the Clinton have a combination of a love and a power arrangement that oscillates between these poles. For months or years the marriage is in phase one and then it reverses to phase two. A seesaw arrangement between Hillary and Bill is the metaphor used by White House counselor David Gergen in his book. Or maybe it's really complicated like osmosis or magnetism or the unconscious.

Sadomasochism, both conscious and unconscious, is the touchstone of the Clinton marriage. These impulses, ubiquitous in marriage, are preponderant in the Clinton's marriage. Their background is in the sections Bill's Sadism and Masochism, Hillary's Sadism and Masochism and Hillary's Moral Masochism and the Monica Lewinsky Porno Flick. But how does their sadomasochism really work?

There is no doubt that Bill's affair with Monica had a sadistic message for Hillary. Sadism is the derivation of sexualized pleasure from pain inflicted on another so the affair has a double thrill for Bill, sexual at the point of production and sadistic in its unconscious meaning. Then he's unmasked by Ken Starr, Linda Tripp and Monica herself, and he suffers public censure, demands for his resignation and impeachment.

Bill was also attacked privately by Hillary, the betrayed wife whose political stock in Clinton & Clinton was declining in value. Now he was a disgraced partner-husband; his sexual affair was over and his credibility was down. Are adulterous husbands victims? Not really, but by then all Bill had left was his masochism, the sexualized pleasure produced by his own pain.

Meanwhile what of Hillary, who, like Bill, is a sadomasochist? She first appeared in the Monica affair as a victim of Bill's adultery and in this role suffered both emotional pain and masochistic pleasure. Then she went into "battle mode" and attacked Bill's accusers as right wing and conspirators. Did she know the truth then or only suspect the worst or was this just plain old denial? One can't be sure, but her attacks on Bill's enemies were a source of sadistic pleasure for her. When the truth about Bill's bimbo eruption emerged there was a noisy confrontation. Hillary slapped Bill hard enough to leave a red mark seen by the Secret Service as Bill emerged, from Hillary's bedroom according to Chris Andersen's book. This was a sadomasochistic response, striking out sadistically and also receiving masochistic pleasure as a victim, maybe helped along by media-enhanced porno images of Bill's affair with Monica.

After Bill's confession, Hillary  says she was"…furious, dumbfounded, heartbroken and outraged…I started crying and yelling." tells Mike McCurry, Bill's chief of staff, that she was "...angry...betrayed...lonely...exasperated and humiliated" Bob Woodward's sources say she told a women friend, "I have to take this punishment...God is doing this, and He knows the reason..."[269]

Theology aside, Hillary is using her ego defenses of intellectualization, isolation, projection and identification with the aggressor against being overwhelmed by her sadomasochism. There is narcissism here, too, although some would take the reference to God to be a surrogate for a punishing Daddy Hugh or an unforgiving Mother Dorothy.

Hillary's response to Monica and to Bill's hundreds of other affairs remained theological a year later. Bill had committed sins of weakness, not malice, according to Hillary as quoted in the Lucinda Franks interview in *Talk* in 1999. In an explanation that goes beyond an analogy, Hillary compares herself to Jesus who was denied three times by Peter, a Jesus who loved Peter anyway. We must look behind Hillary's intellectual facade of conscious grandiosity, narcissism and blasphemy to find her identification with the Jesus who predicted Peter's apostasy. In the New Testament Jesus said, "...I tell thee Peter, the cock shall not crow this day, before that thou shalt thrice deny that thou knowest me." Nonetheless Hillary as Jesus loved Bill the way Jesus loved Peter, who became the Rock on which His church was founded.

Bible history as explained by a scholar, Brownrigg is helpful in understanding Hillary's words when we learn that Peter, like Bill, was "... granite-like.. a man of action and impulse...aggressive...of childlike simplicity...daring...alternating with a weak and cowardly instability."[270]  Both Jesus-Hillary and Peter-Bill performed many miracles before they were crucified. Hillary as Jesus emphases the bisexuality and the feminity of a Jesus who appears in the older mystery religions as a sacrificed Goddess or God. Sadomasochism is significant in legends of the crucified and resurrected God or Goddess whose sacrifice assures growth, fertility, crops and survival, and so it is in Hillary's theology.

"We have love," she says of her marriage. But the love between Hillary-Jesus and Bill-Peter echoes the sadism and masochism of the bloodshed and tribal wars of the Old Testament and their extension into Christianity by the lives of the martyrs, the conversions by sword and fire, the Crusades and the innumerable wars fought in God's name.

The pre-Judeo-Christian origins of this sadomasochism are "...the decisive moments in the life of the female - menstruation, deflowering, conception, and childbearing - are intimately bound up with a sacrifice of blood, the goddess perpetuates life by exacting bloody sacrifices that will assure the fertility of game, women, and fields, the rising of the sun, and success in warfare." This Jungian explanation by Erich Neumann goes on to say, "...the male like the female is impelled by his very nature to sacrifice."[271]


## BILL AND HILLARY'S CHANGE OF LIFE

Why did the Lewinsky scandal happen in 1998, six years after the Gennifer Flowers eruption in 1992 and four years after the Paula Jones lawsuit in 1994, which was based on an incident in 1991? Is this is the perilous midlife passage, the female and male menopause with their dual crises feared and celebrated by Gail Sheehy (later a Hillary biographer) and Daniel Levinson?[272] Another affirmation for both a male and female menopause comes from Isadore Rosenfeld, internist and media health columnist. The male menopause is often called andropause in recognition of the lowered testosterone levels and other physical changes in many males over forty according to the Mayo Clinic, which lists male menopause under Hormonal Conditions on iis website.

The folk meaning of the change of life for both women and men is the loss of sexuality, fertility, and attractiveness. So with the change of life, we see the eruption of old castration and separation fears from unresolved Oedipus complexes and sadomasochism from unresolved pre-Oedipal complexes. For Bill, it was the revival of the sissy, a fat, clumsy little boy with masturbation guilt and anxiety about separation and castration. Bimbo eruptions are his response. Bill's midlife crisis meets a midlife Hillary in her familiar roles: the enabler, the protective wife of an errant husband, and Cinderella, the victim of Monica, the new wicked stepsister.

Hillary and Bill's midlife nest became empty during the second presidential term with Chelsea off to Stanford in 1997. A needy Hillary spoke during the 1996 campaign of a plan to adopt a baby, although it was unlikely then and it has not been mentioned again. Bill adopted Buddy, a Labrador.

Society's traditional response to midlife has been to seek the fountain of youth with powdered jade, potions,  cosmetic lotions and implants of goat's glands. Recently these quests take the form of plastic surgery, spas, estrogen, testosterone, human growth hormone, and Viagra. Midlife is a flexible zone from the late thirties into the forties and through the fifties, but this definition is influenced by our current life expectancy of seventy-five in contrast to 1900 when it was forty-nine years.

The midlife crisis is really a myth according to researchers Hunter and Sundel, who point out that mid-lifers are a remarkably stable group in terms of their statistics.[273]   There is no change in their divorce rate, the frequency and satisfaction of their sexual relations, the number of mental disturbances including their mental hospital admissions, emotional crises, alcoholism, suicide and depression. They remain in much the same jobs, which show the same rate of promotions and levels of satisfaction.

Even more contra-intuitive is the new research which finds that the menopause in women leads to "increased activity, increased excitement, increased overall happiness, a decrease in depression and an increase in pride" after an initial reaction to the empty nest and the loss of biological fertility.[274] These are the words of Betty Friedan, the feminist icon turned gerontologist writing about aging. She summarizes several studies, including one by Bernice Neugarten in 1970 of middle class and working class neighborhoods in Chicago showing that postmenopausal midlife women in their forties and fifties were more satisfied than they had been earlier in their lives.[275] The women with the most favorable outcomes were those who had jobs or careers and were also mothers.

Menopausal zest is the term for this satisfaction. It has been attributed to the adaptiveness learned during a typical women's life of discontinuities: housewife, career, mother, empty nester and widow. The increased vitality of women at the menopause and later on is highlighted when it is compared to men who have more trouble with midlife adjustment and don't live as long. Studies of women in Japan and Israel show similar results. Women have a reduced frequency of impairment compared to men after midlife. This fact is all the more striking because younger women go to doctors more and take more sick leave than men.

Psychohistory is not consensus, and some midlife crises are just like Bill's: the husband has an affair with a younger woman in the office, his job and marriage are threatened, and family life is disrupted. Smoldering midlife crises can be fanned into flames by personal stress like the death of Hillary's father Hugh in April, 1993, followed by Vince Foster' suicide in July, and then the death of Bill's mother Virginia in January 1994. In nine months these were major stresses for both Hillary and Bill according to Bob Woodward in *The Agenda*.

It was during this midlife crisis in 1994 when Bill acceded to the  demands for the appointment of a Special Counsel  which led to the Whitewater investigation and eventually to impeachment saying, "I did it because I was exhausted and I had just buried my mother, and because I had people at the White House who couldn't stand the heat..." [276]

Another point of departure into the Lewinsky crisis is the role of channel fever. Channel fever is the tense, edgy and erratic behavior of the ship's crew in the days before the end of a long sea voyage. The pre-Oedipal maternal security and rhythm of the sea and ship on the journey is exchanged for the uncertainty and hazards of arrival at a port. Another term for such a transition is "the shorts," the anxiety and irritability of long term convicts whose sentence has only a few weeks to run. Misbehavior is more likely in a previously tractable prisoner who is suffering from "the shorts."

The Clintons reached the end of a twenty-year voyage after their eight years in the White House and twelve years in the Governor's Mansion so this was a time of Presidential shorts and channel fever. The visible reason is the pending loss of familiar routines of power and governance for an uncertain future. In the unconscious, this loss is a deprivation of omnipotence like the toddler who suddenly has a new sibling and is no longer an only child or whose parent is lost by death or divorce (See Bill's Separation Anxiety), and so there is depression and mourning. The victims of such a depression use their psychological defenses to cope with the emotions. These defenses may involve the kind of dysfunctional behavior expressed by the Presidential pardon of multi-billionaire tax fugitive Marc Rich and the Clintons' removal of White House furnishings and gifts that were later returned or paid for. There were also accusations of vandalism like graffiti, pulled phone cords and the removal of the W's from White House computers. Later an investigation said the condition of the White House was usual for offices that had been vacated by long time tenants. Still mistakes, practical jokes, confusion and secret deals by the Clintons and their official family have unconscious origins as well as a public face.

I saw something similar in my practice during the midlife crisis of a thirty-something hockey star facing an obligatory retirement from a successful career due to his advanced age for his sport. His future seemed murky as he reacted with irritability, anxiety and depression affecting his marriage and his children. Therapy helped this family and maybe this is a hint for the Clinton family including the brothers of the Presidential Couple and their extended families.


## HILLARY AND BILL'S PSYCHOTHERAPY

The question that tugs at our sleeve from both Hillary and Bill's psychobiographies is what about therapy? Shouldn't they seek self-understanding and personal change as individuals or as a couple? We know that Bill went to family counseling with his mother, brother and Hillary while he was Governor in 1985 when brother Roger was arrested for drug sales. Bill and Hillary were in pastoral counseling for marital problems in 1989 and had counseling again during the Monica Lewinsky crisis.

Hillary's therapeutic White House praetorian guard has consisted of psychologist-philosophers like Jungian Jean Houston and Rabbi Michael Lerner (he will appear later in What About the Rest of Us in Clintonia). The roster also includes Historian Blanche Wiesen Cook who is an Eleanor Roosevelt scholar and Anthropologist Catherine Ann Bateson, who like the others, speaks for a New Age feminism.

The selection of California internist Dean Ornish as a White House physician reflects Hillary's interest in a healthy diet and preventative medicine and perhaps an approach to stress reduction as well. The widely read Ornish program for the rehabilitation from heart attacks as well as their prevention includes diet, exercise, stress management, meditation and psychotherapy.

Both Hillary and Bill use pastoral counseling. In the White House, Hillary consulted with Rev. J. Philip Wogaman at Washington's Foundry Methodist Church, which she attended with Bill. She continues her contact with Don Jones, her Methodist youth leader, now a professor of theology in New Jersey.

President Bill met regularly with three different ministers for Bible reading, prayer, spiritual growth and to stay centered according to a *New York Times* report by Niebuhr. There were weekly phone calls with Rex Horne, his pastor in Little Rock, and monthly visits with Tony Compolo from Pennsylvania and Bill Hybels from Illinois, all Baptist ministers. They describe these sessions using words like "blunt" and "rebuke." By 1998, Bill's "God Squad" included Gordon MacDonald, a Protestant clergyman who had left his pulpit after adultery with a parishioner, Reverend Jesse Jackson, who prayed with Bill and Chelsea in the White House during the Monica crisis and also Hillary's Methodist pastor, J. Philip Wogamon.

A therapeutic alliance between Christianity and psychoanalysis began with the psychoanalytic work of one of Freud's early followers, Oscar Pfister, a Swiss Protestant minister. Although psychotherapy comes in 256 varieties like the colors on a printer, Hillary's New Age explorations and Bill's Bible therapy sound like resistances to the exploration of the unconscious. A resistance is a defense against the conscious awareness of incestuous impulses, murderous rage, masturbation guilt, castration fears, sadomasochism and narcissism, the normal occupants of the unconscious.

There is always more to be said but finally I stopped for help. A friend who read this report refused to comment explaining, "Your analysis of the Clintons will hurt them. I like Bill and Hillary so it would be immoral to help." This gave me hope that there are some secrets here that will illuminate as well as offend.

## IS PSYCHOHISTORY REALLY HISTORY?

How does one know whether the psychohistory of Hillary and Bill is true? Can it be proven? Is Bill at fifty a garden-variety middle-aged satyr, or is he a man with potency problems who is dependent on fellatio, phone sex, and masturbation for orgasms? Is Hillary a masochist who receives unconscious gratification by Bill's affairs, or is she really just a victimized wife? These views are not mutually exclusive but actually complementary.

It has been suggested that psychohistory is just a smorgasbord of anecdotes and events tailored to fit a psychological thesis. Of course it is, but history itself is a series of stories arranged into themes. All accounts of history are selective so the psychohistorian makes choices like other historians. If there is any doubt about the need for themes in constructing history, reading a newspaper from a hundred years ago will show how much context is needed to decipher the meaning behind the words.

It's hard to prove that psychohistorical explanations are right, but the debates about them are invigorating. The emotional nucleus of psychohistory is the communication between the psychohistorian's unconscious and that of the subject, so psychohistorical assertions are metaphors that stimulate the juices of history and life. This encounter in the thicket of psychology and history follows the principles of these disciplines, but such rules don't determine the validity of the conclusions.

The psychohistory of the American Revolution receives a new dimension from Burrows and Wallace, who explain that the Revolution was a family drama in which England acted like a parent while the colonists played the rebellious children.[277] This was just as the colonists themselves were undergoing a change in their patterns of child rearing from England's patriarchal mode to a more autonomous style suited to a frontier society.

Is this psychohistory of the Clintons like the " 'wild' psycho-analysis" which Freud defined as interpretations, which are premature, incomplete and erroneous? He illustrates this aspect by describing a divorced woman with anxiety-states who was told by a physician using his warped version of Freud that she needed sexual satisfaction, so she should return to her husband, take a lover, or satisfy herself by masturbation. Freud concludes that such wild analysis may not be wholly bad because it may stimulate some patients to undertake a real psychoanalysis. Maybe this psychohistory, fierce if not wild, will motivate Hillary and Bill to understand and explain their own behavior or even undertake their own psychoanalysis. The Clinton Library, which will be built in Little Rock, should have a Psychohistorical Wing.

Another perspective is that of psychoanalyst Adam Phillips who says, "I think of Freud as a late romantic writer, and I read psychoanalysis as poetry, so I don't have to worry about whether it is true or even useful, but only whether it is haunting or moving or intriguing or amusing... [278]

Some voices object to the psychohistory of a living president and the first lady because it is an invasion of their privacy. Morality, style, etiquette and the First Amendment enter the argument. Hillary says it is "... mean...the way we strip away everyone's sense of dignity, of privacy..." in her interview in *Talk*.[279] Is there a zone of privacy that is out of bounds to psychohistory? The propriety of the psychohistory of presidents and first ladies may be left to the ethicists and the policy issues to the social scientists, but a taboo here sounds like the prohibitions against childhood curiosity about parental sexuality.

A kind of voyeurism is involved breaching the taboo and violating the parental rule. The flip side to the voyeurism about the personal habits of a president-father and a first lady-mother is exhibitionism. The president and first lady, who are often seen through a beaded curtain, are themselves engaged in selective exhibitionism. This sleight of hand involves not only politics but also their image, their marriage, their child and their life style. All presidential candidates depend on name recognition for their rankings in the polls, for fund raising and then for votes in the primary and the general elections. Perhaps the psychohistorian and the presidential couple have complementary voyeur-exhibitionist roles although they may prefer to see themselves as scholar and statesman respectively. Meanwhile the consumers of this voyeurism are a public who both savor and deplore such exposés.

Revelation about the president remains controversial. When I bought the Starr report from a government office in San Francisco, a clerk told me that he would never read an exposé about President Clinton's private life although he was a presidential history buff.

Psychohistory as an excuse for behavior was raised as a question after Hillary's interview in *Talk* where she calls Bill "...a very, very good man." She says that Bill was the victim in a struggle over him by Mother Virginia and his maternal Grandmother Edith when he was four which "...scarred him by abuse..." and she goes on to explain that he grew up in a violent family with an alcoholic stepfather. Still Hillary says that "He's (Bill) a grownup...He is responsible for his own behavior..."

It is a paradox is that a psychohistorical insight can be wrong and still be productive. Freud's view that Moses was an Egyptian monotheist and his pronouncements (with Bullitt) on Woodrow Wilson whose fear of his father led him to wimp out at Versailles are not the final answers. Thomas Jefferson scholars were of two schools, one that he fathered slave Sally Hemming's children and another that he didn't. Recent DNA tests show that he did father at least one of her children, but the studies of his character and opinions that were done to show that he didn't have a child with Sally do not lose their value for Jefferson scholarship.

Psychohistory, which links author and subject, also connects them to the reader using their conscious and unconscious minds. So hopefully this study is a link to the minds of Hillary and Bill.

## BILL AS SCAPEGOAT IN PERPETUITY

Why is Bill Clinton featured in the news, so long after his presidency? There are interviews, reevaluations of his presidency, his speeches, a meeting with Al Gore, the death of Buddy the Labrador and a handshake with George Stephanopoulos. He was on the cover of *Time* on February 26, 2001, and the cover of *Newsweek* on April 8, 2002. The feeding frenzy in the supermarket tabloids continues with the names of the new bimbos, the transmission of Bill's venereal herpes to Hillary, and the threat of an imminent Clinton divorce.

The reasons for Bill Clinton's persistence in the spotlight through 2002 concern the forces that animate the post-presidential image, his charisma, a current private agenda, the concerns about his legacy, and his leadership of the Democratic Party. It is a meaningless question, a tautology, to ask whether it is the public's interest that leads to the coverage of Bill or whether it is the news about Bill that stimulates the public's attention.

The Clinton charisma was highlighted by charmless George W. Bush and lackluster Al Gore, the candidates in the 2000 election. Bill's instant rapport is an electric communication that registers a sexual charge for both men and women. The sexual emotions of this charisma are explicit in *Dreams of Bill* edited by Judith Anderson-Miller. Of course, charisma was factor in his many elections (he lost two) even though some voters were infuriated by or indifferent to this persona. (Bill's charisma is discussed in Bill's Ego Defenses under Sublimation and also in Monica Talks About Bill.)

Bill's current and unannounced agenda is to procure the Presidency for Hillary and so change America's consciousness about gender. The subtext is Bill's return to the White House as First Somebody. Bill's Sixties' feminism is like Hillary's, action oriented.

Bill's concern about his legacy began well before he left the White House according to pollster Dick Morris, whose memoir Behind the Oval Office recalls the time Clinton spent with Morris speculating about history's verdict on his presidency. Where would Bill rank on a Mount Rushmore of all the American presidents?

Clinton controls the Democratic party with his friends, Terry McAuliffe, the chairman and Al From, who heads the Democratic Leadership Council, while

Clinton raises fund for its candidates and supports their campaigns.

Meanwhile, Bill's major post-presidential activity is his speeches in the U. S. and around the world, some free but many at  $125,000 to $300,000 each. About half the time, he's at home where he is writing a book about his presidency. Newsweek[280] estimates that he is earning twenty million dollars a year, and so he is no longer the impecunious Bill Clinton described in Hillary and Money.

This explanation of Bill's post-presidential prominence requires a study of America's post-Clinton mind and especially its unconscious, the hidden part of our collective psyche.

The unconscious part of our national obsession with ex-president Bill Clinton is fed by our guilt and anger about what happened to Bill as well as what happened to America, not the historical facts but the feelings. These emotions must not be dismissed even though they may not be recognized. The unconscious remains obdurately inaccessible even to the individual who may introspect about it. The hypertropied news coverage is the conscious tip of this unconscious iceberg.

National guilt persists along with anger and depression about the Starr inquiry, Bill's impeachment by the House of Representatives and trial in the Senate. Such emotions in various blends affect both sides of the Clinton divide and the neutrals too. Some Americans believe that Clinton was guilty of high crimes and misdemeanors and so deserved impeachment by the House and should have been removed from office by the Senate. According to other Americans, he was the victim of a right wing conspiracy. This conspiracy is described in *The Hunting of a President* by Joe Conason and Gene Lyons, while one of the conspirators, journalist David Brock wrote about it from the inside in *Blinded By The Right*.

In the psychology of the national unconscious, the Starr investigation /impeachment /conspiracy is a witch-hunt or a lynching. (Hunting of game, witch-hunts and lynching have many common psychological features.[281]) Bill's supporters see this phenomenon as the hunt of a flawed populist hero like JFK or FDR. For Bill's opponents, the quarry is Satanic Bill, liar, adulterer and rapist who is a dangerous socialist and an enemy of American freedom. For the hard-core Clinton haters, he is the murderer of Vincent Foster and the governor who smuggled cocaine for the cartel into Mena, Arkansas.

Bill's image shifted after he left office. Now guilt jostles with righteous indignation. The good times are celebrated. The pleasure of gotcha remains but there is also compassion, atonement and restitution. National forgetting operates too as the emotions and events of Clintonia are excluded from conscious memory and pushed deeper into the unconscious.

Bill as a pop icon is both benign and malign. In the national consciousness or more precisely in its unconscious, nuances and finely reasoned opinions do not exist. In the American psyche, feelings merge in a bouillabaisse whose substance and flavor differs in each season and for every appetite.

Bill is a celebrity, and America has a love-hate relationship with its celebrities, says Steve Coz in *The National Enquirer: Thirty Years of Unforgettable Images*. He describes

"...the needy psyche of American society caught in a tortured love affair with celebrity. We love to feel part of this lifestyle - the privilege, the money, the mansions -but at the same time we want to know there is a price, that after the glory comes the fall...We feel guilty for wanting to see the famous fail, and when they do, we most often want to see them rise back up to new heights of glamour and fame."[282]

The scapegoat is post-presidential Bill's controlling image in the primitive and unconscious mind of modern Americans. A Biblical scapegoat was sacrificed as atonement for the sins of the nation while another goat was led into the wilderness to perish while bearing the nation's sins so punishment would fall on it rather than on Israel.

Scapegoats are a universal legacy, both religious and secular. They are sacrificed to the gods, for better crops, human fertility and victory in war, and to allay human suffering. Scapegoats symbolize communal emotions: guilt, anger and atonement, but also awe, affection, resolution and love. Both the destructive and the sexual instincts are represented. A prototype is Abraham's sacrifice of his son Isaac on Mount Moriah with the last minute substitution of a ram for the son. A consummated Biblical sacrifice was that of Jephthah's daughter after his victory in battle at Mizpeh. In our hemisphere, there was the annual Aztec sacrifice of an esteemed youth after a year of ceremonial preparation during a midnight ritual when a knife-wielding priest wrenched out the youth's heart.

The sacrifice of Jesus by crucifixion is linked historically to the many sacred god-kings who were ceremonially crippled and then crucified when they got old or sick or when they finished their term of office. [283] Jesus' sacrifice is celebrated in the Catholic Church by the mystery of the transubstantiation of the bread and wine at the Mass into the body and blood of Christ.

Eating the body and the blood of Christ hints at an earlier universal human cannibalism that evolved into religious sacrifices.

The first sacrifices were of humans and then animals and crops were substituted. These sacrifices were regarded with emotional ambivalence combining affection, communion and fear according to the psychoanalytic writers Money-Kryle and Sagan. The transition from the sacrifice of humans to animals and later food was a civilizing development in which tribal aggression was sublimated. Sublimation is a psychological mechanism of the individual and the group by which aggression is converted into positive emotions resulting in personal and social good.

These images must be linked to cultural psychohistory if they are to be interpreted. There is a progression from a primal horde to an organized society that leads from a tribe, which sacrifices a human or animal scapegoat to modern political ceremonies like impeachment. The impeachment is the symbolic killing and eating of the tyrannical primal father by the rebellious sons in pursuit the father's power and his women. (See Bill's Impeachment as Psychology.) The ancient subliminal emotions about the scapegoat are still powerful in a twenty-first century nation whose unconscious holds opposites views:  Bill Clinton deserved his punishment, and Bill was a victim.

The nation's Bill Clinton awareness quotient is determined by a balance of emotions that are conscious, unconscious, personal and national. How long will they remain? Will there be new forces? Scapegoat Bill rampant or receding will be determined by the impact of events on America and by Bill's trajectory.


## BILL AND HILLARY FACE THE FUTURE

What's ahead for the Clintons? Psychology is an unreliable predictor of behavior, but some trends are notable.

Hillary was elected to the Senate in New York in 2000, and she may be a candidate for President in 2004 or 2008. A Times/CNN poll of Democrats in 2002 showed Hillary first among the contenders for the presidential nomination in 2004 followed by Senators Kerry, Lieberman and Gephardt after Al Gore announced that he wouldn't run.[284]  Hillary's book is here. Senator Hillary spends her week in her Washington house near Embassy Row leading a life largely separate from Bill, with whom she spends weekends in Chappaqua according to Raymond Hernandez writing in the *New York Times*.

Bill is addicted to politics, so he'll turn to it again after his book and the speaking engagements and perhaps a trophy sinecure. Perhaps he has selected a state like Arkansas where the fundraisers and pols will arrange a Senate seat. The Presidential Library is being planned in Arkansas with an apartment for Bill. Meanwhile the Clintons own homes in New York's Westchester County and Washington.  After John Quincy Adams' term as President in the 1820's, he served seventeen noteworthy years in the House.  Andrew Johnson, the other impeached president represented his state as a Senator after his presidency.

Psychohistory doesn't rule out a divorce as the transition from presidential power leads to more bimbo eruptions. Bill's addiction to casual sex is likely to be more manifest after he leaves the White House and has more time and privacy.

This analysis is focused primarily on Hillary's and Bill's flaws and faults while their virtues and successes remain in the background maybe because the psychological explanation of achievement is more difficult. Maybe psychohistory is like Milton's *Paradise Lost* where Satan really gets all the best lines.

# PART FIVE

WHAT ABOUT THE REST OF US IN CLINTONIA?

"Eros is chaos." Jennifer Stone, *The Morning Show*, KPFA, November 4, 1999

"The mind of man is capable of anything - because everything is in it, all the past as well as all the future." *Heart of Darkness* by Joseph , W. W. Norton, 1963, p. 37.

Clintonia, the place of the Clinton Presidency needs its own psychohistory. To survey this land, the culture of the Nineties must be examined. Hillary and Bill are the symbols for the Nineties as Eisenhower was in the Fifties, Kennedy in the Sixties, arguably Nixon in the Seventies, and Reagan in the Eighties.

A national history is a series of stories with different layers of meaning. To seek the hidden or unconscious meaning of the Clintonian Nineties demands a psychoanalysis of Betty and John Q. Public. This is justified because there are few tools to explain the sometimes strange behavior of societies like the U.S.A. The visible motives of patriots and villains, changes in the biophysical environment, famine, disease, wars, class conflict, self-interest or even the wisdom of economists may be useful but are often wrong, incomplete or misleading. Witness the mysterious demise of major civilizations like the Mayans before the arrival of the Spanish or the Etruscans who lived in Italy before the Romans. A cult of cannibalism led to the near-extinction of the great cliff dwelling Ananazi civilization in the Southwest about 1150 A.D. according to anthropologist Christy Turner.[285] While the psychohistory of individuals from biographical data offers the obstacles mentioned earlier, the study of a national mind is even more dicey. After all, what is a normal nation?

The relationship of Bill and Hillary to the nation can be focused by three questions: Do the United States get the President and First Lady it deserves? What is the relationship between the Presidential Couple and the country? Are both the President and the people really controlled by the forces of history like Manifest Destiny, the Depression, or the Cold War? The answers are, "Yes" to the first, "It's reciprocal" to the second and "Sometimes" to the third question. These answers need elaboration.

William Jefferson Clinton is the President the country deserved because metaphorically, he was the American people. This American Pie is complete with Hillary in the presidential package. "No one gets to run for president on his terms. The terms you run on are set by the American people and that means what the American people are receptive to," says pundit Roger Simon.[286] Bill is the leader "... we have asked for and don't know quite what to make of, " explains writer Stephen Dubner.[287]

The public response in polls showed Clinton's overall presidential performance approval was between sixty and seventy percent during the Monica scandal and the impeachment despite the public disapproval of Bill's behavior with Monica. This was confirmed by the gains of the Democratic Party in the 1998 congressional election. Journalist Haynes Johnson who tracks the polls notes that Clinton's approval ratings were the same as Reagan's during a comparable period in his second term.[288] Chris Matthews in "The Ex-Presidents' Club" tells us that Clinton in 2002 had 50% approval, a level similar to three other ex-presidents, Reagan, Bush and Carter soon after they left office.[289]

The spirit of the Nineties, our zeitgeist, is already the subject of academics, film producers, novelists and pundits but the unconscious part of the national psyche also needs to be examined. Beneath the shores and lagoons of our collective persona are the tectonic and volcanic forces that shape the American mind.

What are these psychocultural landmarks of the Clintonian Nineties?

First and foremost, *sexuality* was the new and noisy issue of the Nineties. This sexuality is not just in the classifieds where men seek women, women seek men, men seek men and women seek women. This is culture wars, a journey into an America polarized into two communities, one which is permissive, pro-choice, tolerant of gay rights, and anti-patriarchal, while another America is fundamentalist, censorious, patriarchal, and opposed to abortion and homosexuality. Conservatives who support the right to privacy are caught in the crossfire. Meanwhile lurking in the erotic wings are the images of Bill's affairs, Hillary's lesbian relationships, her affair with Vincent Foster, and the Clinton's open marriage. The sexuality of the Nineties results in the turmoil between Ken Starr and the White House about Bill's bimbo sexuality, his apology, and Hillary's defense of Bill.

The Nineties are a stage in a sexual revolution beginning with the Pill developed in the Fifties, the liberated Sixties, a gay and a women's movement in the Seventies, and AIDS in the Eighties. For those with a longer memory, the sexual revolution in this century began in the Twenties with the flapper generation, jazz, bathtub gin, and women who smoked cigarettes.

The sexual revolution returned led by Bill and Hillary but also by Gennifer Flowers, Paula Jones and Monica Lewinsky. The immediate effect was Bill's continued high approval rating before and after he admitted he had sex with Monica. His two elections were about the economy, but 1992 was also a referendum on the Flowers affair while his 1996 election discounted the Paula Jones accusation. Hillary's standing by Bill is active, visible and planned like Tammy Wynette, whose lyrics are bittersweet, "Remember, he's only a man." Hillary is a liberated woman who acts according to her own lights. The polls were up for Hillary too as she led on both cultural and political issues during the 1998 campaign and her Senatorial campaign in 2000.

This is a new Nineties' sexuality, not the Fifties' climate control nor the "dope, rock and roll and fucking in the streets" of the Sixties' poet John Sinclair. The Nineties are the time of safe-sex-AIDS-awareness, single parents, gay marriage, and a subdued sprinkling of S and M. Married and unmarried couples often say they are monogamous, but adultery is acknowledged nationally by a third of the married women (the same number as in Hillary's Wellesley class of '69) and half the married men.

The Lewinsky publicity, the prurient Starr report, the chutzpah of Bill's legalistic rebuttal, his apologies, and Hillary's standing by Bill tend to make adulterers feel less guilty. Who could better initiate their forgiveness than President Bill and First Lady Hillary, the Boomers who attend church each Sunday with Bibles in their hands? Maybe Americans will celebrate Bill's August 17, 1998 apology as Adultery Amnesty Day, the first private national holiday.

The new sexuality of Clintonia has a dark side with its unleashing of the forces of sexual repression. The media concentration on the Lewinsky-Clinton foreplay along with the attacks on the right of presidential privacy comes from a long tradition of Puritanism.

Lewinsky-Clinton is Salem Revisited, according to Arthur Miller who points out that "witch hunts are always spooked by women's horrifying sexuality awakened by the superstud Devil...with witch-hunting ministers (who) examine women's bodies for signs of the Devil's marks..."[290] Tens of thousands of women perished in Europe and Salem from a misogyny, which remains alive in our unconscious today.

The prototype is the fear and hatred of an Eve who is held responsible for the expulsion from the Garden of Eden, Biblical sexism. The witch trials were specifically aimed at women's liaisons with Satan who came to them in many guises. The victims of the European witch hunts in the sixteenth and seventeenth centuries were frequently poor or older single women or widows who had worked as lying-in maids for richer, married women after the birth of a baby. The accusers were frequently women whose child failed to thrive or died or those who suffered from other misfortunes. But it was men who solicited the accusations, initiated the trials and then judged and punished the witches. The witch who was hunted, tortured, tried and burned is the prototype for the evil punished by the McCarthyism of the Fifties and now the Star investigation in the Nineties which targeted both Monica and Bill. Like the witchcraft trials, it is directed by men but there are crucial roles for women accusers, witnesses and victims, Hillary, Paula, Monica, Linda, Susan McDougal, Kathleen Willey and Julie Hiatt Steele are examples.

The image of the witch has survived, and today, the world's bestselling author, Stephen King in his novel *It*, informs this fear of women who, "...smell of the monster...a creature which would eat anything but which was especially hungry for boymeat." King acknowledges this fear from the unconscious and myth with unusual frankness when he says that his greatest sexual fear is, " The vagina dentata, the vagina with teeth."

The attack on sexual Clintonia is also directed against the pro-choice position, an openly gay ambassador, art from the National Endowment using sexual images, and even a White House Christmas ornament, probably a fertility goddess called Bertha's Big Butt by author Gary Aldrich, a retired FBI agent. This sexual McCarthyism also invaded the private lives of Republican Representatives Dan Burton, Henry Hyde, Helen Chenoweth, Bob Livingston, Bob Barr and Newt Gingrich with news stories about their adultery. An irony is that Clinton signed a law opposing homosexual marriage, sponsored legislation that makes legal wiretapping easier, and offered proposals for Internet censorship.

Beneath the conscious events of the Nineties is the return of the Goddess, who renews sexuality, fertility, maternity and the earth itself. There is a resurgence of the Yin archetype, the female force in a balance with Yang, the male principle. Yin is earth to Yang's heaven, night to Yang's day, the valley to Yang's mountain and in a more controversial dichotomy, Yin is feeling and receptivity to

138

Yang's intellect and creativity. The Yin forces of the Goddess influence both men and women just as the Yang energy of Zeus also plays on both sexes. Jungians invoke the Chi energy of the unconscious to explain the Yin-Yang balance.

The Goddess reemerges in the Nineties because of increasing threats to survival from pollution, global warming, overpopulation, and the loss of plant and animal species, environmental destruction and nuclear weapons. The Goddess or Great Mother includes both the Terrible Mother sometimes called the Death Goddess, as well as the Good Mother.

The mind of the group is influenced by its collective unconscious where the archetypes hold sway according to Jung and his followers, Neumann and Whitmont. These archetypes are in art, religion, myths, folklore, play and dreams. More controversial is the Jungian idea that such specific archetypes or ideas originate in the racial mind of the species. Freud saw an unconscious continuity with universal mental processes.[291] These issues are still being debated.

Second, *Neofeminism* is pivotal to the Nineties as well as to its government, business, education, culture, law and science. It's "Neo" because it is not the feminism of the Seventies with its attack on the traditional family, women's affinity groups, anti-heterosexual bias and a ban on celebrities. Neofeminism has luminaries like writer Gloria Steinam and entertainer Madonna and a buzz of sex chat and gossip. The Neofeminist avatar is Co-president Hillary  but there are other power centers like the first woman Secretary of State, Madeline Albright, and the first woman Attorney General, Janet Reno. This is a mindset that visualized Elizabeth Dole as a Republican presidential or maybe as a vice presidential candidate in 2000.

In the Nineties, the political power of women voters increased as they played a key role in both Clinton's elections. The gender gap means that women voted for Clinton in a higher proportion then men. Clintonia included the Year of Woman in 1992, when three new female Senators were elected.

Women's concerns include the Democrat's focus on education, health care, the environment and Social Security as well as the traditional feminist causes of gender equity, abortion rights, childcare and benefits for poor women and children. These issues are on Hillary's agenda and were present during Bill's campaigns. It is of interest that the issues of most concern to California voters during an exit poll after the 1998 election were education, 19% and abortion, 16% followed by the economy, jobs and taxes, while the environment, gun control, and the Lewinsky affair trailed in the single digits. The Democratic Party as the Neofeminist engine is a legacy that awaits the verdict of a history that is clouded by Bill's welfare reform with its scuttling of the safety net for poor women and children in his second term.

Another Neofeminist statement from the White House is about the relationship between women and men. Hillary was a successful attorney, a policy leader, and mother who raised a child while married to Governor Bill. Then in the White House she continued her political leadership while mothering teenage Chelsea and being the First Lady. This is a new American homily about the Presidential Family. That their marriage is troubled and that some of the dissension is public gives this neofeminist love story more rather then less credibility.

Bill Clinton's national sexual theater beginning during his 1992 campaign led directly to this Neo-feminism. This was not the plan of the feminists or their enemies, but it happened on Hillary and Bill's watch. It was Bill's in-house sexuality that led to an awareness of the women's agenda in a way that the ERA and abortion rights didn't do. The feminists were pro-choice and for equal rights and the antifeminists were in opposition, but Bill's spectacle was a scream at both factions with a whisper of irony.

National attention was first on Gennifer and Bill, then on Paula and Bill and finally on Monica and Bill, with Hillary completing each of these triangles. National tournaments of prurience, sermonizing and spin reached saturation. Widow Kathleen Willey's case contributed briefly while snitch Linda Tripp and literary agent Lucienne Goldberg had walk-on parts. The power of a sexual platform with Ken Starr, the White House players, the Secret Service, Matt Drudge and the journalists, attorneys William Ginsburg and Bob Bennett, and a cast of hundreds eclipsed issues like campaign finance reform, the sins of the IRS, Iraq's weapons of mass destruction, the survival of Social Security, and even the economy.

Gaia, the first matter to emerge from the void during creation, best symbolizes a separate women's role in the Nineties. A later incarnation of Gaia is Athena, born from Zeus' forehead as the Goddess of wisdom and victory in war for Athens. Androgynous Athena, who invented the ship and domesticated the olive, is a virgin Goddess in a promiscuous Pantheon.

Mother Dorothy, Teacher Elisabeth and Adolescent Guide Don Jones nurture Hillary-Athena, an American Goddess. She faced Daddy Hugh in a love-hate Oedipal struggle from which she emerged with Hugh's dark powers and she continued to contest the oppressors, Daddy Hugh and Husband Bill, and so gives a voice and strength to the Village, especially its women and children. She speaks with fury and sacred curses, a language that is undecipherable to many. The neofeminist legacy from Hillary is served with the salt and pepper of S and M and the hot sauce of anger too.

Third is *nihilism*, which is emblematic of the emptiness, passivity and centrism of American politics in the Nineties and beyond. This is a style of inactivity and moderation that contrasts to the density and activism of both the liberated Sixties and the Reagan Revolution of the Eighties.

The electorate is cynical, apathetic, and uninterested and the number of voters declines in each election. A variety of emotions affect the citizen: passivity, anger at government, loss of hope for a better system, distrust of politicians, and black humor. The public's "...thirst for passivity..." was slaked by George W. Bush's personality and his campaign in 2000 according to Hendrik Hertzberg in the *New Yorker*.[292] "Nobody for President'" is the continuing message of Wavy Gravy.

In addition to public lethargy, there is fear and anger about public service. These emotions are expressed in the suicide note of Vincent Foster, the White House counsel who wrote about a Washington climate where "...ruining people is considered a sport."[293] The same feelings of frustration affect the members of Congress, who increasingly decide not to return for another term, and the citizens who avoid political careers or temporary public appointments. The voters and the politicians feel powerless.

This political passivity and nihilism is Surplus Powerlessness. Psychologist Michael Lerner in Oakland during the Eighties studied groups of stressed workers, which led to the identification of Surplus Powerlessness. [294] As workers and as citizens, most people suffer from real powerlessness leading to their cynicism, passivity and frustration. These workers and citizens who are the victims of real powerlessness blame themselves and this guilt leads to Surplus Powerlessness, a further and crucial increase in isolation, anger, suspicion and alienation that prevents action. Worse still, the victims of Surplus Powerlessness often turn their anger on each other.

People are often unaware of their Surplus Powerlessness because it develops in what Lerner calls the Social Unconscious when the Human Essence is violated. The increase in Surplus Powerlessness during the Nineties can also be explained in Freudian terms, as a regression to the narcissism of childhood so there is oral dependent and passive behavior on a national scale.

The Nineties' preference for centrism and moderation expresses the ambivalence and apathy of the voters who choose a government divided between a Democratic President and a Republican Congress. Bill's ambivalence and indecision and Hillary's pragmatism are the mirror images of the choices made by these Nineties' voters.

The landmarks of Clintonia's domestic program were moderate and centrist: NAFTA, an increased minimum wage, the Brady bill, transferability of health benefits, family leave, subsidies for child care, more police, anti-terrorism laws, welfare reform, a tax increase, benefits for education, a balanced budget and deficit reduction. This is called "The School of Smaller Steps" by Andrea Bernstein. This landscape contrasts with the Himalayan peaks and valleys of domestic policy during the postwar era: McCarthyism, polio vaccine, Medicare, putting a man on the moon, the Civil Rights Act of 1964, and firing the striking air traffic controllers.

International Clintonia was also moderate with its restoration of democracy in Haiti, the Dayton peace plan for Bosnia, the Northern Ireland agreement facilitated by George Mitchell, the White House role in the implementation of the Oslo agreement for the Mideast, and the military intervention in Kosovo. These achievements are important but they are not global events like the Marshall Plan, NATO, a war in Korea and one in Vietnam or the beginning and the end of the Cold War. Other moderate Clinton's policies were the inaction in the thorny human rights issues in the Sudan, China, Indonesia, Rwanda, Nigeria, Afghanistan, and until 1999, East Timor. There were many wars without presidential mediation: Sierra Leone, Liberia, Angola, the Congo, Ethiopia, Eritrea and Chechnya. There were confrontations without resolution between India and Pakistan, both armed with nuclear weapons.

Fourth, the Boomer took the power in the Nineties. The Boomers finally stood tall when the forty-somethings, Hillary and Bill took over the White House from their parents, the World War II Presidents and their First Ladies.

Successions are contentious and tumultuous; the son is often a rebel like the Satan who is pictured by Milton as God's most brilliant angel. Zeus faced his succession problem by swallowing Metis, who was pregnant with his offspring. Zeus' father, Cronos who married Rhea, feared his children and swallowed them, but Zeus escaped to Crete. Cronos, whose father, Uranos had imprisoned him in Hades escaped and used a sickle to castrate his father. The Goddess Gaia began the pattern when she mothered Cronos.

Rebel Oedipus was a son who killed his father and married his mother. He became a King who was punished by remorse, blindness and a life of exile, but eventually he was called to the Pantheon from his death in a Sacred Grove. Oedipus' tragic fate was a divine legend, so despite his behavior there was no personal culpability. Oedipus as a victim and finally transcendent is an imperfect surrogate for Bill but it is a way to see him as a tragic hero who received symbolic punishment, then wandered and finally perhaps will become a hallowed statesman. Like Nixon, who was almost impeached before he resigned, Bill too may be redeemed from impeachment and scandal by history.

The Nineties were the Equivocal Decade because they were formed by the Kennedy Sixties and the Reagan Eighties. A generation in the Sixties was defined by rock and roll, mind altering drugs, and sexual freedom as it struggled for individual and cultural liberation, for civil and human rights, and against the war in Vietnam using civil and sometimes uncivil disobedience.

The Reagan Revolution of the Eighties fought against government regulation and for personal wealth and the freedom of the marketplace. The Sixties' revolution and its attack on authority were answered by a Reagan cabinet officer, William Bennett, who wrote *The Death of Outrage: Bill Clinton and the Assault on American Ideals*.

In the Nineties, there was an uneasy truce between the Sixties and the Eighties in our national character according to political scientist Mark Lilla.[295] Nonetheless, the psychocultural warfare of the Nineties and beyond explains the animus in both the attack and the defense of Bill and Hillary.

The Equivocal Decade found its symbols: Hillary-Athena as the Good and Bad Goddess and Bill as Zeus among the Nymphs.

## AFTERWORD

A psychoanalytic study often ends with an epitome, a kind of summary much as a novel closes with a crucial last line. This inquiry finds that the predominant influences of Bill and Hillary's personalities are their sadomasochism and their unresolved Oedipal complexes. The secondary psychological issues are Hillary's frigidity of character and Bill's narcissistic personality.

Chelsea for whom the evidence is less abundant also has an unresolved Oedipus complex but the role of preoedipal issues like sadomasochism and narcissism remains undefined.

I've said everything about Bill, Chelsea and Hillary's psychology that I know. The Clinton's further life experiences will lead to the amplification of existing emotional themes, shifts in the balances between them and to new trends too. Bill, Chelsea, and Hillary in the twenty-first century will not change their established patterns but new events will uncover more about their ego mechanisms and their unconscious psychological labyrinths. *Living History* by Hillary answers a few questions; Bill's book will be out soon and it's likely that Chelsea will write a book too. Of course, there will be more photos, interviews, speeches, analyses, exposés, tributes and excoriations in the post-Clintonian era as Hillary-consciousness ascends and Bill refuses to fade away.

Psychohistory itself will change as its study and practice continue. The original method of Freud's psychohistory was succeeded by the generation of Erik Erickson; then the contemporary psychohistorians like Robert Jay Lifton; and now, we are in a postmodern phase with work like this.

Psychohistory is like its progenitor, history. It changes when a new generations is ready for a reassessment with a fresh perspective about a leader or an era. New historical information emerges as the hidden diaries of the mind and the hieroglyphics of social currents are retranslated. Clintonstudies will continue as a vehicle of insights about the Clintons, the Nineties and beyond.

BIBLIOGRAPHY

This is a list of all the books, articles and other sources used in preparing this work. Many are mentioned in the body of the text. The footnotes in the text give the page numbers for specific references.

Abram, Herbert. "Desert Storm? or Thyroid Storm? An Inquiry," *PSR Quarterly*, Sept. 1992.

Aldrich, Gary. *Unlimited Access*, Regnery, 1996.

Allen, Charles and Portis, Jonathan. *The Comeback Kid:The Life and Career of Bill Clinton*, Birch Lane Press, 1992.

Allen, Mike. "Clinton Staff Alumni Insist White House Prove Vandalism Claim," *Washington Post*, June 4, 2001.

Allison, Dorothy. *Bastard out of Carolina*, Penguin Books, 1992.

Alter, Jonathan. "Citizen Clinton Up Close," *Newsweek*, April 8, 2002.

Andersen, Christopher. *Bill and The Marriage, William Morrow*, 1999.

Anderson-Miller, Judith and Miller, Bruce, Joshua. *Dreams of Bill*, Citadel Press, 1994.

Appignanesi, Lisa and Forrester, John. *Freud's Women*, Basic Books, 1992.

Arnheim, Daniel and Sinclair, William. *The Clumsy Child, A Program of Motor Therapy*, Mosby, 1975.

Aurelius, Marcus. *The Meditations* (G.M.A. Grube, Trans.) Bobbs Merrill, 1963.

Baker, Peter. "Jones Lawyers Allege Coverup," *Washington Post*, 14, 1998.

Baker, Russell. "Cruel and Usual" *The New York Review of Books*, January 20, 2000.

Barry, Jonathan, Hester, Marianne and Roberts, Gareth (Eds.). *Witchcraft Early Modern Europe*, Cambridge University Press, 1996.

Bellow, Saul. *Humboldt's Gift*, Penguin Books, 1973.

Bennet, James. "First Lady Backs Up Her Man, Once Again," *New York Times*, Jan 25, 1998.

Bennet, James. "Jones vs Clinton Sex Misconduct Suit Appears Headed for Trial," *San Francisco Examiner*, November 9, 1997.

Berne, Eric. *Games People Play The Psychology of Human Relationships*, Grove Press, 1964.

Bernstein, Andrea. "Hillary's Clinton's 'Smaller Steps'" *The Nation*, September 6/13, 1999.

Bertoldi, Andreas. "Oedipus in (South) Africa: Psychoanalysis and the Politics of Difference," *American Imago*, 1998 .

Birnbaum, Jeffrey. *Madhouse The Private Turmoil of Working for the President*, Times Books, 1996.

Boland, Sue Erickson. "Bill Clinton and John F. Kennedy The Dark Side of Charisma," *Psychoanalytic Dialogues*, 2000.

Bonnefoy, Yves. *Mythologies*, University of Chicago Press, 1991.

Brock, David. *The Seduction of Hillary Rodham*, Simon and Schuster, 1996.

Brock, David. "Confessions of a Right-wing Hit Man," *Esquire*, July 1997.

Brock, David. "Bill Bennett, " *Rolling Stone*, November 12, 1998.

Brodie, Fawn. *Richard Nixon The Shaping of His Character*, W. W. Norton, 1981.

Browning, Dolly Kyle. *Purposes of the Heart*, Direct Outstanding Creations, 660 Preston Forest Center, Dallas, 1997.

Browning, Dolly Kyle. "The Complaint Excerpts from Dolly Kyle Browning's Amended Complaint," www.deardolly.com/complaint.htm, 1999.

Brownrigg, Ronald. *Who's Who in the New Testament*, Holt Rinehart and Winston, 1971.

Bruck, Connie. "Hillary the Pol," *The New Yorker*, May 30, 1994.

Brugger, Robert (Ed.). *Our Selves/Our Past*, John Hopkins University Press, 1981.

Brummett, John. *Highwire: The Education of Bill Clinton*, Hyperion, 1994.

Buhle, Mari Jo. *Feminism and its Discontents*, Harvard University Press, 1998.

Campbell, Lewis. "Plato," *Encyclopedia Britannica*. 11th Edition, Vol. 21, Enclyclopaedia Britannica Company, 1911.

Carpozi, George. *Clinton Confidential*, Emery Dalton Books, 1995, 2001.

Cash, W. J. *The Mind of the South*, Vintage 1941.

Cawthorne, Nigel. *Sex Lives of The Presidents*, St. Martins Press, 1996.

Chehrazi, Shahala. "Female Psychology: A Review," *Journal of the American Psychoanalytic Association*, 34: 1986.

Chodorow, Nancy. *The Reproduction of Mothering*, University of California Press, 1978.

Chodorow, Nancy. *Feminism and Psychoanalytic Theory*, Yale University Press, 1989.

Clark, Wesley. *Waging Modern War*, Public Affairs, 2001.

Clinch, Nancy. *The Neurosis*, Grosset & Dunlap, 1973.

Clinton, Bill. "'A Powerful Memory of Constant Love,'" *San Francisco Examiner*, May 10. 1996.

Clinton, Chelsea. "Before and After," *Talk*, December 2000.

Clinton, Hillary. *It Takes a Village*, Simon and Schuster, 1996.

Clinton, Hillary. *The Unique Voice of Hillary Rodham Clinton*, (Ed) Claire Osborne, Avon Books, 1997.

Clinton, Hillary. "Vital Voices Conference on Women and Democracy, Reykjavik, Iceland October 10, 1999" in *Vital Voices* 1997-1999, Washington D. C., PREX 1.2 v 66.

Clinton, Hillary. *Living History*, Simon and Schuster, 2003.

The Clinton Chronicles (Videotape), Citizens For Honest Government, P.O. Box 270, Winchester, CA 92596, 1994

Collins, Nancy. "A Legacy of Strength and Love," *Good Housekeeping*, November, 1995.

Collins, Nancy. "Linda Tripp I'd Do It All Over Again," *George*, December/January 2001.

Cocco, Marie. "What's Behind Hillary Hatred?" *San Francisco Chronicle*, April 13, 2000.

Conason, Joe and Lyons, Gene. *The Hunting of the President*, St. Martin's Press, 2000.

Conrad, Joseph. *Heart of Darkness*, W. W. Norton, 1963.

Coz, S., Introduction, In C. Melcher and V. Virga, (Eds.) *The National Enquirer: Thirty Years of Unforgettable Images*, Talk Miramax.

Clinton, Roger. *Growing Up Clinton*, Summit Publishing, 1995.

Cunningham, Ernest. *The Ultimate Barbra*, Renaissance Books, 1998.

Curiel, Jonathan. "Stripper Charged After Show for Teen Girls in Pleasanton," *San Francisco Chronicle*, November 16, 1998.

Degregorio, William. *The Complete Book of Presidents*, Barricade Books, 1997.

Delmar, Gloria. *Mother Goose From Nursery to Literature*, McFarland & Company, 1987.

Demaris, Ovid. *Judith Exner My Story*, Grove Press 1977.

Diamond, Jared. *Guns, Germs, and Steel*, W.W. Norton. 1998.

*Diagnostic and Statistical Manual of Mental Disorders DSM IV*, American Psychiatric Association Press, 1994.

Douglas, Ann. "The Extraordinary Hillary Clinton," *Vogue*, December 1998.

Dowd, Maureen. "The Privacy Ruse," *The New York*, Aug. 30, 1998.

Dowd, Maureen. "Maldroit Du Seigneur." *The New York Times*, Sept. 30, 1998.

Dubner, Stephen. "Steven the Good," *The New York Times Magazine*, February 14, 1999.

Dunne, Dominick. "Mr. Dunne Goes to Washington," *Vanity Fair*, May 1999.

Efron, Edith. "Can the President Think," *Reason*, Nov. 1994.

Eidelberg, Ludwig. *Encyclopedia of Psychoanalysis*, Free Press, 1968.

Ely, Suzanne, Gould, Martin and Harbour, Maggie. "Clinton and the Sexy Multimillionaire Mom," *Star*, May 1, 2001.

Erickson, Erik. *Identity and the Life Cycle*, W. W. Norton, 1980.

Faludi, Susan. "The Malling of the Media," *The Nation*, May 27, 1996.

Flowers, Gennifer. *Passion and Betrayal*, Emery Dalton Books, 1995.

Flowers, Gennifer. *Sleeping With the President*, Anonymous Press, New York, 1998.

Fenichel, Otto. *The Psychoanalytic Theory of Neurosis*, W. W. Norton, 1945.

Fenichel, Otto. *The Collected Papers of Otto Fenichel*, W. W. Norton, 1953.

Fiscalini, John. "Interpersonal Relations and the Problem of Narcissism," in *Narcissism and the Interpersonal Self*, (Ed.) Fiscalini, J. and Grey, A., Columbia University Press, 1993.

Francoer, Robert. (ed.) *The International Encyclopedia of Sexuality*, Continuum, 1998.

Franks, Lucinda. "The Intimate Hillary," *Talk*, September 1999.

Frazer, James. *The Golden Bough*, Macmillan, 1922.

Frazer, James. *The New Golden Bough*, Criterion Books, 1959.

Freud, Sigmund. *An Autobiographical Study*, Hogarth Press and the Institute of Psycho-analysis, 1935.

Freud, Sigmund. *Moses and Monotheism*, Knopf, 1939.

Freud, Sigmund. *Collected Papers*, Hogarth Press and the Institute of Psycho-analysis, 1949.

Freud, Sigmund. *Totem and Taboo*, Routledge and Kegan Paul, 1950.

Freud, Sigmund. *The Ego and the Id*, Hogarth Press and the Institute of Psycho-analysis, 1950.

Freud, Sigmund. *Three Essays on the Theory of Sexuality*, Basic Books, 1962.

Freud, Sigmund and Bullitt William. *Thomas Woodrow Wilson A Psychological Study*, Houghton Mifflin, 1966.

Freud, Sigmund. *The Standard Edition of the Complete Works of Sigmund Freud*, James Strachey, Editor, Hogarth Press and the Institute of Psycho-analysis, 1953.

Friedan, Betty. *The Fountain of Age*, Simon and Schuster, 1993.

Gabel, Stewart. "Life and Death in the Nursery: A Soft Sell for Hard Lessons," *Journal of the American Academy of Psychoanalysis*, 2001.

Gallen, David. *Bill Clinton as They Know Him*, Marlowe & Co., 1996.

Garchik, Leah. "Personals," *San Francisco Chronicle*, March 17, 2000.

Gathorne-Hardy, Jonathan. *Sex the Measure of All Things*, Indiana University Press. 1997.

Gerth, Jeff. "Clinton Joined S & L Operator in a Ozarks Real Estate Venture," *The New York Times*, March 8, 1992.

Gergen, David. *Eyewitness to Power*, Simon and Schuster, 2000.

Gould, Martin. "Hillary Tells Bill: I want a Divorce As He Confesses We Haven't Made Love for 14 Years," *Star*, September 29, 1998.

Gravel, Pierre. *The Malevolent Eye*, Peter Lang, 1995.

Graves, Robert. *King Jesus*, Cassel London, 1949.

Guinvier, Lani. *Lift Every Voice*, Simon and Schuster, 1998.

Hagood, Wesley. *Presidential Sex*, Birch Lane Press, 1995.

Hamer, Dean and Copeland, Peter. *Living With Our Genes*, Doubleday, 1998.

Hampden-Turner, Charles. *Maps of the Mind*, Collier Books, 1981.

Harpaz, Beth. *The Girls in the Van*, St. Martin's Press, 2001.

Hatfield, Larry and Helm, Mark. "On Tapes, Says Clinton Bemoaned Empty Life, 'Turned Purple' When Angry," *San Francisco Chronicle*, October 2, 1998.

Hefner, Hugh. "The Playboy President," *Playboy*, May 1998.

Hemingway, Ernest. *The Complete Stories of Ernest Hemingway*, Scribner, 1987.

Hernandez, Raymond. "Senator Clinton Settling in as Just One of 100," *The New York Times*, April 13, 2001.

Hersh, Seymour. *The Dark Side of Camelot*, Little Brown 1997.

Hertzberg, Hendrick. "They've Got Personality," *The New Yorker*, November 6, 2000.

Hitchens, Christopher. *No One Left to Lie To The Triangulation of William Jefferson Clinton*, Verso, 1999.

Huffington, Adrianna. *San Francisco Examiner*, Jan. 28, 1998.

Hunter, Ski and Sundel, Martin (Eds.). *Midlife Myths*, Sage Publications, 1989.

Ingraham, Laura. *The Hillary Trap*, Hyperion, 2000.

Isikoff, Michael. *Uncovering Clinton*, Three Rivers Press, 1999.

Jones, Ernest. *The Life and Work of Sigmund Freud*, Basic Books, 1957.

Jones, James H. *Alfred C. Kinsey*, W. W. Norton, 2002.

Johnson, Haynes. *The Best of Times*, Harcourt, 2001.

Jong, Erica. "Hillary's Husband Re-elected!" *The Nation*, Nov. 25, 1996.

Joyce, James. *Ulysses*, Random House. 1986.

Junod, Tom. "You'll Never Look at Hillary Clinton the Same Way Again", *Esquire*, October 1999.

Kaplan, Harold and Sadock, Benjamin, (Eds.). *Comprehensive Textbook of Psychiatry/IV*, Williams & Wilkins, 1985.

Kaplan, Louise. *Female Perversions*. Doubleday, 1991.

Kelley, Virginia. *Leading With My Heart*, Simon & Schuster, 1994.

King, Norman. *Hillary*, Birch Lane Press, 1993.

King, Stephen. *It*, Viking, 1986.

Kinsey, Alfred, Pomeroy, Wardell and Martin, Clyde. *Sexual Behavior in the Human Male*, W. B. Saunders, 1948.

Kinsey, Alfred, Pomeroy, Wardell, Martin, Clyde & Gebhard, Paul. *Sexual Behavior in the Human Female*, W. B. Saunders, 1953.

Kline, Dixie. "High-School Confidential," *The New Yorker*, July 20, 1998.

Klein, Joe. "An American Marriage," *The New Yorker*, Feb. 9, 1998.

Klein, Joe. *The Natural*, Doubleday, 2002.

Knutson, Lawrence. "Transcript Reveals Clinton Blames Himself for Waco," *San Francisco Chronicle*, July 26, 2000.

Kuncl, Tom "Chelsea's Courage," *Star*, September 8, 2000.

Lakoff, Robin *The Language War*, University of California Press, 2000.

Langer, Walter. *The Mind of Adolf Hitler*, Basic Books,1972.

Lant, Kathleen and Thompson, Theresa. *Imagining the Worst*, Greenwood Press, 1998.

Latin, Don. "Presidential Pastor Speaks on Scandal," *San Francisco Chronicle*, Jan. 11, 1999.

Leo, John and Galvin, Ruth. "The Preacher of Narcissism," *Time*, Dec. 1, 1980.

Leonard, John. "Living the Great American Novel," *The New York Times Book Review*, October 15, 2000.

Lerner, Michael. *Surplus Powerlessness*, The Institute for Labor and Mental Health, 5100 Leona, Oakland, CA, 1986.

Levinson, Daniel. *The Seasons of a Man's Life*, Knopf, 1978.

Levinson, Daniel. *The Seasons in a Woman's Life*, Knopf, 1996.

Lewis, Neil. "In Heat of Campaign, a New Report Stirs Old Questions for Mrs. Clinton," *The New York Times*, June 19, 2000.

Lewis, Nolan and Yarnell, Helen. *Pathological Firesetting*. Nervous and Mental Disease Monographs, New York, 1951.

Lilla, Mark "A Tale of Two Reactions." *The New York Review of Books*, March 14, 1998.

Lowinger, Pau.l "Graves Disease" *PSR Quarterly*, March 1993.

Lowinson, Joyce, Ruiz, Pedro, Millman, Robert, Langrod, John, (Eds.). *Substance Abuse*, Williams and Wilkens, 1992.

Lyall, Sarah. "Britain is Becoming, Chelsea Clinton Finds," *The New York Times Sunday Styles*, March 31, 2002.

Lyons, Gene. *Fools for Scandal How the Media Invented*, Franklin Square Press, 1996.

Mack, John. *A Prince of Our Disorder The Life of T. E. Lawrence*, Little, Brown, 1976.

Mailer, Norman. "Portrait - V: Clinton and Dole," *George*, Jan., 1997.

Mansfield, Nick. *Masochism*, Praeger, 1997.

Manson, Marilyn. In "The Clinton Conversation," *Rolling Stone*, Nov. 12, 1998.

Maraniss, David. *First in His Class The Biography of Bill Clinton*, Simon and Schuster, 1995.

Maraniss, David. *The Clinton Enigma*, Simon & Schuster, 1998.

Marquis, Christopher. "White House Vandalism Caper Was Overblown, a Report Finds," *The New York Times*, May 19, 2001.

Masters, William, Johnson, Virginia and Kolodny, Robert. *Heterosexuality*, Harper Collins, 1994.

Matthews, Chris. "The Ex-Presidents' Club," *San Francisco Chronicle*,

June 23, 2002.

deMause, Lloyd. *Reagan's America*, Creative Roots, 1984.

Mayer, Jane. "Following the Trail of the President's Private Eye," *The New Yorker*, Feb. 16, 1997.

Mayer, Jane. "Distinguishing Characteristics," *The New Yorker*, July 7, 1997.

Maynard, Joyce. *At Home in the World*, Picador, 1998.

Mayo Clinic "Mayo Clinic Healthy Living Centers Hormonal Conditions Male Menopause: Does it exist?" www.mayoclinic.com/home?id=MCMC300003.

McLeod, Ramon. "Conservative Voters Sat Election Out, *San Francisco Chronicle*, November 5, 1998.

Meyer, Wayne, (Ed.). *Clinton on Clinton*, Avon, 1999.

Michael, Robert, Gagnon, John, Lauman, Edward & Kolata, Gina. *Sex in America*, Little Brown & Co, 1994.

Miller, Arthur. "Salem Revisited," *The New York Times*, October 18, 1998.

Miller, Arthur. "American Playhouse," *Harper's* June, 2001.

Milton, Joyce. *The First Partner*, William Morrow, 1999.

Money-Kyle, Roger. *The Meaning of Sacrifice*, Hearth Press, London, 1930.

Morris, Dick. *Behind the Oval Office Winning the Presidency in the Nineties*, Random House, 1997.

Morris, Roger. Partners in Power *The Clintons and Their America*, Henry Holt and Company, 1996.

Morrison, Toni. "The Talk of the Town," *The New Yorker*, October 5. 1998.

Morton, Andrew. *Monica's Story*, St. Martin's Press, 1999.

Mullahy, Patrick. *Oedipus Myth and Complex*, Hermitage Press. 1948.

Murray, James. "Medical Care for All American," *New Republic*, July 19, 1944.

Myers, Steven & Stemmata, Eric. "Clinton Seeks to Avoid Acting on Missile Defense System, *The New York Times*, June 21, 2000.

National Institute of Health Consensus Statement *Impotence*, December 7-9, 1992.

Nelson, Lars-Erik. "Whatever Happened to Whitewater," *The New York Review of Books*, August 13, 1998.

Negatron, Bernice. "Dynamics of Transition of Middle Age to Old Age," *Journal of Geriatric Psychiatry*, Fall 1970.

Neumann, Erich. *The Origins and History of Consciousness*, Pantheon, 1954.

Neumann, Erich. *The Great Mother*, Pantheon, 1955.

Nichol, Armand, (Ed.). *The Harvard Guide to Modern Psychiatry*, Belknap Harvard, 1978.

Nyberg, Gustav. "Not All Presidential Advisors Talk Politics," *The New York Times*, March 18, 1997.

Noonan, Peggy. *The Case Against Hillary Clinton*, HarperCollins, 2000.

Oakley, Meredith. *On the Make The Rise of Bill Clinton*, Regency Publishing, 1994.

Olson, Barbara. *Hell to Pay*, Regenery, 1999.

O'Neill, William. *American High*, Free Press, 1986.

Oppenheimer, Jerry. *State of a Union*, Harper Collins, 2000.

Ornish, Dean. *Dr. Dean Ornish's Program for Reversing Heart Disease*, Random House, 1990.

Oremland, Jerome. "Michelangelo's Pietas," In A. Sunlit (Ed.) *The Psychoanalytic Study of the Child*, Vol. 33, Yale University Press, 1978.

Puglia, Camille. *Vamps and Tramps*, Random House, 1994.

Petty, Thomas. "The Tragedy of Humpty Dumpy," In R. Eisner, A. Freud, H. Hartmann and E. Kris (Eds.) *The Psychoanalytic Study of the Child* Vol. 8, International Universities Press, 1953.

Perez, Jane. *The New York Times*, June 2, 1999.

Phillips, Lisa. *The American Century Art and Culture 1950 - 2000*, Whitney Museum of American Art and W. W. Norton, 1999.

Phillips, Adam. *Promises, Promises*, Basic Books, 2001.

Preston, James, (Ed.). *Mother Worship*, University of North Carolina Press, 1982.

Preston, Douglas. "Cannibals of the Canyon," *The New Yorker*, November 30, 1998.

Proznan, Charlotte. *Feminist Psychoanalytic Psychotherapy* Jason Aronson Inc, 1992.

Radcliff, Donnie. *Hillary Rodham Clinton*, Times Warner, 1993.

Ramjug, Peter. "Evangelist: If Clinton is Guilty, I Forgive Him," *San Francisco Examiner*, March 13, 1998.

Rank, Otto. *Will Therapy and Truth and Reality*, Knopf, 1947.

Ray, Robert. *Final Report of the Independent Counsel In Re: Madison Guaranty Savings & Loan Association Regarding Monica Lewinsky and Others*, (March 6, 2002 United States Court of Appeals For the District of Columbia Circuit Division for the Purpose of Appointing Independent Counsels Division No. 94-1) Washington, D.C. U. S. Government Printing Office Washington, D.C.

Redlich, Fritz. *Hitler Diagnosis of a Destructive Prophet*, Oxford University Press, 1999.

Reich, Robert. *Locked in the Cabinet*, Alfred A. Knopf, 1997.

Renchon, Stanley. *High Hopes The Clinton Presidency and Politics of Ambition*, NYU Press, 1996.

Rodham, Hillary. "Children's Rights: A Legal Perspective, " in Virden, Patricia & Brody, Ilene, (Ed) *Children's Rights: Contemporary Perspectives*, Teachers College Press, 1979.

Robinson, Paul A. *The Freudian Left*, Harper and Row, 1969.

Roland, Alan. "Psychoanalysis in India and Japan: Toward a Comparative Psychoanalysis," *American Journal of Psychoanalysis*, March, 1991.

Rosenfeld, Isadora. "What Everybody Should Know About Menopause," *Parade Magazine*, March 21, 1999.

Ross, John. *The Sadomasochism of Everyday Life*, Simon and Schuster, 1997.

Runyan, William, (Ed.). *Psychology and Historical Interpretation*, Oxford University Press, 1988.

Sagan, Eli. *Cannibalism*, The Psychohistory Press, 1974.

Salter, Stephanie. "It's The Love, Stupid," *San Francisco Examiner*, August 27, 1998.

Sandlot, Marc. "Clinton Still Grabbing Front Page," *San Francisco Chronicle*. February 14, 2001.

Sen. Clinton Returns to Health Issues. *USA Today*, July 20, 2001.

Sen. Clinton Ahead of Pack for '04 Race," *San Francisco Chronicle*, December 22, 2002.

Scales, Ann. "Clinton Paints Ominous Picture of World's Future," *San Francisco Chronicle*, May 18, 2000.

Schad-Somers, Suzanne. *Sadomasochism Etiology and Treatment*, Jason Aronson, 1996.

Schaeffer, Bob. "Standardized Tests and Teacher Competence," *School Voices*, Fall 1996.

Schulman, Bruce. *The Seventies*, Free Press, 2001.

Shaker, Arcane. *Khajuraho Orchha*, Lustre Press, M-75, Greater Kailash-II Market, New Delhi-110 048, India, 1997.

Sheehy, Gail. *Passages: The Predictable Crises of Adult Life*, Dalton. 1976.

Sheehy, Gail. *New Passages*, Random House, 1995.

Sheehy, Gail. *Understanding Men's Passages*, Random House, 1998.

Sheehy, Gail. *Hillary's Choice*, Random House, 1999.

Sheehy, Gail. "Cheer and Loathing in New York," *Vanity Fair*, June 2000.

Shogren, Elizabeth. "First Lady Wins Approval With Toned-Down Image," *San Francisco Chronicle*, August 13, 1998.

Simon, Roger. "Clinton" in Brian Lamb *Book Notes Life Stories*, Times Books, 1999.

Smith, Alson. *Chicago's Left Bank*, Henry Regnery Company, 1953.

Smith, Sam. "Arkansas Connections," The Progressive Review, October 8, 1998, http://emporium.turnpike.net/P/ProRev/connex.htm.

Starr, Kenneth. *Referral from Independent Counsel Kenneth W. Starr in Conformity with the Requirements of Title 28, United States Code, Section 595(c)*, (September 11, 1998 Committee on the Judiciary). Washington, D.C., U. S. Government Printing Office.

Stephanopoulos, George. *All Too Human*, Little Brown, 1999.

Sterba, Richard. "Some Psychological Factors in Negro Race Hatred and Anti-Negro Riots," *Psychoanalysis and the Social Sciences*, Rohheim, Geza, (Ed.) International Universities Press, 1947.

Sterba, Richard. *Introduction to the Psychoanalytic Theory of the Libido*, Robert Brunner, 1968.

Steyer, James. *The Other Parent*, Simon and Schuster, 2002.

Stewart, James. *Blood Sport*, Simon & Schuster, 1996.

Stoller, Robert. "The Sense of Femaleness," *Psychoanalytic Quarterly*, 37, pp. 42-55.

Sullivan Andrew. "Psycho," *The New Republic*, March 12, 2001.

Sullivan, Harry. *The Collected Works of Harry Stack Sullivan*, W. W. Norton, 1935.

Survey: Of Kids 15-19, 55% Have Tried Oral Sex, *San Francisco Chronicle*, February 29, 2000.

Thomas, Kenneth. "A Psychoanalytic Study of Alexander the Great," *The Psychoanalytic Review*, December 1995.

Tomsky, Michae.l "Hillary's Turn," *New York*, April 3, 2000.

Tomsky, Michael. *Hillary's Turn*, Free Press, 2001.

Troy, Gil. *Affairs of State*, Free Press, 1995.

Turner, C. and Turner, J. *Cannibalism and Violence in the Prehistoric American Southwest*, University of Utah, 1999.

Waas, Murray. "Sam Dash Speaks Out On What We Won't Be Hearing About Hillary," *The New Yorker*, July 26, 1999.

Weiss, Philip. "Clinton Crazies," *The New York Times Magazine*, Feb. 23, 1997.

Weber, Nicholas Fox. "The Balthus Enigma," *The New*, September 6, 1999.

What Do You Know About Sex, *Seventeen*, April, 2000.

Whitmont, Edmund. *Return of the Goddess*, Crossroad, 1982.

Wickham, Dewayne. *Bill Clinton and Black America*, Ballantine Books, 2002.

Wills, Gary. "The Clinton Scandals," *The New York Review of Books*, April 19, 1996.

Woodward, Bob. *The Agenda*, Simon and Schuster, 1994.

Woodward, Bob. *Shadow*, Simon and Schuster, 1999.

Woodward, C. Vann. *The Burden of Southern History*, Louisiana State University Press, 1968.

Wurtzel, Elizabeth. "Her Age of Innocence," *George*, April 1998.

ENDNOTES

[1] Some of these appear on my website, www.lowingerpaul.com

[2] See the reference to Abram, H.

[3] See the reference to Lowinger, P.

[4] See the reference to Runyan, William, p. 36

[5] In *The Oxford Dictionary of Quotations*, Ed. Elizabeth Knowles, Oxford University Press, 1999, p. 116

[6] See the reference to Faludi, Susan

[7] See the Leonard, John reference, p.19

[8] See the Oppenheimer, J. reference, pp.79 and 81

[9] See the Milton, J. reference, p. 16

[10] See the Oppenheimer, J. reference, p.71

[11] See the reference to Sheehy, G. *Hillary's Choice*, p. 14

[12] See the reference to Sheehy, G. *Hillary's Choice*, p. 318

[13] Most of the biographical material about Hillary's parents and grandparents is from Jerry Oppenheimer's book however some is from Hillary Clinton's *Living History*.

[14] I spoke to a researcher in Chicago who didn't want to be identified  with his characterization of Dorothy's family as "marginal."

[15] See the reference to Oppenheimer, Jerry, p. 70.

[16] These accounts appear in Brock, David *The Seduction of Hillary Rodham*, p.4; Sheehy, Gail *Hillary's Choice*, p. 24-25; Clinton and Clinton, Hillary, *Living History*.

[17] Other accounts of the episode appear in the books by Joyce Milton on p. 13; Jerry Oppenheimer on p. 70; Roger Morris on p. 112; Norman King on p. 7 and Christopher Anderson on p. 91.

[18] See the reference to King, Norman, p. 4

[19] See the reference to Morris, Roger, p. 115

[20] See the reference to Anderson, Christopher, p. 94

[21] The comments by Helen Dowdy are in the Jerry Oppenheimer  book on p. 71 and p. 72.

[22] See Clinton, H. *Living History*, p. 11

[24] See the Appignanesi, L. and Forrester, J. reference, p. 420-421.

[25] See the Chehazi, Shahala reference, p. 149

[26] See Clinton, H. *Living History*, p. 15.

[27] See the reference to Radcliff, D.  p. 37

[28] See the reference to Weber, N.  p. 34

[29] See Bruck, Connie reference, p.65

[30] See Morris, Roger reference, p. 280

[31] See Chodorow, Nancy *The Reproduction of Mothering*, p. 199

[32] See Milton, Joyce reference, p. 24

[33] See Chodorow, Nancy *The Reproduction of Mothering*, p. 199

[34] This appears in "The Dissolution of the Oedipus Complex," *The Standard Edition of the Complete Works of Sigmund Freud*, Hogarth Press and the Institute of Psycho-Analysis, 1953, ed. James Strachey

[35] See the reference to Stoller, R.

[36] See Cherhrazi, Shahala reference, pp. 141-147

[37] See the reference to Freud, S., *The Ego and the Id*, p. 56

[38] See the reference to Oppenheimer, J., p. 81

[39] See the reference to Carpozi, George, p. 343 and p. 361

[40] See the reference to Anderson, Christopher p. 178

[41] See the reference to Flowers, G. *Passion and Betrayal*, p. 41

[42] See the reference to Bruck, C. p. 88

[43] See the reference to Anderson, C. p. 201-2

[44] See the Anderson, C. reference, p. 265

[45] See the reference to Clinton, H. *It Takes a Village*, p. 21

[46] See the Warner, Judith reference, p. 13

[47] See the Morris, R. reference, p. 115-116

[48] See the reference to Schad-Sommers, Suzanne pp.6,7

[49] See the reference to Prozan, Charlotte, pp. 25, 26

[50] See the reference to Bennet, J., "First Lady Backs Up Her Man, Once Again"

[51] See the Anderson, Christopher reference, p. 33

[52] See the Milton, Joyce reference. p. 191

[53] See the Flowers, G. reference *Passion and Betrayal*, pp. 41-42

[54] See the reference to Klein, J. "An American Marriage," New Yorker, Feb. 9, 1998, p. 34

[55] See the reference to Mansfield, Nick p. xii

[56] See the Erickson, E. reference, pp 57-58, 63

[57] See Clinton, H. reference, *The Unique Voice of Hillary Rodham Clinton*, pp. 67-73

[58] See the Erickson, E. reference, pp. 67-73

[59] See the Sterba, R. reference, *Introduction to the Psychoanalytic Theory of the Libido*, pp 35-36, 38-39

[60] See the Campbell, L. reference, p. 816

[61] See the Clinton, H. reference to *It Takes a Village*, p. 43

[62] The person who made this remark did so on condition of anonymity.

[63] See the Clinton, H. reference to *The Unique Voice of Hillary Rodham Clinton*, p. 93

[64] See the Clinton, H. reference to *The Unique Voice of Hillary Rodham Clinton*,

p. 78

65 See the Anderson, Christopher reference, p. 15

66 See the Maraniss, D. reference to *The Clinton Enigma*, p. 21

67 See the Sheehy, G. reference to *Hillary's Choice*, p. 303

68 See the Clinton, H. reference The Unique Voice of Hillary Rodham Clinton. p. 76

69 See the Milton J. reference, p. 343

70 See the Brock, D. reference to "Confessions of a Right-wing Hit Man," p. 52

71 See the Anderson, Christopher reference, p. 179

72 See the reference to Sheehy, G. *Hillary's Choice* pp. 206-207

73 See the reference to Clinton, H. *Living History*, p. 471.

74 See the Bruck, C. reference, p. 74

75 See the Radcliffe, D. reference, p. 259

76 See the Clinton, H. reference to *The Unique Voice of Hillary Clinton*, p. 42

77 See the Clinton, H. reference to *The Unique Voice of Hillary Rodham Clinton*, p. 70

78 See the Bruck, C. reference, p. 67

79 See the Radcliffe, D. reference, p. 35

80 See the Clinton, H. reference to *The Unique Voice of Hillary Rodham Clinton*, p. 74

81 See the Bruck, C. reference, p. 88

82 See the Andersen, Christopher reference, pp. 202-205

83 See the Milton, J. reference, p. 289

84 See the reference to Fenichel. Otto *The Psychoanalytic Theory of Neurosis*, pp. 477-478

85 See the reference to Jong, E., "Hillary's Husband Re-elected," p. 11

86 See the Lakoff, R. reference, p. 188

87 See the reference to Sheehy, G. *Hillary's Choice*, pp. 62-74

88 *Life*, June 20, 1968, p. 28

89 See the reference to Anderson, C., p.7

90 Herz, Steve, Samuels, Jef and Howell, Michele "Hillary in Kinky 3-way Sex Video, *Globe*, May 16, 2000

91 The source for this rumor prefers to be anonymous.

92 See the Oppenheimer, J. reference, pp. 217-218

93 See the Junod, T. reference, p 115

94 See the reference to Garchik, L, p. C-18

95 See the reference to Kinsey, A., Pomeroy, Wardell, Martin, Clyde, Gebhard, Paul where the data is summarized on p. 487

96 See the Francoeur. R. reference. p. 1526

97 See the references to Gathorne-Hardy and Jones, James

[98] See the Horn, M. reference, pp. xv,160-161, 242

[99] See the Morris reference, pp. 227-233 and p. 447

[100] See the Anderson, C. reference p. 226

[101] See the Brock, D. reference p. 54

[102] See the reference to Woodward, Bob *The Agenda*, p. 12

[103] See the Brock, D. reference, p. 61

[104] See the Freud, S. reference to *Collected Papers*, Vol II, pp. 45-50

[105] See the Tomsky, M. reference, p. 8

[106] See the Brock, D. reference to *The Seduction of Hillary Rodham*, p. 152

[107] See the reference to Maraniss, D. *First in His Class*, p. 335

[108] In Freud, S. *Collected Papers* Vol. II, "Character and Anal Eroticism"

[109] See the reference to Bruck, C. p. 89

[110] See the reference to Bruck, C. p. 88

[111] See the reference to Milton, J. p. 19

[112] See the reference to Clinton, H. *The Unique Voice of Hillary Rodham Clinton*, p. 179

[113] See the reference to Sheehy, G. *Hillary's Choice*, pp, 114-116

[114] See the reference to Oppenheimer, J., pp.42-54, 68-88 and 151-161 for details about Hillary's step-grandfather and the Jewish issues for Hillary's mother and Hillary herself.

[115] See the reference to Oppenheimer, J. p. 157

[116] See the reference to Sheehy, G, *Hillary's Choice*, p. 76

[117] See the reference to Oppenheimer, J. p. 77

[118] See the reference to Wurtzel, E. p.118

[119] See the reference to Rodham, Hillary, pp. 21-35

[120] See the reference to Reich, R. p. 166

[121] See the reference to Noonan, P. p. 145

[122] See the reference to Olson, B. pp. 234 and 251

[123] See the reference to Milton, J. p. 90

[124] See the reference to Paglia, C. p. 176

[125] See the reference to Neumann, E. p. 279

[126] See the reference to Tomsky, M., "Hillary's Turn," *New York*, April 3, 2000. p. 28

[127] See the reference to Bruck, C. p. 87

[128] See the reference to Gergen, D. pp 308-309

[129] See the reference to Gergen, D. pp

[130] See Clinton, H. *Living History*, p. 213. 280-291

[131] See the reference to Woodward, B. *Shadow*, pp 474-475

[132] See the references to Clinton, H. *It Takes a Village*, p. 8

[133] See the reference to Milton, J, p. 259

160

134 See the Sheehy, G. *Hillary's Choice*, pp. 182-185. 190

135 See the reference to Joyce, J. p. 292

136 See the reference to Aldrich, G., p. 89

137 See the reference to Harpaz, B., p. 269

138 See the reference of Paglia, C. p. 178

139 See the reference to Harpaz, B. *The Girls in the Van*, p. 152

140 Herz, Steve, Rodack, Jeff and Allison, Lynn "Lonely Chelsea," Globe, August 15, 2000, p. 9

141 Kuncl, Tom "Chelsea's Courage," *Star*, Sept. 5, 2000, p. 12-13

142 See the reference to Clinton, C., p. 100

143 See the reference to Lytall, S

144 See the reference to Freud, S. *Standard Edition*,  "The Acquisition and Control of Fire"

145 See the Clinton, C. reference, p. 142

146 See the Clinton, C. reference, p. 103

147 See the Gabel, S. reference

148 See the reference to Petty, T.

149 See reference to Lytall, S.

150 See the reference to Clinton, B. p. A23

151 The duration of Bill's separation from Virginia is given as two years in Maraniss, D. *First in His Class*

152 See the reference to Weiss, P. p. 34

153 I heard him say this in a talk in San Francisco in 1999 publicizing  his anti-Clinton book listed in the reference to Hitchens, C.

154 See the reference to Oakley, M. p. 23

155 See the reference to Levin, Robert, pp. 10-11

156 See the reference to Anderson, C

157 See the reference to Kelly, V. p. 89. pp. 51 and 59

158 See the Clinton, Bill reference for his column

159 See the reference to Marsalis, D., First in His Class, pp. 21 and    28

160 See the  reference to Sheehy, G. *Hillary's Choice*, p.94-95

161 See the reference to Oremland, J., p. 563

162 See the reference to Kelley, V., p. 152

163 See the reference to Kelley, V. p. 23

164 See the reference to Kelley, V. pp. 19, 24, 29

165 See the reference to Kelley, V. p. 276

166 See the reference to Kelley, V. p. 71

167 See the reference to Stewart, James, pp. 85-86

168 See the reference to Bernoldi, Andreas, pp. 101-134

169 See the reference to Roland, Alan

170 See the reference to Kelley, Virginia, p. 103

171 See the reference to Kelley, Virginia p. 162

172 See the reference to Cawthorne, N

173 See the reference to Browning, D. *Purposes of the Heart*

174  See the reference to Brock, D. *The Seduction of Hillary Rodham*, p. 45

175 See the reference to Flowers, G. *Passion and Betrayal*, p. 41

176 See the reference to Kelley, V. pp. 190-191

177 See the reference to Kelley, V. pp. 292, 192, 199

178 See the reference to Gallen, D. pp. 26-27

179 See the reference to Allen, C. and Portis, Jonathan, p. 18

180 See the reference to Kelley, V. p. 78.

181 See the reference to Clinton, B. p. A23

182 See the reference to Kelley, V. p. 78

183 See the reference to Franks, L. p. 167

184 See the reference to Sheehy, G. *Hillary's Choice*, p. 301

185 See the *Diagnostic and Statistical Manual of Mental Disorders* in the bibliography

186 See the reference to Hamer, D. and Copeland, P. in the bibliography.

187 See the reference to Kinsey, A., Pomeroy, W. and Martin, C., *Sexual Behavior in the Human Male*, p. 203

188 See the reference to Renshon, S., p. 164

189 See the reference to Carpozi, G., p 11

190 See the reference to Kelley, V. p. 100

191 See the reference to Allen, C. and Portis, J. p.15

192 See the reference to Arnheim, D. and Sinclair, W. p. 30

193 See the reference to Marariss, D. *First in His Class*, p. 330

194 See the reference to Kelley, V., p. 83

195  See the reference to Freud, S. *Standard Edition of the Complete Works of Sigmund Freud*, Vol. 5,  Interpretation of Dreams, p. 398

196 See the reference to Allen, C. and Portis, J., p. 5

197 See the reference to Flowers, G., *Sleeping With the President*, p. 93

198 See the reference to Maraniss, D. *First in His Class*, p. 427

199 See the reference to Birnbaum, J. p. 159

200 See the reference to Woodward, B. *The Agenda*, pp. 389

201 See the reference to Woodward, B., *The Agenda*, p.135

202 See the reference to Brummett, J., pp. 13-16

203 See the reference to Myers, S. and Stemmata. E. p. A 10

204 See the reference to Woodward, B. *The Agenda*, p. 397

205 See the reference to Brunet, J., p. 267

206 See the reference to Stephanopoulos, G., p. 284

207 See the reference to Birnbaum, J., p. 7

208 See the Kelley, Virginia reference, p. 151

209 See the reference to Kline, D., p. 7

210 See the Kelley, Virginia reference, p. 151

211 See the reference to Oakley, M., p. xiii

212 See the reference to Brock, D. *The Seduction of Hillary Rodham*, p. 45

213 See the reference  to Browning, D. p. 260

214 See reference to Kelley, Virginia p. 152

215 See the reference to Bloland, S. pp. 287-288

216 See the reference to Leo, J. and Galvin, R., p. 76

217 See the reference to Kelley, V. p. 28

218 See the reference to Gallen, D., p. 90

219 See the reference to Kelley, V., p. 29

220 See the reference to Kelley, V., p. 136

221 See the reference to Freud, S. *The Ego and the Id*, pp. 69-70

222 See the reference to Woodward, C. Vann, p. 19

223 See the reference to Cash, W.J., p. 51

224 See the reference to Morrison, Toni, p. 32

225 Virginia Kelley, Bill's mother, says that her mother, Edith Cassidy, had "Indian blood" in *Leading With My Heart* although nothing is said about a Spanish ori gin for this woman or her family who had lived in Arkansas since the 1800's. David Maraniss in *First in His Class* says that Bill's paternal grandmother, Lou Blythe, who lived on a farm in Texas, between Dennison and Sherman was originally from Ripley, Mississippi.

226 See the reference to Scales, A. p. A4

227 See the reference to Knutson, L., p. A10

228 See the reference to Carpozi, G., pp. 469-470

229 See the reference to Perlez, J. p. A 12

230 See the reference to Fenichel, Otto, *The Psychoanalytic Theory of Neurosis*, p. 58

231 See the reference to Flowers, G. *Passion and Betrayal*, p. 160

232 See the reference to Browning, Dolly, p. 279

233 See the reference to Klein, Joe *Primary Colors*, p. 203

234 See the reference to Kelley, V. p. 86

235 See the reference to Kelley, V. p. 175

236 See the reference to Kelley, V. p. 239

237 See the reference to Clinton, B., p. A-23

238 See the reference to Collins, Nancy "Linda Tripp I'd Do It All Over Again" *George*, p. 56

239 See the reference to Dunne, D., p. 213

240 See the reference to Morton, A. p. 57

241 See the reference to Ramjug, P., p. A-1

242 See the reference to Miller, Arthur "American Playhouse," *Harper's*, June 2001

243 See the reference to Sheehy, G., *Hillary's Choice*, pp. 175-178

244 See the reference to Dowd, M. "Maladroit Du Seigneur," p. A23

245 See the reference to Gould, M. , p. 4

246 See the reference to Andersen, C., p. 201

247 See  the reference to Manson, M., p. 70

248 See the reference to "Survey: Of Kids 15-19, 55% Have Tried Oral Sex," p. A5

249 See the reference to Sterba, R. *Introduction to the Psychoanalytic Theory of the Libido*, p. 32

250 See the reference to Flowers, G., *Sleeping With the President*, p. 59

252 See the  reference to Joyce, James, p. 638

253 See the reference to Klein, J., *The Natural*, p. 196

254 See the reference to Freud, S. *An Autobiographical Study*, pp. 124-125

255 See the reference to Milton, J., p. 396

256 See reference to Woodward, Bob *Shadow*, p. 332 and  to Morris, Dick, pp. 64-65

257 See reference to Carpozi, G., pp. 474-475

258 Sullivan's theories are best read in summaries like the Mullahy, Patrick reference listed in the bibliography although Sullivan's own writings are listed under Sullivan, Harry.

259 Object relations theory is discussed in Chodorow, Nancy *The Reproduction of Mothering*, Chapt. 3

260 See the reference to Woodward, B. Shadow, p. 332 and Morris, Dick pp. 64-65

261 See reference to Johnson, Haynes, p. 259

262 *Life*, June 20, 1969

263 See the reference to Brock, D. *The Seduction of Hillary Rodham*, p. 26

264 See the reference to Oppenheimer, J., p. 7

265 See the  reference to  Andersen, C., p.103

266 See the reference to Maraniss, D. *First in His Class*, p. 247

267 See the to  reference to Salter, S,, p. A-23

268 See the reference to Dowd, Maureen, "The Privacy Ruse" in the bibliography.

269 See the reference to Woodward, B. *Shadow*, p. 451

270 See the reference to Brownrigg, R., p. 346

271 See the reference to Neumann, E. p. 279

272 Three Sheehy books in the bibliography deal with male and female menopause and the midlife crisis which she calls "passages".

273 See the reference to Hunter, S. and Sundel, M.

274 See the reference to Friedan, B., p. 146

275 See the reference to Neugarten, B.

276 See the reference to Klein, J., *The Natural*, p.196

277 See the reference to Runyan,  R., p. 75

278 See the reference to Phillips, A. p. 364

279 See the reference to Franks, L., p. 248

280 See reference to Alter, J., p. 34

281 See the reference to Sterba, Richard "Some Psychological Factor in Negro Race Hatred and in Anti-Negro Riots," pp. 411-427

282 See the reference to Coz , S., p. 4

283 See Graves, Robert *King Jesus* , and Frazer, James *The New Golden Bough* in the bibliography.

284 See reference to "Sen. Clinton Ahead of Pack for '04' Race," p. A6

285 See the references to Preston, D. p. 76 and Turner, C. and Turner, J.

286 See the reference to Lamb, Brian, p. 428

287 See the reference to Dubner, S., p. 31

288 See the reference to Johnson, H, p. 400

289 See the reference to Matthews. Chris, p. D1

290 See the reference to Miller, Arthur, "Salem Revisited"

291 The Freud-Jung differences about the origins and continuity of the unconscious are discussed in Jones, Ernest *The Life and Work of Sigmund Freud*, Volume 3, Basic Books, 1957, p. 309.

292 See reference to Hertzberg, H., p. 37

293 See the reference to Andersen, C. p. 280

294  See the reference to Lerner, Michael. I worked with Lerner at the Institute for Labor and Mental Health in Oakland, CA during the eighties when this research was done.

295 See the reference to Lilla, Mark

# INDEX

Printed in the United States
21333LVS00004B/55